P9-CKP-829

CHRISTOPHER GORE

FEDERALIST OF MASSACHUSETTS

1758-1827

CHRISTOPHER GORE

Federalist of Massachusetts

1758-1827

HELEN R. PINKNEY

Waltham, Massachusetts
GORE PLACE SOCIETY
1969

Printed by The Anthoensen Press, Portland, Maine

Contents

TO

D.H.P.

J.S.P.

D.H.P. III

Preface

IN *Boston, Federalism was a way of life, and Christopher Gore personified it in all its manifestations—social and artistic, literary and religious, legal and educational, economic and political. Through speculation he acquired great wealth, he built a country house that is one of America's finest examples of Federalist architecture, and from the ratification of the federal Constitution until the beginning of the Era of Good Feelings, he applied his talents to shaping the policies of the Federalist party in Massachusetts. In Boston, Washington, and London he defended and promoted the commercial enterprise of his state, and when, between 1807 and 1814, the national government threatened to destroy it, his forceful support of New England's regionalism won him the governorship of Massachusetts and a seat in the United States Senate.*

The Federalist years have frequently been studied from a national point of view. The career of Christopher Gore embraces this period in Massachusetts from the Federalists' beginnings, with their demands for a powerful, central government, to their achievement of a fruitful combination of state and federal interests, through their eclipse by Jeffersonian republicanism and their revival in antinationalism that Gore encouraged and extended, to their disappearance in new political groups.

I thank the following institutions for the use of manuscripts in their collections: Boston Public Library, Dedham Historical Society, Essex Institute, Gore Place Society, Harvard Business School Library, Harvard University Library, Historical Society of Pennsylvania, Library of Congress, Massachusetts Archives, Massachusetts Historical Society, National Archives, New England Historic and Genealogical Society, New-York Historical Society, New York Public Library, Social Law Library, Yale University Library. I also thank James Gore King for the use of typescripts of letters in his collection.

I record my gratitude to Frederick Merk and to David McKibbin, and most particularly to Walter Muir Whitehill for his continued interest and invaluable help, and to David Pinkney for his criticism of the manuscript and his support of my efforts to bring this book to completion.

H. R. P.

CHRISTOPHER GORE

FEDERALIST OF MASSACHUSETTS

1758-1827

I

Christopher Gore, Esquire

ON the morning of June 5, 1809, Christopher Gore, the newly elected Governor of Massachusetts, left his country house at Waltham and, with an escort of several hundred political well-wishers and friends, began the triumphal ride to his inauguration at the State House in Boston. The curious, lining the route to watch him, saw a tall, handsome man impeccably dressed in the blue and buff uniform of the Ancient and Honorable Artillery Company of Massachusetts, riding in an open carriage drawn by four matching bays.[1] His formality held him aloof from the crowd, but his charm reputedly delighted his friends. Throughout the state he was known to be conservative, learned, dependable, rich, and able, and the Federalist party cheered its successful candidate, resplendent in the morning sun, as he moved toward Beacon Street.

The new governor's modest beginning in life gave little promise of his exalted position in the Commonwealth. The only aristocratic symbol in his long family history was the coat of arms of his English ancestors, the Gores of Nether Wallop in Hampshire, England, whose records went back to the early fourteenth century. When Christopher's great-great-great-grandfather died in 1643, his will, probated in the Prerogative Court of Canterbury, carried a seal of the coat of arms of the Gore family and thereby gave to all Richard's descendants the right to use this armorial bearing of three bulls' heads and a crescent; the bulls' heads were an allusion to the family name, and the crescent marked the line of a younger son.[2]

Christopher Gore was born into a family of artisans in Boston on September 21, 1758. His father, John, a painter and color merchant, owned a "shop at the sign of the Painters' Arms in Queen Street," which today is Court Street between Washington and Tremont Streets. The sign bore the arms of the ancient guild of painters of sixteenth-century England and the date "1775," the year John Gore opened his shop at this address. For more than two decades he painted coaches and designed coats of arms for the actual and would-be aristocrats of Boston, an artistic work for which he had great talent; even New Yorkers and Philadelphians employed John Gore to draft their coats of arms. He kept a description of each of the decorations he made, and his roll of arms numbered almost one hundred. John Gore was also a merchant, which in pre-revolutionary

Boston meant that he bought his wares directly from manufacturers in London. Although his trade was profitable enough to justify his son Samuel's continuing it after the father's departure during the Revolutionary War, he was not a rich or powerful businessman. He did, however, steadily improve his family's position in Boston in the years before the war. He owned a pew in the Brattle Street Church, he held minor offices in the local government, and he acquired his own shop and other property, especially in Queen's Street. The addition of "Captain" and "Esq." to his name in the town records shows how close he had come to Boston's aristocracy.[3]

Christopher's mother was Frances Pinkney Gore, a daughter of John Pinkney, who was a shopkeeper in Boston. Quite probably another daughter of John Pinkney was the Mary Pinkney who became Martin Gay's first wife, making Christopher a nephew by marriage of Boston's prominent founder and coppersmith. John and Frances Gore had a large family of at least thirteen children, nine of whom grew to maturity. Christopher, the eighth child, had two older brothers, John, Jr. and Samuel; two older sisters, Suzanna and Rebecca; and four younger ones, Mary, Catherine, Frances, and Elizabeth.[4]

One hundred and twenty-three years before Christopher's birth, his great-great-grandparents, John and Rhoda Gore, and their son, John, sailed from England to settle in Roxbury, Massachusetts. Shortly after his arrival John Gore was made a freeman by the General Court of the colony, which gave him the right to own land. Political privilege in this Puritan community came only with church membership, and these, too, John Gore acquired soon after he became a resident of Roxbury. The Gores left England primarily for religious reasons. Their migration to New England in the 1630's, their settlement in Roxbury, and their early membership in the church, all point to their Puritan faith. The names that the Gores gave to their children were not those of their English forebearers, Nicholas, Richard, and William; they were instead Samuel, Obadiah, and Ebenezer of Biblical literature.[5]

Like his Puritan contemporaries of Massachusetts Bay, the first John Gore was a responsible, conscientious citizen. He served the local government for many years as clerk of writs, and he was one of sixty-three citizens of Roxbury who, "out of their religious care of posteritie," bound themselves and their heirs collectively to pay at least twenty pounds each year for the support of a school.[6] Here education flourished, and in his *Magnalia Christi Americana* Cotton Mather wrote that "Roxbury has afforded more scholars—first for the colledge, and then for the publick of any town of its bigness . . . in all New-England."[7] Although the Puritan John Gore began his life in the new world with only four acres of land, he eventually accumulated 188 acres and ranked among the largest landowners in his township. When he died in April 1657, twenty years after he had set out from England, his estate exceeded the considerable sum of £800.[8]

John Gore established an honorable place for his family in Massachusetts. Although the accomplishments of his great-great-grandson Christopher were of broader and more brilliant design, they were essentially of the same pattern. In his religious thinking one moved from Anglicanism to Puritanism, the other from Congregationalism to Unitarianism; John Gore had pledged himself to the support of Roxbury's grammar school to fit the youth for "publick service bothe in Church and Commonwealth," and Christopher Gore gave half his estate to the "University at Cambridge" for the promotion of "virtue, science, and Literature"; the immigrant had accumulated a sizable estate, his descendant died a very rich man; the elder Gore had served his local government, the younger reached the highest office in the Commonwealth.

The first of Christopher's American-born ancestors was his great-grandfather, Samuel Gore, the tenth child of the immigrant Gores. Samuel married Elizabeth Weld, daughter of John Weld of Roxbury, and lived out his years building houses and barns for the settlers there. Like his father he held local offices, but Samuel also participated in a dramatic overthrow of tyranny. Early in 1689 when Boston heard that the Prince of Orange had landed in England and a new regime was about to begin, some Bostonians gave vent to their hatred of Governor Andros and his despotic rule by arresting members of his government and seizing the fort at Castle William. With the royal governor and his friends out of the way, they reinstated the local magistrates who had been removed by the governor. These patriots of Boston were ably assisted by their neighbors from Roxbury, prominent among whom was Samuel Gore.[9]

The proximity of Boston to Roxbury lured the enterprising son of Samuel, Obadiah Gore, to settle permanently in the larger, commercial town where more opportunities would provide a better living. He came to Boston in 1710, married Sarah Kilby, and worked at the carpenters' trade.[10] His son, John, improved the family's position in Boston and was able to give his son, Christopher, an education in the Latin School and Harvard College that hastened the Gores' rise to prominence.

The importance of learning was deeply rooted in Christopher's environment. The Puritans early set up an educational system to prepare their children for service in both church and state and to perpetuate learning among their posterity. They also believed that a knowledge of the classics had a direct bearing on the standard of virtue in the colony, "It being one chief project of that old deluder, Satan, to keep men from the knowledge of the Scriptures, . . . by perswading from the use of Tongues. . . ."[11] By 1765 when young Christopher entered the Boston Public Latin School, or South Grammar School as it was then called, men devoted less time to reading and interpreting the Scriptures, but the preeminence of Greek and Latin still persisted in the curriculum.

In a culture where education ranked high, the Latin School offered a program that in scope and intensity was very like the course of study in the best grammar schools in England during the eighteenth century. A student was expected to gain a mastery of Greek and Latin and to have more than a passing acquaintance with the best authors in those languages. Boys entered the Latin School at seven years of age, and for the next seven years Master John Lovell, a rigid disciplinarian, put them through a training that was long in hours and exacting in its demands. As a reward for good behavior and academic achievement, he permitted his students to bottle his cider and weed his garden, laughing as loudly as they wished. The Latin School practiced democracy when privilege more often prevailed in Massachusetts; Christopher Gore received as much consideration as the sons of the Sewalls, the Leveretts, and the Cushings.[12]

After spending five years at the South Grammar School, young Gore completed the last two years of preparatory work at the North Grammar School under the tutelage of Master Samuel Hunt, a Harvard graduate who was conscientious, severe, and unpopular. A memorandum from Master Hunt's *Catalogue of the Boston Public Latin School* records the disciplinary arrangement by which a senior student was held responsible for the good behavior of a new boy:

> I, Peter Crequi, engage that Chris. Gore shall punctually observe the rules of this School for three weeks from this date; and sho'd he break them or any of them within this time, I promise to receive peaceably the punishment due to such Offense with the said Christopher.
>
> Peter Crequi.[13]

Some years after Christopher Gore's graduation in 1772, the North

Grammar School ceased to function and children from the northern part of town attended the original Boston Latin School. When that institution celebrated its tercentenary in 1935, Gore was one of the twenty-six men honored in its hall of fame.[14]

At fourteen years of age, his secondary education completed, Christopher crossed the Charles River to begin his higher learning in Cambridge. When he entered Harvard in 1772, antagonisms between the colony and the mother country ran high. Both British and colonial leaders agreed that the teaching of the College shaped the political views of its students, but neither was certain where Harvard stood on the vital issues of the day. Governor Hutchinson thought it leaned well to the Patriot side as early as 1768 and that two Harvard Fellows, Professor John Winthrop and the Reverend Samuel Cooper, were definitely in the radical camp. The presence of the General Court in the "new chapel" at Harvard heightened the political awareness of both students and faculty, especially since the legislature had moved to Cambridge to escape the mobs in Boston. In April 1776 the General Court commanded the governors and instructors of Harvard College to attend the next meeting of the Overseers to be examined "as to their political privileges." The soundings proved satisfactory, and no instructors lost their positions. The College did not deliberately fill its students with radical ideas or incite them to brave deeds in the name of liberty, but indirectly it trained them to be the patriotic leaders they became. The curriculum's emphasis on the classics and ancient political theories and the presentation of orations on justice and morality in government directed the students toward political action.[15]

Public speaking thrived as an extracurricular activity at Harvard when Gore was a student. In 1770 Samuel Phillips, future founder of Phillips Academy, Andover, organized a secret society of upperclassmen called the Speaking Club. About the same time Fisher Ames and a group of students formed the Mercurian Club. The two combined in 1773, and the new organization, retaining the name of the former club, became a training ground for future political leaders. Gore was elected to membership at the end of his sophomore year. When general interest waned, he with Rufus King and a few others revived the club "upon its primitive Foundations." In 1825 it became The American Institute of 1770 and later merged with the Hasty Pudding Club.[16]

The speeches given during Gore's membership reflect a concern with the overthrow of tyranny and the struggle to form an independent state. Orations of Greek and Roman antiquity held first place for recitation, with a preference for Cicero, Tacitus, Livy, Plutarch, and Demosthenes. Gore's speeches were more literary and scientific than political. His first effort dealt with astronomy; others were extracts from Hervey's *Meditations* and a speech by the Bishop of St. Asaphs. The titles of the books that he drew from the Harvard College Library in his junior and senior years, including Fergason's *Civil Liberty* and Voltaire's *State of Europe,* suggest a greater political awareness than the subjects of his orations.[17]

Although the Harvard administration struggled to preserve an academic calm during this period of tension, the Boston Tea Party caused an outburst in the Yard. Samuel Chandler, a college friend of Christopher Gore, recorded in his diary on December 16, 1773, "I hear from Boston that there was a Mob this Evening and the Vessels were borded and ye Tea hove over-bored. Hezza."[18] Other Harvard students on hearing the news threw tea and dishes about the dining room. Trying to hold the Yard safe for scholarship, the president, professors, and tutors passed a resolution that those who had carried tea into the hall should refrain from continuing it and that they and all students "discover a disposition to promote harmony, mutual affection, and confidence, so well becoming Members of the same Society: that so peace and happiness may be preserved within the Walls of the College whatever convulsions may unhappily distract the State abroad."[19]

When the Patriot troops established their headquarters in Cambridge in 1775 and occupied the college buildings, Harvard moved to Concord, Massachusetts, and here Christopher spent his senior year. The sojourn was pleasant enough, but it brought financial problems to the College and little academic profit to the students. Enrollment decreased and instruction proved difficult. After eight months the troops withdrew from Harvard's buildings in Cambridge, and the College was permitted to return to its "ancient seat." The academic year continued one month longer in 1776 because the residence in Concord had prevented the professor of mathematics and philosophy "from carrying the students through his experimental lectures (a very important branch of their Education)." Owing to the "unsettled state of public affairs" in June of 1776, Christopher Gore graduated without the fanfare of a Harvard commencement.[20]

In contrast to Harvard's turbulent history during these years, Christopher's life as a college student was outwardly quiet and inconspicuous. He lived at home during his first year and resided in college dormitories thereafter. He paid only negligible sums for punishment and breakage fines, and as a borrower of books from the Harvard College Library his behavior was impeccable. His name never came before the faculty for bad conduct or because of low or high academic standing; he won no prizes and received no scholarships. Nor did he pursue the frivolous life of his friend Samuel Chandler of the class of 1775, whose diary of his sophomore and junior years is a long recital of sleeping through prayers, sending a freshman to his tutor with excuses for absences, planning and executing frequent trips to Boston when the Charles River had to be crossed by ferry, and wasting hours with a hairdresser for the improvement of his coiffure. Samuel and Christopher were together in a class in anatomy, and Sam with four other Harvard students was entertained at tea one afternoon at the Gores' home in Boston, but Christopher had neither the money nor the inclination to pursue so gay a life at Harvard as did Chandler.[21] John Trumbull, the artist who later painted several portraits of Gore, recalled that when he was a student at Harvard he was so poor and timid that he made only one close acquaintance. "It was with Christopher Gore of Boston, an amiable boy, my junior in years, and in college rank. This was the commencement of a friendship which lasted through life."[22] The college friends whom Gore valued most in his mature years were James Freeman, who transformed the Episcopal King's Chapel into the first Unitarian church in America, and Rufus King, his most intimate friend.

Although Christopher Gore made little impression for good or ill on Harvard, the College held a larger place in the mind of this boy than the records show. As an adult Gore gave years of service to Harvard, first as an Overseer and then as a Fellow of the Corporation, and at his death he left the College the largest bequest it had yet received. Thirty-three years after his graduation, when he was Governor of Massachusetts, Harvard hailed him as a worthy and distinguished alumnus and conferred on him the honorary degree of Doctor of Laws.

The Boston of Christopher's boyhood was charged with the radicalism of Samuel Adams. From the time of the Sugar Act of 1764, the Stamp Act of 1765, and the Writs of Assistance in 1767, he kept the town in a ferment of political strife. The actions of the British government and Sam Adams complemented each other to keep the radicals and conservatives at each other's throats; whenever the British subsided, Adams would ring another "alarum bell" to ward off tranquility. By 1765 he had harnessed the mobs of the north and south ends of Boston to do his bidding against the officers of the crown and the colonists who were loyal to England. Step by step he forced the Bostonians either to put themselves on the side of the British government or to defy it.

When the political lines were drawn in Boston in 1774, John Gore, Christopher's father, stood with the Loyalists. He had not always stood there, however, for at the time of the Stamp Act his sympathies were with the Patriots, and when the Sons of Liberty met at the famous Liberty Tree in Dorchester on August 14, 1769, to celebrate the anniversary of the forced resignation of the distributor of stamps under the Stamp Act, Captain John Gore and his eldest son, John, participated in the revel.[23] But five years later when Thomas Hutchinson, Governor of Massachusetts and hated Tory, was recalled to England, John Gore was among the 120 Loyalists who signed the addresses approving the governor's "wise, zealous, and faithful administration" and pleading with him to make faithful representations in England of the plight of merchants and traders in Boston that they might have "speedy and effectual relief."[24] In the eyes of the Patriots, the addressers to Governor Hutchinson were traitors.

Many a colonist changed his political stripes in the early 1770's, but at that time the usual shift was from the Loyalist to the Patriot colors. John Gore moved in the opposite direction. Why did he become so staunch a convert when the fortunes of the Tories grew more precarious? He was not rich or politically prominent as were Loyalists like the Vassals, Sewalls, Lechmeres, and Faneuils; his services to the government never went beyond the few local offices of clerk of the market and overseer of the poor.[25] As a shopowner he may have viewed the conflict as a battle between the haves and have-nots, in which the latter under cover of patriotism destroyed the property of their more prosperous neighbors. As an importer of English goods he must have protested when the radicals in Boston forced the nonimportation agreement on all the town's merchants. Undoubtedly he preferred a cool-tempered, rational negotiation with the British government to the hot-headed rioting in Boston that followed the announcement of the Townshend Duties. He may have supported the English side because he feared civil war in Boston if the British soldiers were withdrawn.

In spite of the harried existence of a Loyalist in Massachusetts, John Gore stood resolute in his convictions. He signed a protest against the Solemn League and Covenant because it would impose a boycott throughout New England on the sale of all British goods, a tyranny he regarded as worse than that of the king's ministers. John Gore held a commission in the Ancient and Honourable Artillery Company of Massachusetts, and in 1774 during the blockade imposed by the Boston Port Bill, he served with the company to keep order in the town. He helped to administer the money collected in Boston to aid those who "soonest and most severely feel the Effects of Scarcity." When General Gage, the commander of the king's forces in America, retired from the governorship of Massachusetts, Gore was among the ninety-seven who sent him the "Loyal address from gentlemen and principal inhabitants of Boston." He and Henry Caner, Rector of King's Chapel, Colonel Jonathan Snelling, Major Adino Paddock, and Captain Martin Gay were appointed by Lieutenant Governor Oliver to take possession of "the House commonly called the Green Dragon [famous as a meeting place of Sam Adams and his firebrands] and prepare it as a Hospital for the Reception of such Objects as shall require immediate Relief" because of the "long blockade of the Town by the Provincial forces."[26]

These five Loyalists had much in common. They were closely allied in friendship, marriage, and business. Dr. Caner's niece, Sarah, had married John Gore, Jr., and Martin Gay was probably the elder Gore's brother-in-law. Colonel Jonathan Snelling, Commander of the Governor's Guard, conducted a profitable business as a commission merchant. Major Adino Paddock, the principal coachmaker in the colonies, was a family and business friend of the Gores, and when his son drowned in the Charles River during his freshman year at Harvard, Christopher Gore was a pallbearer at the funeral. These men, the rector of the Anglican King's Chapel, a coachmaker, a coppersmith, a commission merchant, and a designer of coats of arms, all enjoyed business or professional contacts with the Tory aristocracy. They were responsible citizens who had risen to the rank of Colonel, Major, Captain, Doctor, and Esquire. They had all progressed to the threshold of Boston's aristocracy, and, as a clergyman, Henry Caner had already entered it.[27]

While Christopher's father signed Loyalist addresses and supported the British government, his brother, Samuel, joined the Sons of Liberty to oppose the tyranny of the mother country. Samuel, a stout-armed artisan, helped to execute Sam Adams' plans for resistance. In the gathering dusk of a winter afternoon on January 16, 1773, he and several hundred other "Mohawks" threw 342 chests of tea from three British ships into the Boston harbor. After the war began, Samuel Gore won special notice for seizing two brass guns called "Hancock" and "Adams" from the gun house on Tremont Street and carrying them to the American lines "under the very eyes of the British."[28]

The realities of Boston's struggle against England bore down upon an impressionable adolescent. With his father a Loyalist and his only living brother a Patriot, young Christopher knew the sharp conflict of divided loyalties. The Gore household lived with tension and anxiety, and although Christopher was in residence at Harvard College, he could not escape the grief for a loved one, hounded and insulted by his fellowmen, and the humiliation he himself suffered from being so closely allied to the despised minority.[29] His father's Toryism was a stigma that pursued him the rest of his life.

John Gore's political alignment was so well known in Boston that flight seemed his only course, and in March 1776 he and eleven hundred other Loyalists sailed from Boston with the British forces under the command of General Howe. Without the protection of the king's soldiers, life in Boston would be too hazardous to risk. John Gore took with him his eldest son's widow and her child, John, but his own wife and family remained behind.[30] Probably Gore thought they would be less terrorized by the revolutionaries if they were in the care of his Patriot son Samuel, and possibly the sympathies of all of them favored the Patriot cause. The evacuation taxed the fortitude of every Loyalist. Leaving his home and family without knowing where he was going or for how long a time was the supreme test of John Gore's devotion to the mother country.

In Halifax, Nova Scotia, the arrival in less than a month of fifty transports crowded with evacuees from Boston strained to the utmost the resources of the town, and, although the governor tried to fix the price of food and lodging, the cost of living rose sharply. John Gore could find no means of livelihood there and, with others in the same predicament, he sailed for London in a ship provided by General Howe.[31]

England could hardly have cared less for the American Tories. Through years of homesickness they dickered with the British government over pensions and compensations. John Gore and twenty-eight other refugees from Massachusetts sent a memorial to George III in which they declared that by their loyalties they had sacrificed their homes and fortunes and they prayed for his favor to relieve their poverty. Some of the Loyalists from Massachusetts formed a club that met at the New England Coffee House in Threadneedle Street to share complaints over their meager allowances, reluctantly granted by the British government, and to pool the scanty bits of news from home.[32]

They learned that the Patriots of Massachusetts, having driven them out of the colony, had banished them by law and confiscated their property. On October 16, 1778, the General Court passed an act that listed the most notorious of the Loyalists, including John Gore, and provided for their arrest and deportation if they should ever set foot in Massachusetts. The major acts of confiscation were passed in 1779 and 1780. If a Loyalist had left his family behind as had John Gore, his estate was probated as if the head of the family were dead. The committee in charge of the administration of estates leased the property at auction and appointed an executor to pay to the family such sums from the rentals as the judge of probate would allow.[33]

In the summer of 1779 Christopher Gore, just beginning his professional career, petitioned the state House of Representatives for the release of the money to which he and his three unmarried sisters were entitled for their maintenance. The General Court ordered the judge of probate to support them out of their father's estate and to permit them to retain the small quantity of family furniture still in their hands. To Christopher went three-fifths of the rent of a brick dwelling house and shop, which annually gave him about £548. Samuel Gore, having the care of his mother in his father's absence, presented accounts to the General Court of the cost of the butter, veal, salmon, mutton, and potatoes he provided for her. In the final accounting the debts charged against the estate exceeded the receipts from the rentals.[34]

In 1785 after nine years of exile, John Gore returned to Boston. His residence in England had convinced him that in spite of his royal partisanship, his first loyalty belonged to Massachusetts. When the fighting ceased and the colonies won their independence, he sought permission to return home. Two years after his arrival in Boston, he petitioned "the honorable Senate and House of Representatives of the Commonwealth of Massachusetts," humbly praying that the honorable Court would be pleased to pass "an act of Naturalization in his favor." He desired to spend the remainder of his life in Boston, "to vest his property" in the laws of the Commonwealth, and to enjoy "the rights and privileges of a citizen of America." Prominent Bostonians of the postwar period, including James Bowdoin, Caleb Davis, Thomas Dawes, and William Phillips, vouched for his good character and worthiness, and on July 2, 1787, the General Court proclaimed John Gore to be a citizen of Massachusetts as if he had been "an inhabitant of the territory, now the Commonwealth aforesaid, at the time of making the present form of civil Government."[35] The service to the Patriots of his elder son, Samuel, and the reputation of his younger son, Christopher, an attorney favorable to the new order, strengthened his case. The influence of Sam Adams, that old radical who began the trouble, helped, too. He told Christopher that out of "pure regard" for him, he was "always willing" that John Gore should return to Boston.[36]

After the restoration of his civil rights, John Gore lived nine years to enjoy the privileges of a government whose inception he had suffered to oppose. When he died in 1796, he left an estate of $2,992 to be divided equally among his seven children and his two grandsons named John.[37] Although the long exile had reduced his wealth, his life had been rich in devotion to the mother country, a devotion that the British government never recognized or rewarded.

Christopher Gore's decision to support the Patriots in the American Revolution was important for his future career in Boston, and, by allying himself definitely and positively with their cause, he helped counteract the effect of his father's Toryism. Several weeks after John Gore's departure with the British army, Christopher joined the artillery regiment of Colonel Thomas Craft, the husband of his sister, Frances, and on October 10, 1776, he became a commissioned officer. From May 9, 1776, to July 1, 1778, while completing his senior year at Harvard and preparing for his professional career, he worked as clerk of Craft's regiment, preparing the payroll and writing the Colonel's letters and reports.[38]

Young Gore also found time in 1777-1778 to join a group of young men fresh from Harvard who frequently met in John Trumbull's rooms at the corner of Court and Brattle streets to discuss politics, literature, and the war.[39] In the club were a number of men, besides Gore and Trumbull, who later achieved eminence: Rufus King, Minister to England and United States Senator from New York; William Eustis, Secretary of War and Governor of Massachusetts; Royall Tyler, playwright and Chief Justice of the Supreme Court of Vermont; Thomas Dawes, Justice of the Supreme Judicial Court of Massachusetts; and Aaron Dexter, Harvard's first professor of medicine.

In deciding upon a career, Christopher turned away from the shopkeeping and small business enterprises of his father, brother, and uncles and chose the law, a profession that was growing in prestige and influence in Boston. Training to be a lawyer in eighteenth-century America was an informal procedure. Gore apprenticed himself to John Lowell, distinguished jurist and founder of the family that helped to shape New England's history for two centuries, and in his master's office he read law and learned the methods of the profession. According to the custom of the time, he paid £100 for his instruction and experience. Few legal treatises and books of cases were available in America, and those that did exist were widely scattered. When Gore first used volume one of Blackstone's *Com-*

mentaries, it had been in circulation only twelve years. Each lawyer started his practice with his own manuscript collection of forms that he had copied as an apprentice and to which he made additions from his own experience. If he were particularly fortunate he might possess a few notes on cases from the courts of the provinces. The Suffolk County Bar admitted only "young gentlemen" who had a college education or its equivalent, and it usually required three years of study with a member of the bar before the student could practice as an attorney before the court of common pleas; two years later he would be allowed to plead causes before the Superior Court of Judicature.[40]

Gore's apprenticeship was shorter than average. After he had read law for only two years, John Lowell was ready to present the necessary recommendations of ability, achievement, and character. In July 1788 the Suffolk County Bar admitted Gore to the status of "attorney." Equipped with as good an education as was then available in America, he opened an office in State Street and began the practice of law.[41]

II
A Young Lawyer-Politician

FOR Christopher Gore, affiable, well trained, and eager to get on in the world, the law as his lifework held a double promise: the achievement of a distinguished professional career and the means to political preferment. The lawyer-politician was common enough in Boston, but this union of interests offered a special advantage to Gore because he began his career when the dislocations of the Revolution offered a rare opportunity to move ahead.

He found the war years a good time to open an office. Some of the best lawyers had left Boston in the evacuation of the Tories, and the pro-Loyalist sympathies of many of those who remained had alienated their clients and given the younger men a larger share of the town's business than they would otherwise have had. Since his practice dealt with cases in probate court, litigation over land titles, and especially with collection of debts for local and distant creditors, Gore's success depended upon the town's economic climate. This, too, was in his favor. During the war Boston's trade increased beyond its former limits and brought general prosperity to the area. In spite of Britain's blockade, privateering accounted for a substantial part of the growing wealth of Boston and the ports on the north shore. The Cabots of Beverly; the Derbys and William Gray of Salem; Stephen Higginson, John Coffin Jones, and Thomas Russell of Boston grew rich as their armed vessels preyed upon the enemy's commerce. Not all lucrative seafaring during the war came from prizes. The Amorys of Boston, to whom Gore was later related through marriage, sent their ships to the Carolinas, Virginia, the West Indies, Holland, and Spain. Some of the cargoes were captured, but enough ships reached their destinations and returned to enrich their owners. The hazards of transportation by sea stimulated the marine insurance business in Boston, where Edward Payne, Gore's future father-in-law, owned a large brokerage. In the midst of this prosperous, wartime activity, Gore's legal practice took root and thrived.[1] Two years after he had opened his office, he wrote to a friend: ". . . C. G. has more business than he had reason to expect. He has maintained himself very comfortably, has argu'd several causes at the bar, and has been much flatter'd, too much, I fear, for his own happiness."[2]

Immediately after the war the expansion of trade pushed Boston's prosperity even higher. Most of the ports of the world were open to ships from

Massachusetts, and more importantly, the normal channels of commerce with England and her empire were again available. The gold and silver currency that was left in circulation by departing British and French armies enabled Americans to buy generously in foreign markets. Firms in London strove to recapture their former customers, and Americans, having found trade with continental countries unsatisfactory during the war, eagerly returned to British merchants and their goods.

Christopher Gore was lawyer and agent for individuals and commercial houses in the United States and Nova Scotia and particularly for merchants in Great Britain. Most of his cases from Nova Scotia dealt with claims of former Loyalists in Massachusetts and the settlements of their estates. For Joy and Hopkins, merchants in London, he collected payments on debts, interest on capital invested in Massachusetts, and rentals from property in Boston. He paid out money that the firm owed locally for deeds, bonds, lawsuits, and debts. On November 20, 1785, Gore registered in his Account Book the receipt of a retaining fee from Joy and Hopkins for ten guineas. He carried on the same kind of legal-financial work for Winthrop and Tod of South Carolina, for Bredell and Ward of London, and for Hugh Mossman of "Edingburgh in Great Britain." He frequently appeared in court to represent Blanchard and Lewis, merchants in London, in suits involving the collection of debts. Gore's largest account came from Champion and Dickason of London; during September 1785 he transacted business for them in excess of £1,665. The firm had an excellent reputation as suppliers to American importers, and rumors circulated that it stood creditor to Boston merchants for over £150,000.[3]

In the 1780's and early 1790's Gore appeared in the Court of Common Pleas of Suffolk County and in the Supreme Judicial Court of Massachusetts as frequently as any lawyer in Boston, and he had better than average success in winning his cases.[4] Although he never swayed a judge or jury by his oratory, his arguments, supported by pertinent legal detail, were logically and convincingly reasoned. He appeared in case after case dealing with controversies arising between merchants and traders of both foreign and domestic residence. In the year following his first election to the state legislature Gore's volume of business in the lower courts advanced markedly. He reported to Rufus King in the summer of 1789 that he had a profitable and honorable practice. "My clients are generally of the class which is able to pay, and I think I can say, without vanity, that my conduct is not dissatisfactory to them."[5]

Having carefully established his professional career, Gore in his twenty-sixth year, with equal care, chose his wife. In November 1785 he married Rebecca Payne and thereby made a fortunate alliance. Rebecca was an alert, attractive, intelligent, warmhearted young woman, whom her brother, William Payne, described as having a mind above the ordinary and a kindness of heart that showed itself in good deeds. Although she was fond of "retirement and domestic quiet," she loved to have her friends about her, and "none could live within the circle in which she moved without being affected by her influence." For the rest of his life Christopher was a devoted husband; his letters tell of his concern for his wife's well-being and of his delight in her company. Rebecca came from a distinguished family in Boston. Her paternal great-grandmother was a Winslow and her mother an Amory; her father, Edward Payne, held an enviable place among the financial leaders of State Street.[6] A few years after the marriage John Quincy Adams described Gore as a "very fortunate man" who had won remarkable success in his profession and whose family connections had "been extremely serviceable to him."[7]

Although the Gores had no children, they were a favorite aunt and uncle to their many nieces and nephews in Boston and affectionately regarded by the children of Rufus King, one of whom was christened James Gore King. William Payne said that Rebecca Gore was mother to the children of two families, his own twin sons and John Gore, the son of Christopher's eldest brother who had died before the Revolutionary War. The Gores later educated young John at Harvard and established him in a successful career in a firm of East India traders.

Fifteen years after Rebecca became Christopher's wife, John Trumbull painted her portrait. He showed a pretty, brown-eyed woman with a rather wistful smile, fashionably arrayed. Her brown hair, styled low on her forehead, her white dress, her grey stole edged with fur and fringe, her long yellow gloves, her earrings, necklace, and brooch reveal a woman attentive to her appearance. In the portrait she creates no dramatic impression, but she sits with dignity and confidence. Alexander Baring, the London banker, called her "a good intelligent little woman."[8]

About the time Gore married, the lawyers of Massachusetts came under serious attack. Never highly esteemed by the ordinary people of the state, in the decade after the Revolution they were even more disliked. Some of their disrepute arose from evils inherent in a profession that was dependent upon the use of English common law and had not had time to develop a legal code better suited to a new and independent country. The lawyers themselves were partly to blame for their unpopularity. The Tory exodus had taken a large number of the eminent members of the bar in Massachusetts and left behind too many of inferior ability and few principles. In his "Observations on the Pernicious Practice of the Law," Benjamin Austin, cordage maker in Boston, condemned the exorbitant fees, the sophistry and cunning of the men at the bar, and he demanded that lawyers be abolished and a system of referees be established to settle disputes. Scores of citizens agreed as they lost their property and faced a debtor's prison.[9]

Fundamentally the problem of discontent was economic. When the postwar boom collapsed in the mid-eighties, Massachusetts sank into the worst depression the state had ever known. The seaboard depended so exclusively upon its income from commerce that when trade slackened in the summer of 1783 because England closed the ports of its West Indian islands to American ships, the whole coastal area felt the pinch. Heavy imports in 1783 put American merchants deeply in debt to their British suppliers; domestic manufacturers, trying to establish small industries, complained of unfair competition; and the distressed in all parts of the state laid blame upon agents of foreign creditors like Christopher Gore.[10] When the Revolutionary armies moved southward, the middle and southern states replaced New England as the chief supplier of foodstuffs. Unable to find new markets, the farmers of Massachusetts saw their produce in oversupply and their incomes shrink.

The seaboard dominated the General Court and enacted legislation advantageous to itself but detrimental to agriculture. The commercial interests won rebates on exports, which made goods shipped out of the country cheaper than those consumed at home, and at the same time they placed an excise tax on domestic goods so that imports could compete favorably in the local markets. The scarcity of cash forced ex-soldiers to sell, for as little as fifteen cents on the dollar, the state certificates in which they had been paid during the war. In the mid-eighties Christopher Gore bought government securities for $3,743 that carried a face value of $25,000 and paid $449.22 in interest. Since most of Massachusetts' debt was due by 1785, the legislature prepared to discharge it by levying high real estate and poll taxes, payable only in specie, and to find new revenue from taxation on farm buildings and animals. Angry farmers besieged the General Court in 1786 and demanded lower taxes, a reduction in the cost of state government, a simplification of the judicial system, a curbing of lawyers' fees and shady practices, and an increase in the money supply through the issue of state bills of credit.[11]

Christopher Gore sat in his law office in State Street and viewed the upheaval with alarm, not because the farmers were losing their land but because the General Court moved too slowly to prepare a military force to protect the creditors and quell any disorders that might arise. "I wish it was generally believ'd that an attack on property and a subversion of the Government was intended, for so great a languor, so little spirit I never knew," he wrote to Rufus King in November 1786.[12] Gore believed that no legislative corrective was necessary or advisable. Deflation should run its natural course, even though "constant complaints are heard for the scarcity of cash and the poverty of trade." He expected that commerce would decline because of the separation from England and "being contracted within a narrowed sphere" would produce advantages to those with large reserves of capital. "Many who retail tape & pins must, as they ought to have done years ago, return to labour."[13]

Gore vented his impatience against the Massachusetts House of Representatives. ". . . tender bills, acts against lawyers, or more truly against law, now occupy their time," he complained to King.[14] ". . . some political wise-acres," who, Gore observed, had never before attempted to speak in that assembly, "are weak enough to think, by sacrificing private contracts, they may support public debts. . . ." He found that men of property placed "little confidence" in the government.[15] When armed farmers, led by Daniel Shays, prevented the courts from sitting in some western and central counties in Massachusetts so that their property would not be seized to pay their debts, Gore was less disturbed by the use of force against established authority than by an attack of debtors against creditors. The rebellion, he feared, would strengthen proposals in the General Court for a fresh issue of paper money and for cancellation of debts. He deplored the apathy of people in Massachusetts because they subscribed only $500 to raise federal troops to support the authority of the state against the insurgent farmers. "Is this not dreadful?" he asked King.[16] Gore was needlessly worried; when the state militia moved into the disturbed area in January 1787, the poorly organized rebellion collapsed.

In the following spring the justices of the Supreme Judicial Court tried the Shaysites accused of insurrection. The court assigned to the prisoners eminent counsel for their defense: Theodore Sedgwick and Caleb Strong for those in the western counties, James Sullivan and Levi Lincoln for Worcester, and Christopher Gore and Thomas Dawes for Middlesex. Each of these men had made public statements hostile to the Shaysites, but in all of Massachusetts there were no neutral lawyers and none who supported Shays. Although the court found the prisoners to be guilty of leading an uprising, the legislature, impressed by General Lincoln's plea for leniency, granted pardon to all who would take the oath of allegiance. The farmers, having failed to improve their situation by rebellion, turned their attention to the State House in Boston.[17]

Gore was dismayed when more farmers sat in the legislature in 1787 than in any previous session and when, with some support from the seaboard area, they enacted relief bills to aid the agricultural counties. They reduced both land and poll taxes, limited the duration of imprisonment for debt, and prescribed that for the next six months creditors must accept goods as well as currency in payment of debts.[18] Gore complained to King, ". . . our Govt. is weak and languid and inefficient to support the great objects of civil institutions and personal liberty and property of the subject."[19] Although bills to regulate lawyers' fees and to forbid the practice of champerty failed to pass, the charges against lawyers inspired a greater concern in the Massachusetts bar for higher standards of conduct. During the rebellion members of the legal profession held strategic positions in Governor Bowdoin's administration and as a group were an important force in suppressing the disturbances. "Lawyers are growing into consequence," Gore wrote in June 1787.[20]

The uprising of the farmers and the political distemper of the General Court having convinced Gore that property must be guarded against the attacks of radicals, he joined those in Massachusetts who wanted to increase the power of the national government so that it could vigorously support the interests of business, prevent the enactment of legislation dangerous to the economy, and exert its authority over all the American states. He wrote to Rufus King at the Constitutional Convention in Philadelphia, "You of the federal Convention, must invent some plan to increase the circulation at the heart and thereby dispense heat and vigor to the extremities—if you do not, we shall descend to anarchy and disgrace."[21]

In Massachusetts the chief support for the Constitution came from the professional, commercial groups and from the farmers along the Connecticut River and the seaboard. Although some artisans and mechanics gave approval, the lawyers, clergy, bankers, manufacturers, merchants, and shipowners composed the majority of those favoring the new form of government. The supporters in Boston, having direct contact with the State House and dominating the local newspapers, exerted influence out of all proportion to their numbers. Many of them had risen to prominence during the Revolution, moved to Boston if they were not already there, and become important citizens. William Phillips, John Coffin Jones, and Thomas Russell, all delegates to the ratification convention, had grown rich in interstate and foreign commerce and their holdings of government securities exceeded those of any other delegates. The men who had recently acquired their wealth aggressively sought political action to protect and increase it. Although the trade of Massachusetts had steadily improved since the depression of the mid-eighties, the commercial interests wanted a central authority strong enough to enforce uniform trade regulations throughout the states, negotiate with foreign governments, pay the domestic as well as the foreign debt, encourage capital investments, and protect the rights of property. These nationalists envisioned themselves as the controlling political force in such a government, and they were willing to wage a fight to secure their advantage.

The bulletins from Gore to Rufus King, who represented Massachusetts in the Continental Congress, first report confidence that the Constitution would be widely approved in Massachusetts and later anxiety that some counties might fail to accept it. A few days after the first copy of the new document arrived in Boston and appeared as an extra edition of the *Massachusetts Centinel* on September 26, 1787, Gore wrote, "The federal plan is well esteemed, and as far as can be deduced from present appearances, the adoption will be easy."[22] Those in favor of the Constitution were only more quick to give their approval than those in opposition were to denounce it. Small property holders, men of lesser social and economic status, and most farmers from the interior of the state gradually took their positions against the adoption of the federal plan either because it would not benefit them or because they believed it held dangers for the country. Discouraging reports came to Gore from the western counties, and he told King that Worcester would generally oppose the plan.[23] Almost all the towns that had sympathized with Shays' Rebellion stood against the Constitution.

The voters of Boston elected Christopher Gore, twenty-nine years of age, to be a member of the state convention that would meet on January 9, 1788, to accept or reject the proposed plan from Philadelphia.[24] In this election, which marked the beginning of his political career, Gore received the least votes of Boston's twelve delegates, and his candidacy attracted the opposition of three zealous Patriots and democrats: Charles Jarvis, physician and aristocrat, Benjamin Austin, ropemaker and enemy of lawyers, and Sam Adams. Gore complained to King that falsehoods of every kind were "loudly declared," and the "lowest and meanest acts of deception made use of to effect their purposes. This being the case, and I being the only one they opposed, I feel as honourably elected as any one of the delegates."[25] The opposition to Gore stemmed from his father's Toryism and his own antidemocratic reputation, his connections with British merchants, and his known support of a strong federal government.

As Gore considered the Constitution's prospects for ratification in Massachusetts, he worried about the silence of Sam Adams, and the longer he waited for Adams to declare whether or not he would support the Constitution, the more anxious he became. Although his influence had dwindled since the Revolution, Adams was still a force to consider. Not to elect him to the convention would be unwise, Gore reasoned, for resentment would prompt him to come out against the Constitution and "endeavour to make proselytes," and "the rumour of his opposition wou'd weigh more than any real objections he cou'd raise in convention." The Boston voters chose Adams to be a delegate not knowing whether he was for or against a change of government.[26]

Before the opening of the convention James Bowdoin invited the delegates of Boston to his house for dinner and suggested that they discuss the Constitution. Gore hastened to Bowdoin to protest. For those in favor of adoption to announce any plans for achieving ratification "would be to expose ourselves to A. [Adams] & possibly others, and inform them how they might best counteract our intentions—. . . ." Gore surmised that Adams himself had proposed the discussion so that he might determine the strength of the opposition within this group of delegates. If the Federalists were forewarned, Gore thought, they would not "be entrapt by the craft of A."[27] All the delegates from Boston attended the dinner except John Winthrop, merchant and suspected critic of the Constitution, and Governor Hancock, reportedly ill with gout. Here, fully and positively, Adams revealed his opposition. He believed that the American states were too large an area and too diverse in their interests to form a successful centralized government, and he feared that the liberties of the people would disappear when the states relinquished their sovereignty.

The Antifederalists, assuming that the tradesmen of Boston would follow Adams' leadership, called them together on the evening after Bowdoin's dinner party to organize their resistance to the proposed plan of government. The supporters of the Constitution, however, had no reason to fear the outcome of that session. They had worked so thoroughly to convince the tradesmen of the benefits of ratification and were so certain of having committed them to it that Gore could write to King: ". . . there is no doubt they will express their sentiments as highly favourable to the plan, and their great anxiety that it should be adopted—they may possibly have effect on Mr. A, if not—it will effect his E—[Excellency, i.e. Hancock] who wavers. . . ."[28] On the opening day of the convention, the *Massachusetts Centinel* carried the resolutions of the "Tradesmen and Mechanicks of Boston" approving the Constitution because it would safeguard their liberties and improve their trade and employment. They declared that in electing delegates to the convention they had voted for "such only, as would exert their utmost ability to promote the adoption of the proposed frame of government in all its parts, without any conditions, pretended amendments, or alterations whatever."[29] The Federalists could not have wished for a statement better calculated to dampen Sam Adams' fire. Adams had scarcely any following among the farmers in Massachusetts, and when the tradesmen in Boston stripped him of his usual support, he was helpless. "He is too old not to know that his dependence is more on the people than theirs on him," Gore wrote to King.[30]

In the convention the Federalist delegates with their youth, enthusiasm, energy, and purpose held conspicuous advantages. The younger men like Gore had grown to maturity after the signing of the Declaration of Independence, and they saw weaknesses in the Articles of Confederation more vividly than they remembered the centralization of the British colonial system. The leading enemies of unconditional ratification, on the other hand, were older Patriots like Sam Adams and Dr. Charles Jarvis, who had vigorously promoted independence from England and held a personal aversion to a strong central government. Although the Antifederalists included a few lawyers, security holders, and merchants, most of them were farmers, uneducated and unknown. Jeremy Belknap, minister of the Federal Church in Boston, found their speeches "clamorous, petulant, tedious, and provoking."[31] The talents of the Constitution's supporters more than balanced the numerical superiority of the Antifederalists. Not only did the Federalists add force to their arguments by their greater learning, but they spoke with persuasion and displayed a flair for skillful compromise.

As soon as the convention began its debate on the Constitution, section by section, the Antifederalists leveled their guns on the provision for biennial elections of the representatives to Congress. They argued that a one-year term would better safeguard the people's liberties and that since annual elections had always been the practice in Massachusetts, why change? Gore, like other Federalists, favored the longer term to give the representatives more independence from their constituents, but he defended it for more conciliatory reasons. In reply to General William Heath of Roxbury, who quoted from Montesquieu that the delegation of great power should be balanced by short duration, Gore, well read in the political philosophy of the eighteenth century, rose to make his first speech at the convention. Declaring himself in general agreement with Montesquieu, he denied the application of his statement to the Constitution because the governments he described neither defined nor balanced their powers. Gore argued that because senators had been given a long term of office, members of the House, who more directly represented the people, should have "a permanence in their office, to resist any operations of the Senate, which might be injurious to the people."[32]

In fighting to reserve for the states the power to lay and collect taxes, the Antifederalists compared the authority given to Congress by the Constitution with a similar power assumed by the British Parliament in taxing the American colonies. Gore declared that no comparison existed because members of Congress would be elected by all the people of the United States and could impose no burdens that they would not share with their fellow citizens; nor could senators and representatives hold additional offices that would make them independent of their constitutents. What if the United States should need large sums of money to wage war? Gore asked. At best the states provided their apportionments slowly, and if they refused they must be coerced by arms with all the horrors of civil war. To the argument of those who said the United States had no enemies, Gore countered, "Let the gentlemen consider the situation of our country; they will find we are circumscribed with enemies from Maine to Georgia."[33]

The judiciary power proposed for the new government aroused more fears among the Antifederalists that Congress would abuse its power. Wearied by petty obstructions, Gore observed to the convention that opponents of the Constitution maintained that whenever administrators would have a chance to do wrong, they would do so, that they would take away trial by jury, and, because the Constitution did not expressly provide for an indictment by a grand jury in criminal cases, every man's life would be in jeopardy. "If the gentlemen would be candid and not consider that, wherever Congress may possibly abuse power, they certainly will, there would be no difficulty in the minds of any in adopting the proposed Constitution."[34]

By the latter part of January the Federalists despaired of securing an unqualified ratification. They had failed to allay the mistrust of delegated powers, to resolve the conflict between the commercial and agrarian interests, and to end the fear that the lawyers and men of education and wealth would "get all the power and all the money into their own hands, and then they will swallow up all us little folks, like a great Leviathan. . . ."[35] Too many delegates still believed that consolidating a democracy into one government equated an attempt "to rule Hell by Prayer."[36] Searching for a harmless maneuver that would bring enough of the opposition into their camp to make a favorable majority, the Federalists conceived a clever strategem.

They secretly drew up nine amendments that Massachusetts would recommend to the future Congress for adoption after the Constitution had been accepted. Probably written by Theophilus Parsons, distinguished lawyer from Newburyport, the propositions enumerated various states' rights and personal safeguards.[37] To assure the success of the scheme the Federalists persuaded the popular Governor John Hancock, who had been conveniently ill with gout, to appear and present the amendments. Gore reported to his college classmate, George Thatcher, that for this service the Federalists agreed that Bowdoin's friends would support Hancock in the next gubernatorial election, and, if Virginia did not ratify the Constitution, Hancock would be considered "the only fair candidate for President."[38] The wily delegate from Boston found the bargain appealing, and Rufus King wrote joyfully to Henry Knox, "Hancock has committed himself in our favor and will not desert the cause."[39]

The Federalists carried the ratification through the convention with a majority of nineteen among 355 votes. The proposed amendments even won over Sam Adams, and all the delegates from Boston declared themselves in favor of the Constitution.[40] Seventy-eight per cent of the lawyers at the convention voted for ratification; the commercial group supported it by two and a half to one, and the maritime interests by more than twenty to one.[41] Several days earlier Gore had written to George Thatcher that "integrity, abilities & patriotism seem to declare for adopting the constitution—while vice & poverty, with few exceptions, make the opposition.—"[42] The "few exceptions" to Gore's censure of the unconverted included eighteen security holders; William Widgery, shipbuilder and owner; Samuel Nasson, lawyer and property holder; and Amos Singletary, proprietor of grist- and sawmills, who feared the "great Leviathan."

The ratification convention provided a favorable beginning for Gore's political career. It identified him with the men who fought hard for the

Constitution and who, after their victory, would assume the Federalist leadership in Massachusetts; and it offered a propitious circumstance where Gore could demonstrate his charm and intelligence that would make him a likely candidate for future political office.

Exuberant over their victory for the Constitution, the Federalists in Massachusetts determined to control the state election in 1788. Although they had promised to support John Hancock for governor, they had freedom to nominate their own candidate for lieutenant governor. Three men wanted the office: James Warren, who had sympathized with the distressed farmers while opposing their disorder, Benjamin Lincoln, who had led the militia against them, and Samuel Adams. Gore favored the conservative Lincoln and worked to elect him because, if Hancock became president or vice-president of the national government, Lincoln would then be acting governor and well placed to win the governorship at the next election. When the votes were counted and none of the three had won a majority, the election moved to the state legislature, and that body chose General Lincoln to be lieutenant governor. In Boston Hancock won all but ten votes for governor, proving that the Federalists stuck to the bargain they made at the ratification convention. The supporters of strong government controlled the legislature of 1788-1789 and judged its members to be "able and honest men."[43]

One of these was Christopher Gore, whom Boston elected to fill a vacancy before the General Court began its second session.[44] During this critically important sitting, the legislature would set up machinery to implement certain provisions of the Constitution pertaining to relations between the state and national governments. Gore had definite opinions on how this should be accomplished, and he eagerly took his seat in the House of Representatives.

The radical legislation that followed Shays' uprising had convinced Gore that the national government must be safely removed from popular control, and this conviction determined his action, when, at the beginning of the legislature's session, he became a member of the committee to consider the resolve of Congress that provided for the choice of electors for the President and Vice-President of the United States and for the selection of senators and congressmen to represent Massachusetts in the national government. In 1788 before the rise of political parties, the electors chose the president and vice-president according to their individual preferences. Gore's committee recommended that the electors from Massachusetts be chosen by joint ballot of both legislative houses. Samuel Nasson and William Widgery from the district of Maine and Charles Jarvis of Boston declared the plan unconstitutional because the right of election belonged to the people. Christopher Gore pointed out that the Constitution provided that the electors should be appointed in such manner as the state legislature should direct, and Theophilus Parsons added that not enough time remained before the convening of the electoral college to hold an election by the people. Jarvis contended that time would permit an election by plurality, which was preferable to election by the legislature.[45]

When neither side convinced the other, a subcommittee proposed an amicable settlement, and the General Court adopted its recommendations. It gave to the people in each district the right to vote for two candidates, and from the two candidates in each district having the greatest number of votes, the legislature would choose one elector; to represent the state at large, the General Court would appoint two more electors from the candidates submitted by the voters.[46] In establishing the electoral college, the framers of the federal Constitution had placed the choice of the president and vice-president one step beyond a popular election; in Massachusetts Gore's committee had attempted to place it yet another step beyond the people's control. Failing this, it recommended a compromise that was adopted and gave to the General Court the final judgment on the people's choice of the state's electors.

The conflict between the rural, debtor counties and the creditor seaboard flared again over the division of Massachusetts into voting districts for the state's representation in Congress. Gore's committee proposed that the state be divided into districts in such a way that without dividing the counties each district would contain one-eighth of the voters and elect one congressman. Protests came immediately from legislators from the western and northern parts of the state, areas of scant population where several counties would have to be combined to make one district. They fought in vain, however, against the populous, creditor towns to the east, whose representatives, remembering the radical proposals that came to the Massachusetts legislature in 1786 and 1787 from the western counties, stood firm in support of the proposed plan for districting, and on this issue they controlled a majority of the legislators' votes.[47]

Antifederalists maintained that the choice of representatives in each district should be limited to persons resident in that district. Gore argued that a legislature had authority to prescribe the time, place, and manner of election but not the qualifications of the candidates. The provision passed, however, and ended the political career in Massachusetts of Gore's good friend, Rufus King. After King's marriage to Mary Alsop, the daughter of a rich merchant in New York City, King spent much of his time there. Although Gore urged him to reestablish his residence in Massachusetts and King tentatively considered buying property in Cambridge, he decided to make his political career in New York.[48]

The method of electing senators to the national government produced the hottest battle of the General Court's session. The Constitution provided that the legislature of each state should choose two senators, but Gore's committee tried to reduce further the public's influence by recommending that each branch of the legislature be given a veto power over the other. The more democratic House favored a joint ballot, but the Senate clung to the privilege of a veto. In a speech to the House, Gore referred his opponents to the Constitution of Massachusetts, which declared that the legislature consisted of two branches acting on each other through a negative. He changed no votes. To break the deadlock a representative from Hampshire County moved that the House should originate the choice of two senators and send their names to the Senate for approval; if the Senate did not concur, the House would choose again for the Senate's approval, and this process would be repeated until the selection was made. The motion carried and thereby enabled the Federalists, in the election of senators to the national government, to restrain the more popular will of the House through the negative vote of the conservative Senate.[49]

The Federalists soon demonstrated the worth of their victory. Although the Senate quickly approved the proposal of the House to appoint Caleb Strong, a Federalist lawyer from Northampton, to be a United States Senator from Massachusetts, it refused to concur in the selection of Charles Jarvis as the second senator and substituted the name of John Lowell of Boston. When the House would have nothing to do with Lowell and the Senate three times refused to approve Jarvis, they briefly considered Nathan Dane, whom Gore viewed unfavorably because he had opposed the Constitution. Finally the Senate sent down the name of Tristram Dalton, a rich Federalist from Essex County, and on the second vote the House confirmed him.[50] The negative voice of the Senate had given the Federalists their margin of safety.

When the legislature adjourned early in 1789, Gore was on his way to becoming a leader among the conservatives in Massachusetts. He had wielded more influence as a member of the General Court than as a delegate to the ratifying convention, and his judgment and dependability were becoming known and appreciated. Although every election brought forth two opposing groups, one led by Hancock and the other by Bowdoin, no organized political parties had yet appeared in Massachusetts. Gore referred to his opponents as Antifederalists even though they were not always the same men who had opposed the Constitution. Quietly and out of public view he promoted the candidacy and election of men who would serve the interests of Massachusetts as he saw them, and he plotted the defeat of those who threatened or opposed them.

John Hancock was one of these. Gore scorned the Governor's repeated ruse of ill health, his great vanity, his questionable means of holding his popularity. In the summer of 1788 before the officers of the new national government had been chosen, Gore feared that Hancock might work his way into the presidency or vice-presidency of the United States. He "thinks himself equal to the first place . . . and disdains the second," Gore wrote to Theodore Sedgwick, an elector from Massachusetts. "Suppose you should give the hint to Bowdoin as Vice President—it would at least divide the vote so that Hancock cou'd not attain his views to the first chair."[51] Ten days later he reported to Sedgwick that on a visit to Portsmouth he had found "the sober part of the community were desirous that John Adams should be Vice President. . . . The other character (H) acts with such capriciousness that every man of reason and virtue is afraid of him."[52] To Gore's relief the electors from Massachusetts gave Hancock no votes for either office.

After several futile attempts, the conservatives of Massachusetts abandoned their hope of dislodging Hancock from the governorship and directed their efforts toward opposing him in the legislature. Their first conflict arose over Governor Hancock's refusal to give Lieutenant Governor Lincoln, a Federalist, the emoluments from the garrison at Castle William, which was the customary remuneration for that office. A House committee recommended that a group be appointed to inquire of the Governor whether he had commissioned anyone to be captain at the Castle, for if the vacancy were filled, the legislature would find other support for the Lieutenant Governor. Against Jarvis and Widgery, who argued that the legislature had no authority to question the conduct of the supreme magistrate, Christopher Gore maintained that the General Court had every right and indeed an obligation to inquire into the condition of the state's defenses. The House adopted the committee's report, but it failed to spur Hancock to appoint Lincoln. The Governor replied that as commander in chief of the army he was in command of Castle William, an arrangement that saved the taxpayers' money.[53]

When the legislature convened in January 1789, Gore was one of a joint committee to determine a salary for the Lieutenant Governor. In the preamble to its report the committee explained that since the Lieutenant Governor did not receive for his support the fees from Castle William that usually came to that office, it recommended that he be given a salary of £300 for one year. Dr. Jarvis at once objected to the validity of the preamble's contention that Lincoln should receive the emoluments. Gore declared that the statement was essential to explain to the taxpayers the purpose of the additional expense and to make clear to them that the Executive, who alone had power to name the captain of the Castle, had refused to appoint Lincoln, who would then have received the fees for his income. Because of the implied criticism of Hancock, the House refused to accept the preamble. When the legislature debated the amount of the Lieutenant Governor's salary, Gore argued that it should be large enough to support the position of the second ranking officer of the state. Widgery and Jarvis convinced the legislature, however, that £160 adequately paid the Lieutenant Governor for his services.[54]

Gore's first term in the state legislature ended on February 17, 1789, and he questioned the advisability of seeking another because he did not believe that the interests of the public, the Federalists, or his friends required his presence in the House. He did, however, stand for reelection, becoming a candidate because he believed that if he should win he would be in line for an "honourable advance" in his political career. His plans almost miscarried. He lost the first election but won in the second, which was held to fill three vacancies of members who had resigned.[55] Although Gore frequently lagged at the polls, his weakness in 1789 came from his adherence to nationalism, which placed him in opposition to the voting trend that gave a sweeping victory to Hancock and the supporters of state sovereignty.

Near the end of his second term in the House, Gore was the center of a controversy over whether a member of the General Court might hold a federal office and at the same time retain his seat in the legislature. In September 1789 President Washington appointed him the United States District Attorney in Massachusetts, and, although several members of the state legislature who had accepted appointments in the national government had resigned their seats, Gore saw no conflict in his simultaneously holding a state and a federal office. The legislature, hostile to a strong central government, thought differently, and Charles Jarvis moved that the House conduct an investigation. In defending Gore's position, the

Federalists asserted that nowhere did the federal Constitution forbid a man to hold office at the same time under state and nation, and they argued that the smooth performance of both governments demanded close cooperation between the two groups of officials, that vesting two offices in one man would enhance the effective administration of each. The Federalists hoped to lessen the evils of radicalism in Massachusetts by extending the arm of a conservative, national government to check the imprudences of the state legislature. The Antifederalists maintained that dual officeholding would upset the balance of power between the state and national governments and that a legislator who accepted a federal appointment would no longer stand in the same relation to his constituents as he had at the time of his election. When the issue came to a vote, the House ruled by 137 to 24 that a person could not retain his place in the legislature if he held an office under the United States government that was similar to the offices declared by the Constitution of Massachusetts to be incompatible with holding a seat in the General Court. The Jarvis group pointed its finger at Gore and declared that the position of United States district attorney for Massachusetts was similar to that of attorney general of the state.[56]

Gore, however, did not interpret the decision of the House to mean that he had been asked to leave his seat, for the question as it was phrased for the voting covered a general policy rather than a specific instance. But when the House took no further action to clarify his position, Gore submitted his resignation, and in a letter to David Cobb, Speaker of the House, he defended his right to hold an appointment under the federal government and to retain his seat in the legislature. The offices, he wrote, that would disqualify him for membership in the House were expressly named in the Constitution of Massachusetts and were only those under the jurisdiction of the state; in assuming the right to extend disqualifications by analogy, the legislature had threatened the liberty of the people and their freedom of elections.[57] Gore's resignation was a victory for the Antifederalists, whose efforts had prevented an encroachment of the national government upon the Commonwealth of Massachusetts and had destroyed forever the Federalists' dream of enlarging their power through a combination of state and federal offices held by a single individual.

III
A Man of Property

CHRISTOPHER Gore was ambitious to be a rich man, not because he enjoyed the acquisition of wealth but because he coveted its attributes of esteem, leisure, elegance, and power, and in the expanding economy of the postrevolutionary decades he found opportunities to shape a handsome fortune. War had shifted the ownership of capital from aristocratic Loyalists to less distinguished merchants and traders and to the lawyers with whom they were associated. Gore allied himself to experienced financiers with big ideas, and he operated in the congenial climate of a government trying to win the support of men of wealth.

His early financial ventures were highly speculative because in eighteenth-century America no channels existed for profitable, stable investment. Men gambled in public lands and government securities, they played risky games with bankrupt paper, and they invested in long voyages to China or shorter hauls to a blockaded coast. Their profits might be lavish or nothing, and while some prospered spectacularly, others met disaster. Gore's legal practice gave him a small working capital, which he may have enlarged, with his father-in-law's help, through buying shares in trading vessels. But Gore was intrigued by speculations of bolder and more intricate design, and through his work as a commercial lawyer he became involved with Andrew Craigie, Daniel Parker, and William Duer, all devotees of the big deal.[1]

Andrew Craigie, a Bostonian, had been Apothecary General of the continental forces during the Revolution and at the end of the war had established a medical supply house in New York. Gore's business association with Craigie began in the early 1780's when he became Craigie's legal-commercial agent in Boston.[2] Daniel Parker, a merchant who was an army contractor during the war, was a client of Gore and a partner of Craigie in speculation.[3] A larger operator than either of these, although his career was brief, was William Duer of New York. He gave distinguished service to the Patriots in the early days of the war, and in 1782 he became an army contractor in New York. The dealings of Parker and Duer were extensive; not only did they supply the army directly, but they subcontracted goods to contractors in other states and sold supplies to the French soldiers fighting in the Revolution. Gore was not a close business friend of Duer, but he was impressed by him. Duer was secretary to the

Board of Treasury and friend of Washington and Hamilton; he lived in magnificent style and entertained his friends extravagantly; he promoted his financial schemes with daring and imagination.

Gore, with little experience in speculation, had great faith in the wisdom of Craigie and Duer. "You can but judge when is the proper time to dispose of our sum," he wrote to Craigie when the two men were anticipating the sale of their securities. "All these matters I fully confide to your discretion. . . ."[4] At the end of his letters to Craigie, Gore often sent greetings to William Duer. "If you see Colo. Duer, pray tell him, that I sincerely and heartily wish him & Lady Kitty every thing that can encrease, & ensure their felicity."[5] Several months later he was even more cordial, "God bless Duer—may he possess an earldom in honor & profit,"[6] and in excitement over the speculation in public securities, Gore wrote, "God bless Duer—I wish he had a golden apostle—and if I could transmute the family of Appletons' into gold, his warrants might produce specie. . . ."[7] Gore laid the foundation of his fortune by speculating in government securities with Andrew Craigie.

A large quantity of continental bonds and certificates that had been issued to finance the Revolutionary War remained outstanding after 1783 to weaken the credit of the new nation. Some of them bore interest and all of them were depreciated. Rumor held that the government might refund this debt at some percentage of its face value, but the fact and the time were tantalizingly uncertain. Christopher Gore gambled on the government's paying its domestic debt, and as early as 1783 he held twenty-eight certificates with a total face value of $3,412.[8] By the time he was speculating heavily, Congress had adopted the dollar as the money unit of the United States, but in practice that action affected money of account rather then money of exchange. Because an equivalence between the two was necessary for the conduct of business, the dollar was reckoned at a given number of shillings. The standard varied from place to place. In New England the dollar was worth six shillings, in New York, eight shillings, and in Georgia, five. The face value of the certificates that Gore bought was listed in dollars, the medium of exchange was chiefly in pounds, and the price paid was a given number of shillings in the pound, according to the current market. In Boston, where six shillings equaled $1, $3.33 equaled £1.[9] Activity in government bonds accelerated in 1788 because the ratification of the federal Constitution increased the possibility of refunding the debt.

Gore and Craigie secretly agreed to buy government securities until they had accumulated a total face value of $100,000. In January 1788 Gore wrote to Craigie: "I cou'd purchase 20 or 30,000 finals at 4/ and 4/5—say between these sums—shall we speculate?"[10] On August 12 he informed Craigie that he had "already paid and agreed to pay nearly £3,000 and dared not risk himself in further engagements for cash at present—. . . ."[11] In early September Gore contracted with his broker for $10,000 finals at 4s.6d. to be paid in a month.[12] "Be so obliging as to let me know how many finals you have purchased on our account in N. York and what is the probability of their rise," he wrote to Craigie. "If my recollection is just we shou'd stand near 60,000 Dollars bought in this place and I am desirous of seeing our round 100,000 Dollars completely in our hands."[13] Securities totaling $61,310 in face value had cost Craigie and Gore £4,298, or about $14,309.[14] Anticipating that the value of certificates would rise sharply, he urged Craigie to buy with dispatch. On October 4, Gore reported that the joint account stood at $87,390, for which they were obligated £6,078.16s.5d. Since Gore and Craigie wished to keep their speculation a secret, they had to pay a broker to purchase their securities. This expense plus the interest on borrowed money "will amount to something considerable," Gore wrote to Craigie. He advised that they make every effort to hold their securities until they could dispose of them at six shillings in the pound. Gore assured Craigie that he could "most always" command £1,000, and at three weeks' notice he could probably raise £3,000 with the aid of the bank.[15] By October 26, 1788, the two men had topped the $100,000 goal. Gore had certificates in his possession listed at more than $90,000 for which he had paid £6,166, or $20,641.78, and Craigie had purchased securities with a face value of $11,000. Gore believed that the market would soon rise sharply, and he suggested to Craigie that they might purchase $40,000 or $50,000 more if Craigie could get the money for the investment.[16] Before the middle of November, however, government securities were so scarce in Boston that Gore doubted whether one could buy $100,000 within four months.[17]

The price of certificates did not rise as rapidly in the autumn of 1788 as Gore had anticipated. He wrote to Craigie that if they could not sell at more than five shillings within the next eight or ten weeks he would part with their securities for less, but he preferred to hold them for six shillings and "worry through the want of money."[18] He repeatedly urged Craigie to wait for higher prices. ". . . sale at a distance of two or three months might net us a handsome profit. The approach of the new government will undoubtedly give a Spring to public credit. . . ."[19] Rather than sell at a discount, Gore would suffer "embarrassment for want of cash," at least until February or March.[20] Craigie had difficulty in paying his share of the cost of the speculation, and on March 1, 1789, after some of the securities had been sold, Gore told Craigie that he "shou'd like well to command the balance of cash due for our securities . . . for I am under such acceptances that if I do not, I shall greatly suffer both in my purse and reputation."[21] By the end of March the two men were closing their joint account and discussing another speculation of fifty or a hundred thousand "on safer grounds than we ventured before."[22] They did not reveal in their correspondence the selling price of their securities, but it was probably between five and six shillings in the pound.

Although Gore and Craigie did not again speculate jointly in public funds, Gore continued to purchase for his own account. He invested his wife's legacy of $7,000 from her father's estate, and told Craigie that he "wou'd willingly turn all like property I possess into the public funds."[23] The available registers of the funded and assumed debts for Massachusetts show that he was a heavy investor. Late in 1789 the price of securities rose to seven and eight shillings in the pound. The appointments of Hamilton as Secretary of the Treasury and of Duer to the second highest position in the Treasury were partly responsible for the upward swing, for both were known to favor refunding. The expectations of the speculators soared.

Finally the great proposal came. Early in 1790 Secretary Hamilton recommended that the national government pay the domestic debt at its full value and assume, also at full value, the debts of the individual states. Hamilton's plan provided that both debts would be funded by issuing negotiable bonds to the creditors in return for their certificates of indebtedness, without determining the original owners, the total depreciation of the old securities, or the difference between the real and nominal value of money at the time the certificates had been issued. Hamilton's plan exhilarated those who had been rich enough to keep their certificates or to purchase those of less fortunate citizens who, needing money, had to part with theirs at considerably less than face value. When the bill to refund the domestic debt appeared before Congress and some members opposed it, Gore sent letters of vigorous protest to King and Ames against the shortsightedness of the perverse lawmakers.

"The creditors are numerous and important, and are so attach'd to property that we have reason to fear they would change sides rather than lose any share of the blessing . . . ," he told King on January 24, 1790.[24] In early May Gore reported that ". . . all order of men in the populous towns, are outrageous in their exclamations against Congress for delaying to fund the Continental debt, until the State debts shall be assumed." Funding the debt, he explained, would not only put more money into circulation, it would revive trade and stop complaints against the import duties. By the end of the month Gore was alarmed because many in Boston "who have heretofore been considered as rational men & men of understanding" were opposed to the funding bill because it did not discriminate between the original holders and the speculators who had bought the securities for a fraction of their face value. Gore wrote to King that if the new government were to flourish men should be bound to it by strong pecuniary ties not obvious to the public view. ". . . and let me ask you, what other chain [would be] so binding as that of involving the interests of the men of property in the prosperity of the Government. . . ."[25] The proposal of the Senate that the government should pay a "bare 4 per cent" interest on the debt was contrary to the expectations of the "real friends" of the country. ". . . the odds to Massachusetts in point of real property between this and the Secretary's report will be so great, that I think our members ought to hazard everything rather than accede to such schemes."[26]

Gore supported a public program that spectacularly enhanced his private advantage. He believed in the political benefits of allying the rich to the central government. He defended Hamilton's plan for assumption and refunding while his own investment in depreciated securities totaled thousands of dollars. He approved the subordination of the individual states to the federal government, which was implied in the proposed payment of their debts by the national authority. He saw wisdom in Hamilton's recommendation to meet part of the interest and capital payments on the national debt by taxing imports, the bulk of which came from Great Britain; Gore had important clients among British merchants and American importers, and any government policy that depended upon a high volume of imports and upon friendly relations with England could not fail to help him. In Congress Fisher Ames worked hard for Gore's point of view, which was also his own, by making frequent and repetitious speeches. Thomas Jefferson wrote that Ames's concern with speculation had not been for himself but for his friends Jonathan Mason, a merchant in Boston, and Christopher Gore.[27]

In the early summer of 1790 Gore feared with good reason that Congress might not approve Hamilton's recommendation to assume the state debts. This part of the Secretary's program created a division even among the Federalists. Massachusetts, having one of the largest state debts, had much to gain from assumption, but some conservatives like Stephen Higginson of Boston, who had been a strong supporter of the Constitution, hesitated to add $21,500,000 to the new government's debt. Gore believed that the Antifederalists wanted Massachusetts to retain its war debt "that thereby their own importance may be increas'd, & the national government embarrass'd."[28] He disdained the bargain in Congress that would trade agreement to assumption for establishment of the government's headquarters in the South. Virginia had already discharged a large part of its war debt and was unwilling, without compensation, to be taxed for the benefit of northern speculators.

Congress finally accepted Hamilton's plan both to pay the foreign and domestic debts at par and to assume most of the debts of the states, and on August 4, 1790, the funding of the continental and assumed debts was legalized in three new security issues of 3 per cent, 6 per cent, and 6 per cent deferred. By December 1791 the 6 per cents had risen 60 per cent, the 3 per cents, 85 per cent, and the deferred, 120 per cent.[29] The speculators had made a killing.

How much did Christopher Gore make? John Quincy Adams heard that Gore's speculation in public funds brought him a fortune and made him the richest lawyer in Massachusetts. The only records of Gore's ownership of securities are in the registers and journals of the funded and assumed debt for Massachusetts. Because the volumes are incomplete and because investors often failed to record their transactions in the heat of speculation, the official record gives only a suggestion of his holdings. On September 1, 1791, Gore's securities were listed at $104,986 in 3 per cents and at $30,631.86 in 6 per cents in the funded debt. This investment, with a face value of more than $135,000, represented the peak of his holdings that are listed in the loan records. He purchased the securities at anywhere from five to twelve shillings in the pound and disposed of most of them in the early months of 1792 when they were selling above par and before the panic of that year depressed their value. After the price of securities fell, he made a new purchase with a face value of more than $36,000 and sold it in 1793 when the market had recovered.[30] Undoubtedly Gore was a successful speculator, and he probably made the fortune in public funds that John Quincy Adams attributed to him.

Gore believed that the really big speculations in the United States could be financed only in Europe, and in 1788 he joined enthusiastically with Craigie, Duer, Parker, and their group to promote the sale of American land and securities to European bankers and, since they believed the war debt owed by the United States to France would be repaid with interest, to arrange a transfer of that debt to themselves. With Duer a high officer in the Treasury, the associates were optimistic about the success of their schemes. Their first need was a European agent to represent them abroad. When Brissot de Warville, a French financier and politician, arrived in the United States in 1788 with introductions from Daniel Parker, who was abroad selling public securities, he was warmly welcomed by Duer, Craigie, and Gore. Brissot had come to the United States as the result of an agreement with certain French, Swiss, and Dutch bankers to learn the amount of the domestic debt of the federal government, its market value, and the probability and time of repayment.[31] In Boston Brissot was received by Craigie, who wrote to Parker that he hoped the Frenchman would "think well of our Funds and our lands."[32] Brissot thought well of Boston, reporting that he found everywhere "in this charming town" hospitality and friendship for France.[33] Here he met Christopher Gore who became a financial associate. In October 1788 Duer and his group formed an association with Brissot and his European financiers to obtain from the Court of France a transfer of the debt "due to the crown from the United States," and to purchase as large a proportion as possible of the domestic debt of the United States to sell abroad at not less than sixty per cent of par.[34]

Christopher Gore became involved with the international speculators when he provided $10,000 of the $109,350 that the association raised to purchase securities to sell in Europe. Brissot gave him a draft on Etienne Clavière, a Swiss banker, for the amount of the investment, and on April 25, 1788, Gore wrote to Craigie: "I hope no . . . demur will attend Warville's bill—if there shou'd be my reputation and property will be greatly injured." Ten days later he learned from a banking house in London that Brissot's draft on Clavière had not been accepted because the Swiss banker was waiting until the securities should be transferred to his name before honoring the draft. In alarm Gore told Craigie that Clavière's failure to pay the draft "has caus'd me very great uneasiness."[35] Craigie tried to solve the difficulty by transferring the certificates to Clavière's name, but William Seton, cashier of the Bank of New York, which stood as security for Gore, refused to let them leave his hands until the bill was paid. Two months later Craigie told Brissot that he was closing the accounts "with Mr. Seton and Mr. Gore."[36] Gore's experience had been worrisome and unprofitable, and it showed that in 1788 he had not yet accumulated enough capital to participate in prolonged and complex international speculations.

The negotiations of Duer, Brissot, and their associates to buy up the American debt to France ended in failure. A rival American group, working for the same objective under the direction of Robert Morris, joined Duer to accomplish the transfer. They calculated abundant profits for all if only the deal could be made. In January 1790 while Brissot and Gouverneur Morris tried in Paris to negotiate with the French government, they learned that the Van Staphorsts of Amsterdam had contracted directly with the United States government to loan £3,000,000 to pay part of the debt to France. The Dutch bankers with their established prestige, unified organization, and large capital easily won out over their Franco-American competitors.[37]

The desire to buy the remainder of the debt to France stuck with Gore after Craigie and Duer had lost interest. In May 1792 he proposed to Rufus King that a company be formed to get control of the debt, which then totaled nearly $6,000,000. "If there is no political objection to the plan, I think the measures may be so adopted that no other risque need be feared, than the loss of a sum necessary to defray the expences of that person who may undertake the operation in Europe in case his endeavor shou'd be unsuccessful." Gore believed that because the internal affairs of France were "deranged" and the government lacked hard money to support its paper currency, the French would be willing to part with their demands against the United States for cash equal to the value of that credit in their own paper. Gore discussed the plan with John Coffin Jones, a merchant in Boston, and then wrote to King to learn his opinion of the proposal and whether he would be interested to join the enterprise. King endorsed Gore's letter: "ansd. that two attempts having already been made, I doubted the expediency of a third."[38] With that rebuff Gore dropped the subject.

In the postwar years claims against insolvent estates were an attractive speculation. In 1788 Duer, Craigie, and Parker, with Gore as investor and lawyer, became involved in such a venture while closing the affairs of Daniel Parker & Co., a partnership between Parker and Duer. Gore was frequently consulted. "Mr. Gore is now here," Craigie wrote to Parker who was in Europe, "and promises to write you. I shall engage him as council and shall while he is here endeavour to make a settlement of your affairs with the Creditors."[39] An important asset of the company was a claim against De la Lande and Fynje of Amsterdam, which Parker had purchased after the Dutch firm was bankrupt. De la Lande and Fynje had traded with companies in North America, especially with merchants in Boston and Philadelphia.

When Craigie was in Europe pursuing Parker's claim against De la Lande and Fynje, he discovered that the United States government also had a claim against the Dutch firm. He learned, furthermore, that De la Lande and Fynje had provided three-fourths of the capital of its London branch and had loaned to it United States securities, making the claims of Parker & Co. and the United States government particularly attractive to Duer and his associates.[40] Craigie's findings increased the complexity of Gore's participation in the case because Gore was also attorney for Samuel Rogers, proprietor of the residue of the London branch of De la Lande and Fynje after the British creditors had been paid. "I will do everything in my power to expedite a settlement of De la Lande's affairs," Gore wrote to Craigie on April 13, 1788.[41]

As Roger's attorney, Gore sent a memorial to Congress explaining his client's connection with the English branch of De la Lande and Fynje and suggesting that since few assets would remain after the English creditors had been paid, the United States government agree to a compromise of its attachment on the assets of the English branch for the debt owed to it by the parent firm in Amsterdam, which at the beginning of its bankruptcy was $43,009. A congressional committee authorized the Treasury Board to negotiate and settle with the Dutch firm for the claim which the United States government held against it, and through the influence of Duer, the Board assigned its collection to Christopher Gore.[42]

Negotiations for a settlement crawled on with ever more frustration for Gore. On November 16, 1788, he wrote to Craigie, "Can we get nothing from the De la Lande and Fynje estate, that is to say to acct. of the Claim of the United States—if I knew any means to obtain an adjustment of that demand and my proportion I cou'd afford to keep my moiety of the public securities."[43] Success depended upon attaching certain goods of American debtors of the Dutch firm and upon a favorable settlement of the assets in London and Amsterdam. Gore advised Craigie to trust no longer the promises of "these slippery men," the American debtors, but to come to terms with Daniel Babcock, the agent in London of the bankrupt firm.[44] Although Babcock admitted the claim of the United States in full, "which will be 16,000 or 20,000 $ more than probably could be otherwise recovered," Craigie wrote, the final settlement dragged on for several more years.[45]

When Gore's appointment as district attorney of Massachusetts was pending in the national government, he learned that an unknown source had told Hamilton that while Gore was pursuing the claim of the United States against De la Lande and Fynje, he was also serving as attorney for the British creditors of the Dutch firm. Gore wrote in haste to Rufus King, requesting him to show to Hamilton certain papers concerning Samuel Rogers and the assignment of the residue of the London branch that would clear him of any unethical implications. Gore told King that when the subject of the United States claim was before Congress he had "uniformily avow'd" a compromise of the attachment, and he had "particularly mention'd to Hamilton the advantage that wou'd accrue to Dan'l Parker & Co. if the purchase cou'd be effected."[46] King convinced Hamilton of the validity of Gore's position and received a grateful acknowledgment from Boston: "I am much obliged by your kind attention to the business with Colo. Hamilton. I shou'd suffer great distress if I suppos'd he had any just cause to think as he did."[47]

Gore was not associated with Duer, Craigie, and other "principal characters" in the famous Scioto land speculation. Duer said that those who held shares were "for the most part those who had much influence in the formation of the Company of the Ohio at Marietta or in the Legislature or Executive branches of the government." Craigie joined the enterprise to strengthen his connection with Duer, and he persuaded investors here and abroad to purchase land.[48] Although at the time of the Scioto land deal Gore had joined Craigie in the speculation in public securities and was promoting his friendship with Duer, no conclusive evidence points to his participation in the venture. Nor did he speculate in land in New York and Maine where Duer and Craigie were heavily and unprofitably involved.

Gore was not as large an operator as Duer and Craigie, but he was a more successful speculator than either of them. He showed his astuteness, for example, in taking no part in the big land deals that drained the resources of many of his contemporaries. He risked his capital with a more realistic appraisal of the outcome than Duer and Craigie, and he restricted himself to no more projects than he could carefully follow. Both Duer and Craigie neglected their correspondence. "I pray you to answer some of my epistles . . . ," Gore wrote to Craigie when the two were partners in speculation.[49] Duer's financial ruin stemmed in part from his failure to keep his agents informed. Reluctant to discuss a major business transaction in writing, Gore tried whenever possible to arrange a direct conversation.

In the spring of 1788 he told Craigie that if he could not leave New York for a long time, "I will with pleasure meet you at any middle place."[50] Gore promoted his interests away from the public view; Craigie, when the funding bill was before Congress, took up residence in New York in the same boardinghouse with influential senators and representatives. In March 1789 Gore told Craigie that although he would like to come to New York to see his friends, "to be at the seat of Federal Gov't at this time, wou'd, though very unjustly, subject my political character at least, to many imputations, either of seeking preferment for myself or plotting some plans which wou'd be said unworthy."[51] When Craigie chided Gore for not introducing him to his powerful friends in the new government, Gore replied: "If I had thought your interest or pleasure wou'd have been encreased, by an acquaintance with any members of the new congress, who are among my friends, I shou'd most readily have embrac'd an opportunity of recommending them to your civilities—but I did not think thus. You will therefore pardon me."[52] Gore's financial dealings could stand closer scrutiny than those of Duer and Craigie. While Craigie hid from the sheriff and Duer sat in jail for his debts, Gore grew increasingly rich.

Without credit readily available to him, Gore could not have been a speculator. He depended upon the Massachusetts Bank for capital to buy government securities and to finance other ventures, and his participation in the bank's affairs as a stockholder and a director enhanced his reputation in Boston's financial circles as a worthy, ambitious, young lawyer.

The Massachusetts Bank developed out of the need of businessmen in Boston for more credit for mercantile expansion. Their demand exceeded their supply of credit, and by pooling their resources in a bank they hoped to increase the availability and quantity of capital. The organizers of this bank were merchants and insurance underwriters, men who had money to lend and knew the promising enterprises for investment. Six Bostonians, all but one a merchant, successfully petitioned the General Court for the establishment of the Massachusetts Bank, and on July 5, 1784, it opened for business in the remodeled Manufactory House on Tremont Street, the first bank to be chartered in Massachusetts.

Its character was clear from the beginning. The legislature limited the capital to £500,000 so the operations of the bank would not become large, and it permitted only £50,000 of the capital to be held in real estate so the bank would be kept commercial. The stock sold for $500 a share, commercial paper was not discounted for less than $100, and all loans had to be paid in thirty or sixty days, provisions which excluded from the bank's service the small tradesmen, consumers, and farmers. Although its management and ownership were private, the bank was closely associated with the state of Massachusetts. It issued notes from $1 to $100 that carried the seal of the Commonwealth, it received the government's deposits, and in the granting of loans it treated the state as a favored customer; in 1787-1788 the bank's loans helped the state militia quell Shays' Rebellion. The establishment of the bank extended Boston's financial independence by providing, for the first time in the city's history, a market for commercial paper. No longer need the transactions of lending on paper be centered in London. From its earliest days the Massachusetts Bank was a prestigious institution in Boston. Its president had the right to a seat on the rostrum at Harvard commencements, and while conducting his business in the bank a customer stood with his head uncovered.[53]

Gore's relationship to Edward Payne hastened his rise at the Massachusetts Bank, for his father-in-law was one of the chief figures on State Street and one of the bank's most important directors. Payne owned eighteen shares of stock in his own right and forty shares in the name of his insurance office. He devised the bank's system of keeping accounts and shaped its internal organization, and, on two occasions when the president was absent, he presided at the stockholders' meeting. Although Gore owned only one share of stock in 1785, the board, possibly in need of legal skill, elected him a director. In 1791, a year before he withdrew from the bank, Gore bought eight more shares at $500 per share.[54] The other members of the board included distinguished Bostonians, Thomas Russell, Jonathan Mason, John Lowell, Thomas Dawes, Edward Payne, and William Phillips, the powerful, conservative president.

These men were concerned with all the details of operating a bank. Each of them, serving in rotation, took charge of the bank's affairs for one week and was known as the "sitting director." The major function of the board was lending money to business and professional men by discounting promissory notes and bills of exchange. Twice a week the directors met to consider applications for discounts. A black ball dropped in a box in a corner of the room, with no reason given, prevented a would-be borrower from getting his loan. Shortly before Gore became a director, the bank, in an effort to tighten its operations, withdrew 311 of its 511 outstanding shares of stock, thereby ridding itself of those stockholders who were primarily interested in borrowing from the bank and were slow to repay. Gore was one of a committee of three directors, with Edward Payne as chairman, who revised the bank's regulations along more conservative lines. The directors insisted that loans must be paid when due, and if they were not, the board would initiate a lawsuit within two weeks. This rigidity did not make the directors popular with some of their customers, but it made the bank a more stable and profitable enterprise than it had been in the first two years of its existence. By enforcing punctuality in the payment of loans, the directors were able at all times to keep their capital unimpaired.[55]

From 1784 until 1792 Gore made good use of the services of the Massachusetts Bank. He kept his money there, and his deposits and withdrawals were in substantial sums. Of greater value, however, was the credit he received from the bank to expand his financial operations. His discounts varied from several hundred dollars to more than $2,500 when $3,000 was the bank's limit, and they often occurred three or four times a month.[56]

Although the avowed purpose of the Massachusetts Bank was to promote the economic welfare of Boston and not to enrich a few individuals, the stockholders expected profits. Banks were among the most successful of late eighteenth-century business corporations, and the Massachusetts Bank was no exception. From 1784 to 1792, when Gore owned stock in the bank, its dividends averaged 12.35 per cent, the highest in its history, and during the last three years they were 21.75 per cent, 19 per cent, and 29.26 per cent.[57] The bank continued under its original name until 1903, when it merged with the First National Bank of Boston. In 1791, however, its position was challenged by the appearance of a national competitor.

When Congress, on the recommendation of Alexander Hamilton, established the Bank of the United States, the Massachusetts Bank, anticipating a system of interlocking interests with the national bank, authorized the purchase of 250 shares of stock, to be paid for from its own capital, and appointed Christopher Gore and Jonathan Mason to attend a meeting of the stockholders. Contrary to the expectations of the Massachusetts Bank, the stockholders of the national bank voted to open branches in the commercial cities of the country, and the Massachusetts Bank soon found itself with a competitor in Boston who lured its cashier and raided its board of directors. Gore, Russell, and Mason resigned as directors of the Massachusetts Bank when the board of the Bank of the United States appointed them directors of the Boston branch, a coveted position of prestige and power. Within a few months Gore sold his shares of stock and left the Massachusetts Bank forever; he was committed intellectually and financially to the Bank of the United States.[58]

Before the shares of the new bank were available for purchase, William Payne, Gore's brother-in-law, traveled to Philadelphia with orders from subscribers in Boston. Gore told King that "the most respectable men" in Boston had instructed Payne to buy for them, but unless there were enough stockholders east of Philadelphia to balance the influence of that city, they would not wish to purchase the stock. He suggested that the subscribers in Boston and New York participate jointly and if King thought that Massachusetts "shou'd be more deeply interested," Gore would endeavor to increase the subscription. When the books were opened in Philadelphia on July 4, 1791, for the purchase of the bank stock, the issue at $400 a share was oversubscribed within an hour. Gore purchased 200 shares, which made him a large stockholder.[59] Through control of the assignment of shares to subscribers, Secretary Hamilton was able to distribute the stock geographically to New York, Boston, Philadelphia, Baltimore, and Charleston.

Gore wished for a merger of all banks with the Bank of the United States. "Its advantages are so many, and so exclusively belonging to the corporation," he wrote to King, who was a director of the bank, "that other institutions of the like kind cannot do business to a great profit, if the national Bank be sufficient for the property and commerce of America." He believed that no banks "under State patronage shou'd exist—that they shou'd gradually decline in their profits and find their advantages in surrendering their corporate rights."[60] His vigorous statements for the centralization of banking through the control of all bank stock by the national bank stemmed from firmly held opinions.

Moneyed men should be bound to the union, he believed, and the elimination of all banks except the national one and its branches would help to achieve this end. He feared the loose, unpredictable policies that the state legislatures would impose upon the state banks and the rivalry of these banks with the conservatively operated Bank of the United States. When Gore heard that the Bank of New York was scheming with the state legislature to prevent the opening of a branch of the Bank of the United States in that city, he feared that a similar connection might be made between the General Court of Massachusetts and the Massachusetts Bank in Boston. Should the movement to establish state banks quicken, Gore reasoned, it would be difficult to stop because every state legislature would be anxious to share the prestige of Congress in having a bank under its patronage with the power to issue circulating notes.[61] The effort to centralize banking failed, and time showed that an expanding economy contained room for banks under either state or federal control.

Within a month of their election, the directors of the Boston branch held their first meeting and dispatched a letter drafted by Gore and Mason to the parent bank. They reported that their "Banking house" would be completed within a few days and they were ready for business. They urged an "immediate establishment" of the Boston branch because of the small quantity of money available in the area and the need for larger discounts than those permitted by the Massachusetts Bank. The letter argued that discounts were especially necessary because New England stockholders of the Bank of the United States were too far from Philadelphia to use the services of the parent bank and they, therefore, needed the branch bank to help them "furnish the specie proportion of their second payment" for stock in the Bank of the United States. The directors threatened that unless an office of discount were opened "very soon," the stockholders would "shift their interest" and seek to incorporate a state bank with a capital of $500,000 to $1,000,000.[62]

The Boston branch of the Bank of the United States opened in the spring of 1792 when the branches in New York, Charleston, and Baltimore began their business. The central board in Philadelphia assigned a specific capital to each bank, appointed the directors and cashier, set the limits for discounting and for the issuing of notes, required a weekly financial statement, and transferred specie from one branch to another as the need arose.[63]

Gore brought influence and experience to the Boston branch and used both in the selection of the bank's officers. Through his efforts Peter Roe Dalton, cashier of the Massachusetts Bank, was elected cashier of the new bank, but Stephen Higginson, who Gore thought would not increase the popularity or the business of the bank, received no "compliment" whatever. Gore also opposed Judge Lowell for the presidency and reported to King that Lowell's influence on the Massachusetts Bank had "occasion'd loss to the corporation, and evils of no moderate degree to the trade and business of the commonwealth."[64] Thomas Russell, Boston merchant and former director of the Massachusetts Bank, was Gore's choice for president, and he won the election. Two years later Gore resigned his directorship in the Boston branch, informing the central board that his professional duties took him away from Boston too frequently to make his service valuable to the bank.[65]

By the time he was thirty-four years of age, Christopher Gore had accumulated a fortune. Socially, professionally, and financially he stood in the front line of distinguished Bostonians. The achievement prompted John Adams to comment to his cousin, Samuel, "You and I have seen four noble families rise up in Boston,—the Crafts, Gores, Dawes, and Austins. They are as likely a nobility in our town as the Howards, Somersets, Berties in England."[66]

The possession of money permitted style and elegance. In 1789 Gore and his wife bought a large, three-story wood and brick house on the south side of Bowdoin Square in Boston's fashionable west end and staffed it with four servants. The spacious property, appraised at $20,000, included stables, wood house, and separate kitchen.[67] Highly sensitive to the appropriate accouterments, Gore searched for fine horses to pull his carriage. "If you can purchase me a pair of good horses you will really oblige me," he wrote to Rufus King in New York. "My expectations from Virginia are at an end and there are no good horses in or near this town. I shou'd prefer bays or chestnuts in colour to any other. . . ."[68]

This Boston in which Gore moved with distinction had a population of better than 18,000 inhabitants in an area that could easily be covered by foot. Excepting a few streets devoted to business, the most important of which was State Street, the town still looked quite rural with its open areas and shade trees.[69] In the early 1790's Boston prospered as never before; four to five hundred ships riding the harbor on any given day proclaimed its far-flung trade. Brissot reported in 1788 that the town's preoccupation with commerce left little time for the encouragement of the arts, except those pertaining to navigation. "But let us not blame the Bostonians," he cautioned, "they think of the useful before the beautiful. They have no brilliant monuments, but they have neat and commodious churches, they have good houses, they have superb bridges, and excellent ships. Their streets are well illuminated at night. . . ."[70]

Although an appreciation of the fine arts lagged in Boston, the enjoyment of literature flourished among the educated. Collecting a library of Greek, Latin, and English history and literature delighted Gore throughout his life. He read the volumes and pondered their ideas. He had, furthermore, esteem for writers and scholars, and as a rich man, he felt concern for their wellbeing. In reply to a request for aid from Jeremy Belknap, minister of the Federal Street Church and author of *History of New Hampshire*, Gore wrote: "That men of genius and study should be comfortably situated, and at ease to improve the world, while they indulge their own minds, is the warmest wish of my heart—to assist such characters in any degree, is the first object of my ambition." He sent Belknap a loan of £50.[71]

Like most Bostonians of 1790, Gore attended a church and contributed to its support; his distinction was in joining the most unorthodox church in town, making religion his one conspicuous departure from conservatism. Although he had been baptized in the Brattle Street Church and had attended it with his parents and although this church ranked as the wealthiest and most fashionable in Boston, Gore chose to become a member of King's Chapel, where James Freeman, a college friend, led his Episcopal congregation to repudiate the doctrine of the Trinity and to counter the Calvinist idea of human depravity with a more modern concept of man as essentially good. In the light of Gore's own achievements and aspirations, the worthlessness of man must have rankled as a false image, and like others who reflected on man's relationship to God, he found appeal in the theology of James Freeman. Gore and his wife owned the fifth pew in King's Chapel, and for twenty years Gore was a vestryman.[72]

In the same year that he bought the house on Bowdoin Square Gore also acquired fifty acres of land at Waltham, an area of well-cultivated farms ten miles from Boston, where he and his wife spent their summers. The purchase of a country estate as a part-time residence had become fashionable among Boston's merchants, physicians, and lawyers. Gore soon increased his acreage to 300, and in 1793 he built a house on the property.[73] William Bentley, minister of East Church at Salem, recorded in his diary that he had seen the "splendid seat belonging to Gore. The right wing was not completed but the whole formed a fine object."[74] "My farm at Waltham," Gore unpretentiously called his land, and on it he lavished his time, his concern, his energy, his money; as Gore Place developed and prospered it found few rivals in all of Massachusetts. Although from time to time Gore sold one town house and bought another, nothing could tempt him to part with Gore Place.

As soon as he took possession of his farm, he searched for ways to improve the soil and increase its production, and this pursuit opened to him the exciting world of agricultural experimentation. Exhausted soil, clumsy implements, few varieties of fruits and vegetables, and inferior specimens of domestic animals characterized New England's agriculture in 1790. The poverty of the farming economy drove Gore and a few other progressive landowners in 1792 to organize the Massachusetts Society for Promoting Agriculture. The trustees, of whom Gore was one until 1806, resided in Boston and came together once a month for an all-day meeting. Most of them were Federalists, and none pushed his own plow, although some like Gore ran their farms for profit.[75]

Although the founders were motivated by a desire to improve the production of their own land, they also felt an obligation as educated men to dispense information and promote experimentation for the good of all farmers in the state. Nearly every issue of the Society's *Massachusetts Agricultural Repository and Journal* invited "practical farmers" to submit pertinent information and assured them that grammatical defects would not hinder publication. The trustees offered prizes of $50 or a medal of distinction for outstanding results from new techniques, they gathered information from travelers and from correspondence with agriculturalists in England, and they subscribed to foreign and domestic publications from which they extracted information to use in their own *Journal.* The Society's efforts in its first twenty-five years, however, made little impression on the practices of agriculture in the state; to most of the yeomanry who knew anything at all about the organization its members were a set of gentleman farmers who bred cattle in their libraries.[76]

The Society's success came at a higher intellectual level. In 1801 it gave $500 to establish a professorship of natural history at Harvard, and in partnership with the University it established the Botanical Garden in Cambridge. The money to finance its work came from its members; Gore gave $800 in the form of two shares of stock in the Bank of the United States, a generous gift that showed the extent of his interest.[77] In 1793 when William Bentley drove past Gore's cultivated fields, he noted "the advantages derived from an agricultural society which had induced Gentlemen of taste to attend to the extensive experiments made to facilitate the management of the farm."[78]

The hard work of acquiring money and building a professional career compelled Gore to forgo the leisure he craved. "I am as much jaded as ever in my life," he wrote to Craigie in September 1788. ". . . the importance of my causes in court and the weight of other concerns equally important outside of court harass me beyond what is pleasant."[79] While still in his early thirties he looked toward the happy future when he could retire to the "calm retreats of mild philosophy" and to his farm at Waltham. Politics interrupted this reverie to challenge his energy and his talents.

IV

A Defender of the Faith

DURING the organization of Washington's administration, Rufus King, who had recently become a United States Senator from New York, inquired of Christopher Gore whether he would like to be United States District Attorney for Massachusetts. Gore replied that "although the appointment wou'd be gratifying—the appointment of another wou'd neither mortify, depress or disappoint me."[1] As a young, active Federalist, however, Gore deserved some consideration from the new government, and on September 24, 1789, President Washington named him District Attorney for Massachusetts.[2] During the seven years in which Gore held this office, the national unity that had developed around the new government gave way to strife and division. As resistance grew to Washington's foreign policy, Gore came forth as its vigorous defender, and in this capacity he established his kinship with the conservative faction of Massachusetts Federalists.

The French Revolution produced disturbances in the United States that aroused Gore's concern. Remembering French aid in his own country's recent struggle, he applauded the first reports from Paris that despotism had been overthrown. He lost his enthusiasm, however, when he learned of the execution of Louis XVI and of England's joining the coalition of kings to crush the revolution. The excesses of republican France repelled him, and in support of sanity and order he took the side of Great Britain. He viewed the French upheaval as a threat to Federalist positions in the national government and to the security of property. Although Americans already possessed the most essential of the reforms that the Jacobins sought—republican form of government, separation of church and state, widespread ownership of land—Gore feared that the revolt in France would precipitate a drive for extended liberties in the United States.

And indeed the cheers of many Americans for the new republic in France carried simultaneous protests against a limited democracy at home and against a government that seemed to have little concern for the welfare of its ordinary citizens. Discontented farmers, sailors, artisans, and laborers complained of the frittering away of the liberties they had fought to win in the American Revolution. Frontiersmen, attacked by Indians, called for federal protection; settlers, robbed by land speculators, resented the tolerance of corruption; and landowners, jealous of their political influence, protested the excessive power of the national government at the expense of the states. Many Americans felt the sharp injustice of the whiskey tax and of the funding and assumption of domestic and state debts. Those who disliked England hailed France: traders and manufacturers restricted by British regulations and competition, seamen impressed for service under the Union Jack, frontiersmen harassed by England's illegal occupation of the military posts on America's northwestern frontier. In the United States the French Revolution drew to its standard those who sought some means to challenge economic privilege, to claim political power for the many instead of the few, and to put the English to rout.[3]

The French declaration of war against England in February 1793 placed the United States government in a dilemma. Although all members of Washington's cabinet held that the United States should take sides with neither belligerent, they could not ignore the nation's treaties signed with France during the Revolutionary War. In exchange for loans, troops, and ships, the American states had promised to defend the French West Indies and to give French privateers and prizes the exclusive right to enter American ports, and they had agreed, also, to prohibit the enemies of France from fitting out privateers in American harbors. Jefferson thought the government was bound by the treaties; Hamilton advised that they be suspended.

Washington's solution set the country upon a neutral course. On April 22, 1793, the President announced that henceforth the United States would be friendly and impartial in all its relations with the belligerent powers, and American citizens who engaged in contraband trade would be liable to prosecution in the federal courts.[4] In an exuberant letter to Tobias Lear, the President's secretary, Christopher Gore wrote that "nothing cou'd have been more fully adapted to gratify the friends of America, than the proclamation of our revered president," who did not waver from the line of rigid justice nor become subject to the influence of the pseudo-patriots. "Would to God he cou'd be immortal."[5]

Gore applauded Boston's substantial support of the policy of neutrality. He reported to Lear that when the town's democrats and French sympathizers, led by Benjamin Austin, "most furiously inveigh'd against the impositions of Britain and the pusillanimity of the government in bearing them, their outburst was attended by no other consequence than a general hiss." The prosperous merchants hailed the proclamation with enthusiasm, and at a meeting chaired by Thomas Russell they passed a resolution that anyone who armed a vessel to cruise against France or England should be punished.[6]

To affirm neutrality was easier than to enforce it. As district attorney, Gore found his chief difficulties to be a lack of definition of what constituted a violation and the disinclination of Governor Hancock to perform his duty. In the summer of 1793 a group of Bostonians, directed, Gore believed, by the French Vice-Consul, Antoine Duplaine, fitted out the privateer *Roland*. After the vessel had chased ships in the harbor for several days and returned to its berth, Gore served warrants for the arrest of the two Americans aboard. Beyond this he had no clear course of action. In reporting the incident to Attorney General Edmund Randolph, Gore inquired whether any agreement with France authorized Frenchmen to purchase vessels and equip them as privateers in American ports. If the procedure were illegal, Gore wanted to know who should "take cognizance of such violations of the laws of neutrality." Refusing to bind their future action by hasty commitments, Washington and his cabinet moved slowly in the summer of 1793 to establish regulations of enforcement. Although they early agreed to prohibit both the French and English from fitting out privateers in ports of the United States, they carefully discussed every incident that might be a violation to determine the government's action. On August 3, after considering Gore's report on the *Roland*, they agreed to ask the governor of Massachusetts to "suppress" the privateer.[7]

Before Governor Hancock received this instruction from the federal government, Gore had informed him that the *Roland* was about to sail and asked him to stop the vessel before it left Boston harbor. Hancock then requested an opinion from James Sullivan, Attorney General of Massachusetts, who advised him to detain the sloop until he could receive an order from the President of the United States, and, furthermore, since equipping a privateer in an American port was a breach of neutrality, the French vice-consul in Boston should pledge his word that the ship would remain in the harbor until instructions arrived from Philadelphia. If the French officer refused to comply, Governor Hancock should take the ship into custody and so inform Secretary of State Jefferson. Hancock refused to heed Sullivan's advice, and the *Roland*, "arm'd, equipped, and commissioned as a privateer against the enemies of France" sailed from the harbor without hindrance. The governor, Gore reported to Lear, did not "chuse to interfere."[8] To Rufus King, Gore confided that Hancock might have followed Sullivan's advice except for the bitter opposition of that French sympathizer, Lieutenant Governor Samuel Adams.[9]

The failure to hold the *Roland* brought further displeasure to Gore because he had hoped to prove that Duplaine and Juteau, Chancellor of the French Consulate in Boston, had ordered the ship to be equipped as a privateer. Gore believed that no immunity could save them from action of the courts, and, although prosecution of members of the French diplomatic corps would create a furor, it would focus attention on the illegal operations of the French government. Hancock destroyed Gore's opportunity to publish the names of the violators of American neutrality; the governor had permitted the ship to leave, Gore believed, because "an hatred of the Union prevailed over even the love of power, or an exercise of sovereignty."[10]

While cruising in waters off the Massachusetts coast, the *Roland* took possession of the British schooner *Greyhound* with its cargo of 95,000 mackerel and brought its prize to Boston harbor. The owners of the captured ship sought recovery in court on the grounds that their vessel had been seized within the jurisdiction of the United States. When the federal deputy marshal, following the usual procedure in such a case, tried to take custody of the *Greyhound* and to arrest the Americans on board the *Roland*, a French armed guard took him prisoner, and, by order of Duplaine, the *Greyhound* was moved near a French ship of war.[11]

Washington and his cabinet learned of Duplaine's conduct through Gore's report to Tobias Lear on August 24, 1793. On the same day Stephen Higginson informed Alexander Hamilton that Gore had tried to prevent the French privateer from leaving but had received no cooperation from the customs officers and the officials of the state government. Secretary of State Jefferson directed Gore to prosecute Duplaine on whatever charge would be most likely to bring conviction, and he requested Gore to send him evidence, taken under oath, of Duplaine's part in the incident. Gore faithfully carried out these instructions to try the French vice-consul for opposing by arms the enforcement of United States law, but he accomplished nothing. Three times he brought charges against him, and three times the Boston jury of French sympathizers failed to sustain them. The President and his cabinet then considered the case and on Gore's evidence Washington expelled Duplaine from the country. He, with the notorious Genêt, was the only French officer in America who was specifically named in a decree of the French Committee of Public Safety that ordered the arrest and return of Frenchmen guilty of misbehavior in office.[12]

By early winter in 1793 the enforcement of neutrality in Massachusetts had become clear and firm. Washington and his cabinet determined that the territorial jurisdiction of the United States would extend three miles from the coastline and that the decision would apply to the prizes then being held for settlement. With this announcement the Administration answered the last of the puzzling questions that concerned the implementation of its policy. Also by the end of 1793 District Attorney Gore had become experienced in recognizing acts of violation and in bringing offenders to trial.[13]

Although Gore had only contempt for the new regime in France, he did not disdain all Frenchmen. A year after his difficulties with the *Roland*, the French statesman Talleyrand arrived in the United States to await the day when the French Convention would revoke its decree against him. Persecuted in France by Marat and Robespierre and driven from England by Pitt, he found hospitality in the United States among high-ranking Federalists. Gore entertained Talleyrand when he visited Boston, where he was "very much esteemed" and cordially welcomed. ". . . he dined with me . . . when I introduced [him] to the most respectable and liberal of our society," Gore wrote to King.[14] Talleyrand was not impressed. Although the people of Boston had an aristocratic polish, he reported, they bored him as much as they respected him.[15]

A proper man of upright character, Gore cared what important people thought of him. He was especially concerned with the impression he made upon Federalists in the upper echelons of Washington's administration who could advance his political career. On one occasion, however, when he visited Philadelphia in 1794 with his friend Joseph Russell, Jr., a Boston merchant, he flung decorum to the winds. The report came back to Boston from David Cobb, a Federalist congressman from Massachusetts, who in 1809 was lieutenant governor when Gore was governor. Cobb, a wit, wrote amusing bulletins to his friends about life in the capital of Philadelphia.

> Last Wednesday evening our friends Gore and Russell arrived here. . . . These fellows . . . have come on here only to play the devil. They are drinking in one house, frolicking in an other, and I suspect wh—g in a third. Last evening they lost their hearts with Mrs. Bingham, having yesterday dined with her husband and went from thence drunk to Mrs. Washington's drawing room and clos'd the evening at Mr. and Mrs. Morris's. God only knows when or how they got to their quarters. They are already

> engaged to dine and spend the evening twice in every twenty-four hours during their continuance here. Indeed, the whole city is in an uproar, and their conduct is such that I am fill'd with my fear that they will disgrace their families and their country. They certainly go to bed drunk, if they git up sober. Do tell their good families, that my example and precepts shall momently be impressed upon their husbands, so that if it is possible they may once more return to them in safety and honor.[16]

Gore's major concern in England's war against France was the state of Massachusetts' commercial prosperity. In December 1793 he wrote to King that "there never was a time when our harbors were so crowded with vessels as at the present day, and never a time when we had half so many out on charter."[17] As the war progressed reports came to Boston of pirates loose on the Atlantic, seamen impressed, and cargoes seized. The Algerians preyed upon American ships because the British government, needing aid from the Portuguese against the French, had released Portugal from a truce with Algiers that held the pirates in check. In November 1793 the British announced that all shipping to and from French colonies would be subject to their seizure, an order that struck at the heavy American trade with the French West Indies. As the British confiscated American ships and cargoes while enforcing their wartime decrees to cripple the French economy, Gore reported to King in the spring of 1794 that Boston's merchants showed "great moderation and temper." Knowing that their losses would be much increased if the United States went to war against England, they were "unremitted in their efforts to convince others of the fatal consequences of such a step."[18]

Gore directed his political efforts toward reviving the commercial prosperity of Massachusetts. Reporting to King that the marauding Algerians affected the economy of Boston adversely, he urged Congress to make a bold offensive against the pirates. Against England, however, he recommended a more conciliatory approach. Gore sent to King a proposal from the Boston merchants that the United States should present a claim to the British government that would show not only the amount of the losses and the circumstances under which they were incurred but would make clear the scrupulous attention of the merchants to the obligations of neutrality. Gore believed this action would produce an indemnity. "The whole force of those British merchants, who trade to this country, I am well convinc'd, cou'd easily be brought to act in concert with the American Minister in support of such a claim."[19]

Gore's plan to deal with Britain's interference in American commerce was in sharp contrast to the proposal for retaliation that James Madison presented to Congress in January 1794. These resolutions stemmed from a report that Thomas Jefferson had submitted to the House of Representatives in which he showed that Great Britain was the only country with whom the United States had extensive trade but no commercial agreement. Madison proposed to win better treatment from Britain by placing higher duties and additional tonnage on the goods and vessels of all nations with whom the United States had been unable to negotiate a commercial treaty, and he directed his resolutions particularly to New England in the hope that Britain's seizure of American ships would bring the trading interests of the northeast into the Republican camp.[20]

Gore was aware of the threat, and the welfare of the merchants and shippers became a dominating concern to him lest their losses drive them to Madison's side before the government would come to their aid with a more moderate plan of dealing with England. Gore told King that while most Bostonians realized that strong measures against England would aggravate their situation, "such a temper cannot be expected to continue for any length of time in those, who from the most elevated state of affluence, are thrown into poverty and bankruptcy." Gore had little faith in the merchants of Salem, who had not "that spirit of forebearance, which operates on those of this place."[21]

Even in Federalist Boston dissension ran strong. Jarvis and Austin, local leaders of Republicanism, called a town meeting ostensibly to learn the opinion of the people about retaliation toward England, but their true purpose, Gore believed, was to play upon the hatred against England, to overrule the mercantile interests, and send recommendations to their congressmen to support Madison's resolutions. Although Gore reported to King that the meeting "ended in a compleat overthrow of those who advocated the interference of the town," Jarvis and Austin almost succeeded. The Federalists managed to hold their own through the arguments and parliamentary skill of Harrison Gray Otis and John Coffin Jones, and on the second day they were able to carry a motion for adjournment before a resolution supporting Madison had come to a vote. Aware that reports of Boston's anti-British demonstration would soon reach Philadelphia, the Federalists hastily collected a vote of confidence in England's good faith and sent it to congressmen Ames and Goodhue, who fiercely opposed James Madison.[22]

As British seizures of American ships and seamen in the West Indies continued, Gore proposed to King in March 1794 that a special envoy be sent to England to settle the commercial difficulties before the two countries came to armed conflict. He believed that a special deputation would be the most effective, but if the government thought this an "unnecessary expense," Thomas Pinckney, the American Minister to Great Britain, could present the case "in a manner the most flattering to British pride, most soothing to their wounded spirits, at the same time, most alarming to their apprehensions." Gore firmly believed that if the United States presented a claim for damage to its commerce, the British government would not "hesitate to afford a satisfactory reply to so just a demand."[23] Gore accurately appraised England's sentiments. The British government could not risk war with the United States while fighting France, and under the guidance of William Pitt and Lord Grenville the rigid policy of no compromise with the United States shifted in 1794 to one of conciliation. Like their American counterparts, English merchants and traders urged concession.[24]

When President Washington on April 16 nominated John Jay, Chief Justice of the Supreme Court, to be an envoy to England, Gore was jubilant, not only because he believed that negotiations with England would restore the commerce of Massachusetts and keep the merchants loyal to the Federalist party, but because he had great esteem for the Chief Justice. Four years earlier when Jay had visited Boston, Gore wrote to King that Jay had so delighted the people there and they had considered his manners "so perfect as to believe that New York stole him from New England."[25] Most Republicans assailed Jay's mission to England as a sharp maneuver of the Federalists who, frightened over the support that the middle states and New England had given to Madison's resolutions in the House, were determined that commercial relations should be put under the control of the executive and Senate by means of a special mission and a treaty.[26]

Even before the controversy over Jay's Treaty, Federalist opponents, inspired by the French Jacobins, organized associations called Democratic or Republican Societies. Although these clubs did not develop into the Republican party nor ally themselves with the anti-Administration faction of the capital, they effectively advanced the growth of liberal, anti-English, Republican attitudes. By publicizing their opinions in newspapers, by discussing and clarifying issues among ordinary men who had shown little interest in government, by proposing candidates for office, and by bringing out voters who previously had not voted, these pressure groups aroused a popular interest and participation in government that had not existed before. The leading members of the societies were craftsmen, laborers, farmers, seamen, civil servants, small merchants, and some intellectuals; more than a third of the membership belonged to the "lower order of men." They were quick to draw distinctions between themselves and the aristocratic Federalists, and they found little in the existing state of affairs to claim their allegiance. The societies showed their greatest activity in the middle and southern states. Excepting the frontier organizations in Maine and Vermont, the only club of importance in New England was the Constitution Society organized in 1793 in Boston.[27]

The Boston club so alarmed Gore that it drove him to public opposition. Directed by his old enemies Dr. Charles Jarvis and Benjamin Austin, the society had as its president Perez Morton, a prominent lawyer. Gore scorned them all.[28] In his concern for national stability and unity he saw only evil in the counterattack of the Democratic Societies. Not only did he consider the opposition of social and economic inferiors to be improper, but he feared that in mobilizing the dissenting elements of the population the societies threatened, through the peaceful elective process, to replace the Federalists with a new set of rulers. He observed that on every public issue the associations presented a contrary point of view. Gore felt the bite of their popular disapproval when he tried to enforce neutrality in Boston against the French sympathizers. He wrote to Lear in September 1794, "We have here madcaps enough to set the world in confusion. Their disposition is strong and it requires all the forces of good men to keep even Massachusetts in tolerable order."[29] In the same month over the signature of "Manlius" Gore wrote eight articles for Boston's *Columbian Centinel* in which he denounced the Democratic Societies and all Americans of anti-British, anti-Federalist persuasion.[30]

Reprinted in pamphlet form and widely circulated, Gore's articles gave satisfaction to many Federalists. Fisher Ames wrote from Philadelphia that he had the "pleasure to see an edition of Manlius piled up in Fenno's office for circulation among the heathen in the back parts of this State. . . ."[31] As a statement of Gore's political belief, the series shows a contraction of his view from its ebullient nationalism during the ratification of the Constitution to an anxious provincialism in 1794.

"Manlius" first struck at the patriotism of the Democratic Societies. While urging the United States to fight England, these democrats plotted to keep the country defenseless. They opposed Washington's declaration of neutrality, they unlawfully induced citizens to equip privateers for the

French government, and they urged the French Minister Genêt to appeal for aid directly to the people in defiance of the President's authority. Gore believed that disloyalty flourished because the clubs were a mixture of a few unworthy "sons of America" and the "scum of Europe," and he disdained particularly the immigrant Irish.

The protection of Boston's commerce concerned "Manlius" most of all and led him to denounce any belligerence toward England. In trying to humble Great Britain, Madison's resolutions would destroy New England's shipping, and in cutting off the trade with Britain, they would end the import revenues on which the United States government depended for its credit. The societies opposed Jay's mission to England, Gore believed, because they wanted war, and while they would not attempt a pacific settlement with one of the most powerful nations in the world, they would "crouch to supplicate a peace with the barbarians of Algiers." Although Theodore Sedgwick of Massachusetts had introduced the bill for the embargo of 1794 in the House of Representatives and it had passed with the support of the Federalists, Gore had never approved it. Now he blamed the societies for the harm the embargo had brought to the economy of Massachusetts. While idle seamen disturbed the peace of coastal towns, 20,000 tons of shipping decayed at Boston's wharves, and scores of workers in industries related to navigation lost their jobs.

Gore's concern for New England led him to attack the South. He believed that Virginia had pressed for Madison's resolutions out of jealousy for Massachusetts' prosperous commerce. He wrote that the people of the South were willing to risk war in order to withhold the payment of their just debts to English creditors. The citizens of New England, whether rich or poor, had equal representation in Congress, but the South sent twelve representatives for a slave population that had no vote. Fisher Ames shared Gore's view of Yankee superiority. He wrote to Gore, "I take more and more pride in the comparison of our merchants and people with those of the South. You praise the former very justly for their coolness and steadiness."[32]

The charges of "Manlius" in the Boston *Centinel* drew a counterattack in the rival *Independent Chronicle,* which in Gore's opinion was a sheet of impudence and falsehood. A "Consistent Republican" declared that Madison had drafted his resolutions not to destroy American commerce but to show England the value of its trade with the United States, and he contrasted the wide approval for the embargo of 1794 with the meager opposition of a few Anglophiles. What success would Jay have in his negotiation in London, the Republican wanted to know, when "Manlius" publicly declared "that the United States gains more than she loses by Britain," and that "no nation treats us so well as Britain?" Although "Manlius" calls himself a federalist, he cannot bring unity by calling Virginia a "set of bankrupts and slave-drivers." Reminding "Manlius" that Madison had been one of the chief authors and supporters of the Constitution, he asked whether the charge of seeking large benefits for particular friends should go to Ames or Madison. When the subscription for the federal bank was opened in Philadelphia, he asked, were the "numerous Coaches, Phaetons, and Horses . . . from Virginia or Boston?" The Republican cautioned that "Manlius" with his immense property in public funds should be quiet, for that Federalist's particular attachment to the British was explained by his investment in public securities and in stock of the United States Bank, investments that depended for their profits upon the tariff revenues arising from imports from England.[33]

If the treaty that Jay secured in his negotiations with the British was a disappointment to Gore, who had put so much faith in England's reasonableness, he never admitted it. Although many northern Federalists had misgivings and even Washington was dismayed when he read the text, Gore unequivocally defended every provision. In the final agreement between Jay and Lord Grenville, England promised to evacuate the military posts on America's northwestern frontier, to arbitrate the debt, seizure, and boundary disputes, and to permit the United States to trade with the colonies of the East Indies and, under certain conditions, with those of the West Indies; England refused to give compensation for the slaves taken during the Revolution, to end the impressment of American seamen, or to accept the American interpretation of the rights of neutral commerce. In June 1795 before publication of the contents had produced a furor of controversy throughout the country, the Senate, pressured by Hamilton and supported by Washington's name, ratified the treaty. Most of the southern members voted against it, but only two senators from New England failed to give their approval.[34] Gore hailed Jay's work with enthusiasm because he believed it would avert a catastrophic war against England and because it would bring distinct advantages to the commercial interests of Massachusetts.

To his despair he heard among Bostonians a swelling protest against the treaty's fair and reasonable terms. On July 10, 1795, in Faneuil Hall Dr. Charles Jarvis presided over a meeting of 1,500 people, all of whom voted their disapproval of the treaty. Not only did they oppose its specific arrangements as being too favorable to Britain, but they believed the treaty would offend republican France and ally the United States to class-conscious England. Gore reported to King that Governor Sam Adams, led on by Boston's mob, was "one of the loudest bawlers against the treaty and the boldest in proposing schemes of opposition to the federal government."[35] The Federalists, aware that the opponents of Jay's Treaty challenged their economic and political leadership, campaigned to enlighten the uninformed, convince the wavering, and rally the defectors. In recalling this period some months later Gore wrote to Sedgwick: "There was in . . . July three more gloomy weeks than I have ever known in our political hemisphere."[36] Jay's supporters in Massachusetts covered the state with their arguments, enlisted the help of the clergy, prevented hostile town meetings, solicited resolutions from dependable local organizations, and everywhere proclaimed that the treaty was better than war.

At the height of the campaign Gore wrote a series of four articles for the *Centinel* to prove to his fellow Bostonians that Jay's Treaty would be neither injurious to their commerce nor "derogatory to their national honor and independence."[37]

The maritime provisions were his chief concern. Gore publicly announced that England, in admitting the United States to trade in Europe on the most-favored-nation basis and in offering commendable terms for trade with its Asiatic and North American colonies, was more generous to the United States than any other nation. In return for these advantages the treaty understandably required the United States to give the most-favored-nation treatment to Britain. The unrealistic critics of this provision, Gore declared, could never induce the British to bind themselves to give the United States the same terms that they gave other nations yet leave the Americans free to impose discriminatory measures against them.

When Jay departed for London he carried an instruction to obtain permission for American ships to trade with the British West Indies, which to American merchants were the most valuable part of the British Empire. Jay did secure this privilege for ships of limited size, but the Senate rejected it because the British would permit American ships to bring Caribbean goods only to the United States. The provision was designed to prevent the Americans' capturing from the British merchant marine its profitable carrying trade in tropical produce. To the American demand for freedom to reexport, Gore answered that the right of a parent country to exclude foreigners from a direct trade with the mother country was not only universally acknowledged but had been expressly recognized by the United States in its trade with the Netherlands and with France.

When Britain granted Jay's request for American ships to enter its territory in the East Indies, it required the payment of a tonnage duty, which Gore declared was no higher than the duty paid by British vessels in American ports. He assured his countrymen that in spite of the tax, they could purchase East Indian goods from 30 to 50 per cent more cheaply than in European markets, and he noted that although the Netherlands had imposed restrictions on American ships that entered the Dutch East Indies, the United States had enjoyed a lucrative trade.

Gore denied the charge that Jay's Treaty permitted England to direct the commerce of the United States as though the nation were a colony, for American trade could go without restriction to any country or people. He gave little concern to the impressment of American seamen, and he refused to condemn Britain's unwillingness to accept the United States' liberal interpretation of the rights of neutral commerce. How could anyone expect that England, in the midst of a war against France, would agree to revise its maritime law? Although the treaty preserved Britain's protective system, it did not sanction any new restrictions. No American had been more exasperated than Gore by Britain's illegal seizures of American vessels in the West Indies, but he had confidently maintained that England could be induced to make adequate settlement for the losses. Jay's Treaty vindicated his position. Article VII provided that American claims would be arbitrated by an Anglo-American commission, to which Gore was later appointed. The British promised that henceforth all goods not generally contraband would no longer be confiscated but instead would be preempted with an adequate profit for cargoes and an allowance for freight. By moderating Anglo-American conflicts, the treaty in Gore's opinion would enable both countries to develop policies of mutual benefit.

The upper echelons of the Federalist party appreciated Gore's defense. George Cabot wrote to Rufus King that "the explanation given by Gore in the newspaper and those circulated in private conversation had so well aided the investigation of individuals [in Massachusetts], that the subject is pretty well understood and its friends increased in a corresponding ratio."[38] A "Constitutionalist" writing in the *Independent Chronicle* called Gore a sophist, but to Ames and Cabot and King he was a clear-headed realist who saw that "the elixer of national credit" depended upon trade and friendship with Great Britain, which war or even commercial hostility would destroy.[39]

Early in August Gore wrote to King that "the many sober, but unreflecting, men who first joined with the opponents were endeavoring to return to their old friends: they had been ensnared; they saw it, but many had not magnanimity enough to declare their conviction, without some good apology." If President Washington would quickly sign the Senate's ratification of the treaty, these people would gladly return to the Federalist fold. A week later Gore wrote again to King urging more strongly than before that the President be prevailed upon to sign the treaty immediately.[40] The Federalists clung desperately to the prestige of the great Washington to bring them victory, and they were not disappointed. On August 14, 1795, the President put his signature to Jay's Treaty. Although Washington usually stood above partisan strife, the agreement with England brought him under serious attack for the first time. Nor was opposition to the treaty confined to the American side of the Atlantic. Although in the London newspapers the signing of the agreement passed with little notice, in the House of Commons the Pitt ministry was forced to defend itself against charges of pro-Americanism.[41]

Five years after Jay's Treaty had been in force, the commercial prosperity of the United States proved the soundness of Gore's defense. Between 1795 and 1800 the value of all American exports to the British Empire rose by 300 per cent, and during the same years the United States purchased more goods from England than did all of Europe combined. Without Jay's Treaty to lessen the conflicts, this prosperity of American commerce would have been impossible. Although the Senate threw out the treaty's provision for trade with the British West Indies, during the Anglo-French war annual proclamations of colonial governors permitted American ships to carry provisions to most of Britain's Caribbean islands.[42] In setting up joint commissions to settle international disputes, the agreement with England inaugurated the modern process of arbitration and began a new development in international relations. How appropriate that Christopher Gore should represent the United States government on the Anglo-American claims commission established under Article VII of the treaty.

V
A Diplomat in London

WHILE Gore upheld the neutrality of the United States and defended the foreign policy of the Washington administration, he looked about for a more responsible and prestigious political appointment. To King in Philadelphia he wrote that although his "task" as district attorney for Massachusetts had been a humble one and had precluded him from more conspicuous offices in the state, he flattered himself "that a centinel though guarding only a small port wou'd be entitled to some consideration if he performed his duty with fidelity."[1] Gore sought a diplomatic appointment, and in spite of frustrations and contrary proposals he resolutely held to his course.

After Washington's selection of James Monroe as Minister to France, Gore wrote to King, "It seems to declare to me in most absolute terms, that under the present administration all public employment shall be refused to your friend, C. Gore."[2] The next year, however, offered more prospects: Edmund Randolph resigned as Secretary of State, Attorney General William Bradford died, and nominations would soon be made for commissioners to England under the seventh article of Jay's Treaty. Henry Knox, Federalist from Boston and Secretary of War, in suggesting men to fill the cabinet vacancies, told Washington that Christopher Gore was an excellent copy of Edward Rutledge, whom he had described, "in point of manners, information, head and heart," as everything that could be wished. "His [Gore's] fortune is handsome, and he has no family but his wife. Perhaps he would make a proper alloy, General."[3]

King knew that the office of attorney general had little appeal for Gore but that appointment to the Anglo-American Board created by Jay's Treaty would gratify his wishes, and the sensations he would "suffer at being neglected, wou'd be painful."[4] Both Stephen Higginson and George Cabot pressed for Gore's deserved promotion, and Henry Knox, writing another letter to his close friend President Washington, described Gore's abilities as respectable, his fortune handsome, his manners engaging, and his integrity unquestionable.[5] On March 31, 1796, Gore won his case. Washington appointed him a commissioner under Article VII of the Treaty of Amity, Commerce, and Navigation between Great Britain and the United States, with an annual salary of $6,667.50. So highly did the

Administration regard the London Commission that at one time Washington had considered naming to it Alexander Hamilton.[6]

During the next eight years Gore lived in London and represented his government on the five-man, Anglo-American board that determined the validity of the American claims against the British for the capture of ships and cargoes and of the British claims against the United States for losses of goods and vessels through American violations of neutrality. To Gore the mission offered a pleasantly challenging occupation: he would support the claims of American merchants and shipowners, whose interests he had long championed, against a foreign government whose reliability and integrity he not only respected but had vigorously defended. When he learned that his dearest friend, Rufus King, was the newly appointed Minister to Great Britain, his good fortune seemed rich indeed. He quickly wrote to King, "As circumstances prevent our living near each other in our own country, I rejoice exceedingly that we are destined to be neighbors in a foreign land."[7]

Federalists generally approved Gore's appointment as a reward for ability and effort. In a letter to William Pinkney, the other American appointed to the Commission, Henry Knox wrote that the selection of Christopher Gore had given entire satisfaction to the interested groups in Massachusetts "as well as to the public who had any knowledge of his character." Few persons, Knox continued, had contributed more than Gore to explain the government's policies in a safe and forcible manner and to harmonize the public mind. "The amiableness of his manners, the purity of his morals, and his political conduct, render him highly beloved by his acquaintances and cause him to be esteemed as an ornament to his country."[8]

Although William Pinkney of Maryland was an able lawyer who would bring distinction to the Commission, the Federalists found less to admire in his politics. Chief Justice Marshall had said that Pinkney was the greatest man he had ever seen in a court, that he could be unmerciful in debate and eloquent as an advocate.[9] At the Maryland ratification convention, however, Pinkney had voted against the federal Constitution, and later as an avowed Republican, he held appointments in the administrations of Jefferson and Madison.

In the spring of 1796 when Gore prepared for his departure to London, the Federalists rode high in Massachusetts. Even Madison conceded as much in a letter to Jefferson: "Such have been the influence and exertions of Aristocracy, Anglicanism, and Mercantilism, in that quarter, that

Republicanism is perfectly overbalanced, even in the town of Boston."[10] Death had finally removed Hancock from the governorship, and although Sam Adams succeeded him the time was rapidly approaching when purely personal leadership in the politics of the state would give way to direction by men representing national parties and programs. Gore impatiently awaited the demise of Adams. On a day officially set aside in Massachusetts for fasting and prayer, Gore wrote that it would be a day of real joy and thanksgiving to him if he were assured that Sam Adams would never have an opportunity to appoint another. "After beseeching the Almighty to prosper our husbandry, and our fisheries . . . I will most devoutly pray, that his Servant Samuel may be relieved from the burthens of government. . . ."[11] Despite his contempt for Adams, Gore thought well of the rest of this state government. He advised Theodore Sedgwick at Philadelphia to dismiss his fear respecting Massachusetts, "for you may be confident there never was a time, when the general government was so much and so generally admired as now, and its administration so universally and sincerely approved."[12] Adams retired from office in the spring of 1797, and at the next gubernatorial election the Federalist candidate, Increase Sumner, carried every county but the Republican stronghold of Middlesex.

Having settled their affairs for a probable absence of three years, Christopher and Rebecca Gore sailed from Boston in May 1796 aboard the *Minerva*. After a voyage of almost six weeks they arrived at Dover, and on the following day they reached London, where they established their residence at No. 1 Great Cumberland Place across the street from Hyde Park in a fashionable part of the city.

In London Gore and Pinkney learned that their English counterparts on the Commission were John Nicholl and Nicholas Anstey, well-known experts in maritime law. The fifth member, chosen by lot from among the four English and American nominations, was the American painter, John Trumbull, who had been Gore's college classmate and Jay's secretary during the treaty negotiations with Lord Grenville. Although Trumbull had no legal training and little business experience, the commissioners thought him a fair-minded umpire. Through the efforts of Gore and Stephen Higginson, the United States appointed Samuel Cabot of Boston to be its assessor on the Commission. He with England's Alexander Glennie determined the value of each claimant's loss and compensation. Both men were merchants, and Gore believed that since Cabot had participated in the West Indian trade he would well represent and protect the commercial interests of Massachusetts.[13]

The British government received Gore with even a spark of warmth. Lord Grenville, the Foreign Secretary, wrote to John Jay that Gore seemed a sensible and moderate man, and that he, Grenville, would find pleasure in facilitating the "public objects of his mission" and in showing him "any private attention and civility that may be in my power."[14] Benjamin West, a prominent American artist in London and a favorite of George III, told Rufus King that England was moving toward friendship with America and that King George had spoken "in a very pleasing manner of Mr. Gore." Both Grenville and Pitt, deeply involved in England's war against France and impressed by the rapidly advancing economy in the United States, saw wisdom in developing better relations between the two countries. Their conciliatory attitude guided their choice of England's members for the Commission; Grenville wrote to Jay that both Nicholl and Anstey were known to some extent in the United States, "and I trust the appointment has proved the spirit in which it was made."[15]

Before the Commission began its deliberations in its office at No. 5 Gray's Inn Square on October 10, 1796, Gore heard discouraging predictions from Americans in London that the British would construe the seventh article of Jay's Treaty to preclude all jurisdiction of causes that could be settled by English courts, and that the United States would encounter delay, condescension, and the practice of any device to prevent a decision on its cases. Gore remained hopeful. He believed that the presence of John Nicholl, who had often represented American claimants in British courts, ensured a more favorable climate; ". . . there is good reason to hope from his general character for integrity, candor & soundness of intellect, that he may not be unfavorable to a true & liberal exposition of the rights of neutral nations—"[16]

Article VII of Jay's Treaty provided that when American claimants could not obtain in English courts adequate compensation for their losses, England would make full and complete payment if the five commissioners received the claims within eighteen months after taking their oaths and approved them. To all English claimants who could not obtain compensation under the terms of Jefferson's letter of September 5, 1793, the United States would pay the sums determined by the Board. The awards of the commissioners, or any three of them, would be final and conclusive, "both as to the Justice of the Claim and the amount of the Sum to be paid to the Claimant."[17]

The United States admitted that British subjects had suffered losses through the capture of ships and cargoes within its jurisdiction and through seizure by vessels originally armed in its ports, and the government agreed that restitution should be made. Many of England's claims against the United States arose from unlawful seizures by cruisers fitted out in American ports by French diplomatic officers and their sympathizers. French Minister Genêt refused to return the captured vessels, even when he had taken them within the territorial limits of the United States. In a letter to Secretary of State Jefferson on September 14, 1794, he had boasted that privateers fitted out in the United States had seized fifty vessels flying the Union Jack, and George Hammond, British Minister to the United States, informed Grenville that from the outbreak of hostilities between France and England to August 1, 1794, seventy-five British vessels had been brought into American ports and of these, forty-six had been captured by ships that had been armed and equipped in the United States.[18]

Although at the beginning of Genêt's high-handed conduct the American government had neither statutes nor precedents on neutrality, Washington's Proclamation of April 22, 1793, set the general policy, and Jefferson's letter to Hammond on September 5, 1793, developed it into specific responsibilities. This letter, which Jay and Grenville incorporated into their treaty, promised that the United States would: 1. restore vessels captured within its jurisdiction (the three-mile limit), 2. restore vessels captured on the high seas and brought to American ports by cruisers that had been armed there, if such vessels were captured and brought in after June 5, 1793, and 3. pay compensation in cases in which the government had not used all its means to fulfill its two obligations. Jefferson's letter to the British Minister presented an advanced, liberal interpretation of the obligations of a neutral government, and Grenville, to balance the claims of American merchants against the British government, had shrewdly included it in the treaty.[19]

The Board under Article VII granted awards to only nine English claimants against the United States. The first obligation of American neutrality, to restore vessels captured within the three-mile limit, presented no problems of interpretation, but the second, to restore vessels captured on the high seas and brought into American ports by cruisers that had been armed there, provoked controversy. The British claimants contended that if their ships had been captured by French vessels fitted out in the United States, regardless of place of seizure or efforts of the United States to prevent such arming, they should be entitled to compensation. In its decision on the *Jamaica,* which Gore presented, the Board accepted the interpretation of the American commissioners: while holding Jefferson's letter to Hammond to be the test of its responsibility, the United States could not admit that a claimant should be entitled to compensation merely because the cruiser that captured his vessel had been armed in an American port; the claimant must also prove that the United States had connived at such arming or had failed to use all means to prevent it. Since the *Jamaica* had not been brought within American territory and since the owners of the ship could give no evidence of United States forebearance, the Board ruled that the claim merited no compensation. In the eight years of the Board's deliberations only three English claimants won awards on grounds of United States' failure to perform the two obligations set forth in Jefferson's letter.[20]

American claims against the British government were not only more numerous but far more complex than England's against the United States. The first of the "humiliating incidents" of disagreement between the English and American commissioners threatened to end their deliberations when they had only begun. The British maintained that if the High Court of Appeals, the last resort of judicial redress in England, had refused compensation to an American claimant, the Board had no jurisdiction to examine, review, or reverse the decision. Gore, in his opinion on the *Betsey*, declared that "power to decide whether a claim preferred to this board is within its jurisdiction, appears to me inherent in its very constitution, and indispensably necessary to the discharge of any of its duties." Although he and Pinkney agreed with their English counterparts that the Court's decision should stand, they argued that it should not be the final judgment, that the Board should rectify through compensation any injustice to the claimant. Both sides postponed further discussion while their governments searched for a settlement. On the advice of Lord Grenville, Rufus King discussed the Commission's deadlock with Lord Chancellor Loughborough, who worked out a compromise that appeased the British and upheld the interpretation of the Americans. The Commission, the Lord Chancellor advised, had power to examine cases on which the High Court of Appeals had made decisions and it could, furthermore, give redress, not by reversing decrees already made but by ascertaining the damage sustained by the claimant and awarding compensation. The Board resumed its meetings and eventually allowed £6,700 to the owners of the *Betsey*.[21] "One difficulty is at an end," Trumbull wrote to Oliver Wolcott, "but new ones like young Hydras are daily multiplied around us."[22]

In the summer of 1797 another conflict of Anglo-American interests brought forth a debate among the commissioners of vital concern to American merchants and shipowners. At stake was the legality of Britain's Order in Council of April 1795, which directed British privateers and warships to stop all vessels carrying flour, meal, or corn to France or any territory occupied by French armies, and to send the ships to an English port for the sale of the products to His Majesty's government. The ships would then be released and the owners paid the invoice price of the cargo plus a ten per cent mercantile profit and allowance for freight charges. The case that occasioned the Board's great debate was the ship *Neptune*, which was seized while carrying rice and other foodstuffs from Charleston to Bordeaux. The claimant, dissatisfied with the compensation allowed in the British courts, appealed to the Commission for an adjustment, estimating his loss to be the difference between the allowance granted by the English court and the price he would have received at Bordeaux.[23]

Nicholl and Anstey defended the Order of April 1795 by arguing that when their government issued its decree the favorable prospect of reducing France by famine justified the ruling that all provisions bound for ports of the enemy were contraband. Their second argument declared the Order of April 1795 to have been necessary because Great Britain at that time was threatened with a scarcity of food.

Trumbull, Pinkney, and Gore destroyed the British defense. Maintaining that France was self-sustaining and not dependent upon imported food, Trumbull challenged England's hope of defeating the enemy by famine and concluded that the capture of provisions bound for French ports not under blockade could not be justified.[24] To England's argument that the Order of April 1795 had been issued because of the scarcity of provisions, Pinkney replied that the maintenance of England's food supply had not necessitated the seizure of neutral ships. If the situation had been so desperate, England should have offered better prices than France, and he reminded the British commissioners that sometime after the Order of 1795 had been in force, England had granted a bounty for the importation of scarce articles that attracted so many neutrals with the desired provisions that the market became overstocked; this inducement, Pinkney counseled, should have been offered at an earlier time.[25] Gore argued that since the *Neptune* was illegally captured, the claimant was justified in demanding the price at which he would have sold the cargo at its intended destination, where it undoubtedly would have arrived but for its seizure by the British.[26]

In June 1797 the British accepted the American position, and the Commission ruled that the Order of 1795 was not a legitimate exercise of belligerent rights and that the owner of the *Neptune* should receive the net value of his cargo at the time it would probably have reached Bordeaux. During its eight-year existence the Board granted more compensation to American merchants and shipowners under this decision than under any other, and the English government's willingness to pay the larger awards demonstrated its good faith.[27]

When the case of the *Sally* came before the commissioners, they faced a more heated controversy: did the Board have power to examine evidence and determine awards in cases on which the High Court of Appeals had not yet rendered a final decision? The Americans declared the Board's powers equal to any exigencies; their English colleagues clung to a literal, limited interpretation. Both sides agreed that an underlying cause of the difficulty was time. The British government had pledged in Article VII to pay the American claims awarded by the seizure commission only when compensation could not be obtained in the ordinary course of justice, but on April 10, 1798, when the claimants' time for introducing petitions to the Board expired, 390 cases still awaited action in England's courts, as well as cases of other claimants trying by judicial means to collect restitution already ordered. Although the American commissioners admitted that the halting pace of the judicial process stemmed in part from the lack of "clear and unquestionable" information that should have accompanied every account, England's slow moving judicial procedures caused even more delay. The issue of the Board's power to examine claims still before the courts moved Gore to present a strongly worded opinion.[28]

Since the Anglo-American treaty had authorized the Board to consider all cases in which compensation could not be obtained in ordinary judicial proceedings by the date of the treaty's ratification, Gore argued that the same power should enable the Board to make awards on cases lacking a judicial decree at the expiration of the time for receiving petitions. He accused the English commissioners of "arresting the progress of the board" by their failure to fulfill the promise of the British government to provide compensation when, "for whatever reason," it was unattainable in the ordinary course of justice. To Gore the limit of eighteen months during which the Board might receive petitions, applied to the testimonies of the claimants, not to the obligation of the Board to judge the merits of the cases and make awards. He refused to admit any interpretation of Article VII that would leave to the discretion of the promising party the choice of whether or not it would fulfill its promise. As the tension of the Board mounted, the British commissioners threatened to secede if the Americans insisted upon hearing cases that had not exhausted the judicial remedies of the English courts even though the time allowed for such review had run out.[29]

Several weeks later the British government considered the problems of the deadlocked claims Commission. Under pressure from Downing Street, the Lords Commissioners of Appeals modified the presentation of evidence to quicken the movement of claims cases through the courts. The British members of the Board announced to their American colleagues that their government would permit them to examine cases in which restitution had been ordered but not collected; for this concession they expected the American commissioners to refrain from any consideration of claims still before the courts. Although the compromise offered less than they had demanded, Trumbull, Pinkney, and Gore, eager to move on to other cases, accepted it.[30]

Two and a half years with the claims commission weakened Gore's opinion of England's good intentions. Exasperated by delay and obstinacy, he wrote to Cabot during the controversy over the *Sally* that if a nation like England, "professing . . . a character for integrity, and desirous of sustaining that character, shou'd, under the existing circumstances, be disposed to cavil, and fritter down the provisions of a treaty," the United States in any future agreements should permit no vagueness of language that would allow the British to evade their commitments.[31] To Secretary of State Timothy Pickering Gore reported that every time the Commission met the Americans were told "that it is owing to the great condescension of the British Government that the Board is permitted to examine and decide on Cases after a final determination of the Lords of Appeals, not only on the merits, but on the account to be paid."[32] Irritated by the "tediousness of the process" and "the delays of the Courts," Gore felt unhappy enough in London to seek a change. In March 1799 King wrote to Pickering that if the President "should think of sending a Minister to Constantinople" to negotiate a commercial treaty, "I know of no one . . . , more capable of conducting the negotiations than my early and worthy friend, Mr. Gore." Cabot sent a similar suggestion to Oliver Wolcott, but nothing came from either effort.[33]

At the end of July 1799 the British commissioners announced that at His Majesty's command they would decline to attend any further meetings of the Board until the commission in Philadelphia, established under the sixth article of Jay's Treaty, should resume its deliberations on the claims of British creditors against American citizens for debts contracted before the Revolutionary War. Reversing the attitudes of their countrymen on the London claims commission, the American commissioners in Philadelphia maintained that judicial remedies should be exhausted in the courts of the country before a case should come before the board, and when the British commissioners refused to accept this limitation, the Americans angrily withdrew. Other reasons also explain the board's failure: the sum England claimed was nearly double the annual American budget, and Republicans in Congress accused the British of deliberately imposing a huge burden on the American government. Even so strong a supporter of England as John Jay believed that British interpretations of the treaty had augmented the claims after his negotiations with Grenville. The emotional encounters of Secretary Pickering and Robert Liston, England's Minister to the United States, further aggravated controversies that demanded coolness and moderation. In London Lord Grenville, regretting the "state of affairs so injurious to the subsisting friendship between the two Countries," compared unfavorably the conduct of the diplomats in Philadelphia with the conciliatory interventions of Rufus King and himself in the jurisdictional problems of the seizure commission.[34]

Gore sent to Pickering for his use in reaching a settlement at Philadelphia an instructive survey of the London Commission's experience with the pursuit of judicial remedies in England's courts. He wrote that without qualification the Board under the seventh article had admitted no case in which the claimant had failed to apply to the English courts for redress; unless the complaining party proved that he had sought redress in the courts of the country, the commissioners dismissed his case. All the experience of the London Board refuted the contention of the British commissioners in Philadelphia that the legal remedies in the United States need not be exhausted before a case could enter the Board's jurisdiction.[35]

The commission under the sixth article never resumed its deliberations. In a compromise negotiated by Rufus King and Lord Hawkesbury, Grenville's successor, on January 8, 1802, the Philadelphia Board ceased to exist, and the United States government, on condition that the London Commission would again take up its work, agreed to pay £600,000 to settle the prerevolutionary debts that American citizens owed to British merchants.[36]

The suspension of the work of the claims commission in London during the dispute in Philadelphia gave Gore a respite to return to the United States in the spring of 1800 to attend to his personal affairs. Reaching New York on April 23 aboard the *Arabella*, he went immediately to Philadelphia to report to President John Adams. Then he hurried home to Boston.[37] During the preceding year fire had destroyed part of his house at Waltham, and Gore was anxious to determine the extent of the damage. Also he needed more money for the remainder of his stay in England, and this he hoped to raise through the sale of real estate in Boston. He had few misgivings about the disposal of his office in State Street, but he regretted having to part with the house on Bowdoin Square. Reluctantly he put it on the market, and in November Theodore Lyman bought the property for $24,000.[38]

Gore found Boston society in a gay whirl of balls, cotillions, and immense dinners. They all depressed him. He reported to King that he did not have the means nor, since his thirtieth year, the desire to vie with his neighbors in their modes of ennobling themselves and pursuing enjoyment. He found the great dinner parties, "with all their accompaniments of conversation and amusement," a task at which he was unwilling to labor. The company of a few friends, "who have had considerable converse with the world and with books," offered to Gore the most enviable pleasure.[39]

Cabot and Ames brought him up to date on the Federalist party. Division in its national leadership accurately described its condition; those who followed Hamilton showed no loyalty to the President, and John Adams disdained the council of those he could not trust. "Pickering, Hamilton, and Higginson he seems to hate without any modification," Gore reported to King in London. "Cabot and Ames are not behind in his estimation nor does he seem to think better of Wolcott. . . ." In spite of the hostility between the President and influential Federalists in New England, Gore believed that in the coming presidential election Adams would win a unanimous vote in Massachusetts.[40]

"What did Gore think of England?" his friends wanted to know. Cabot, displeased with the rumors of what Gore thought, wrote to King: "Our friend Gore . . . is quoted as having found by experience that the English do not merit so much respect as the damned british faction . . . are disposed to pay them. . . ."[41] This idle talk he attributed to Jacobin sympathizers, but, if Gore's alleged report required an explanation, Cabot offered his opinion that English greatness was better seen abroad than in the British Isles.[42] Anticipating that the claims commission would soon resume its work, Gore returned to London in the summer of 1800 only to find that the English commissioners still refused to continue the Board's deliberations because of the problems of the Board in Philadelphia.

Taking advantage of the enforced vacation, Christopher and Rebecca Gore left England in May 1801 to visit the Continent. They traveled in Holland, Belgium, and Switzerland, and for six months they established themselves in Paris, where they rented a town house, the Hôtel de Carramon, on fashionable Rue Saint Dominique, and acquired a carriage, coachman, and footmen.[43] The Gores were captivated by the charms of the city, "and it surely has many for all tastes," Gore wrote to King, "especially for those who are delighted with viewing specimens of exquisite skill and beauty, who desire to improve in the arts, or to study chemistry, mineralogy, and natural history."[44] He found the French more to his liking than the English and told King that "there are hardly two things in nature more different than the human species on the different sides of the Channel." Gore could read and write French and presumably he could also speak the language. At the request of Rufus King, he and his wife investigated schools in Paris to which King might send his sons who were then at Harrow, and they discussed with an architect their wish to build a distinguished country house at Waltham. They strolled in the Tuileries Gardens, sipped ices at Frascati's, attended the theater, viewed the great art at the Louvre, and sent their impressions to King.[45] "The Apollo Belvidere is really alive, and a God. . . . The Sculpture is beyond what I have ever before observed. . . ." Gore was less enthusiastic about music. "My avocation is not much, you know, for these amusements, least of all for Opera Music. . . ."[46] From Holland he reported that while he had no desire to remain long or to return, he had found the country "more a work of art and industry" than he had anticipated. Whenever the Gores traveled in Europe, Paris like a magnet drew them back to France; but even there they missed the Kings and wished for the pleasant evenings at Great Cumberland Place when Gore reviewed for King the salient points of a "Gray's Inn Debate" and listened to the Minister's account of a "Downing Street Conference." As weeks passed without a summons to resume the meetings of the London claims board, Gore feared his Commission would never complete its obligation to American merchants; on December 17, 1801, however, he sailed back to England hoping to begin another term of work.[47]

When the Board took up its duties at No. 5 Gray's Inn Square on February 15, 1802, it immediately considered whether or not the British government should pay interest to American claimants for the time of the Board's suspension. John Swabey, who had succeeded John Nicholl, doubted the justice of increasing the amount Britain should pay, and he also questioned the Commission's authority to demand it. Gore declared that the subject fell within the Board's competency to decide, and since the United States had given full satisfaction under Article VI in the payment of claims to British merchants, his government would expect the British to do equally well under Article VII. Pinkney convincingly argued that the claimant had lost for the time of the suspension not only the amount of his principal but also the interest that otherwise would have come to him. Even if England allowed a sum for the interruption, he would still have sustained a loss because he had been denied the use of his money at the time when commercial capital was particularly active. Pinkney declared that the British government, having the use of both principal and interest during the suspended proceedings, had realized a gain that was at least coextensive with the claimant's loss. Unable to reach an agreement, the Board referred its dispute to the Lord Chancellor, who upheld the opinions of Gore and Pinkney by ruling that the British government must pay 6 per cent interest to the American claimants for the time of the Board's recess.[48]

After this settlement the work of the Commission went steadily forward. In July 1803 Gore reported to Pickering that, excepting a few cases before the English courts, they had completed their decisions on all the American appeals.[49] By the end of August they had also cleared away the few remaining British claims against the United States for violations of neutrality. For the next five months the Board convened only occasionally.

Having chafed under the Commission's long and recurring delays, Gore could scarcely tolerate the reported rumor from Boston that the Board would long since have ended its deliberations except for his determination to extend them. "You know better than any man," he told King, ". . . all the contest I have had in my own mind for the last five years between a sense of duty which . . . constrained me to remain and endeavour to perfect what I have undertaken, and a desire to return, a desire prompted by the strongest interests which called me home, and rendered extremely ardent by constantly experiencing the mortification and disgust over so inglorious a station."[50] King attributed the slander to "the malignity and envy of some falsehearted Jacobin," and urged Gore to forget it.[51]

During slack periods in the Commission's proceedings, the Gores also toured parts of England and Scotland. They traveled in crowded, horse-drawn carriages whose drivers paused en route at every ale house, and they stayed in inns that failed to "afford any satisfaction to a gentleman." On one trip Gore vowed that when he returned to London he would walk more, "for this constant riding increases my flesh much." In the summer of 1798 he and his wife visited Margate, a fashionable seaside resort where the bite of the flies reminded them of home, and the following year they were in the Lake District and described its beauties as "beyond description."[52] In Scotland Gore found the people sober, industrious, and informed, "without any marks of the new philosophy, or rage of democracy," but the poverty of the country depressed him, with its uncultivated land around Glasgow, women without shoes, and everywhere accommodations that were "sorry and not remarkable for cleanliness." In a letter from Edinburgh he told King that neither he nor his wife would "voluntarily take another journey into North Britain, wild, beautiful, and sublime as it is."[53]

In England the Gores found their best friends among Americans—the Pinkneys, the Higginsons, John Trumbull, Samuel Cabot, and especially the Kings. They lived near the Kings in London and frequently visited them at their country place in Leatherhead, Surrey; in 1802 they spent two months there as guardians for the King children while their parents vacationed on the Continent.[54] Bostonians traveling abroad often visited the Gores, especially the young whose families recommended a stop at 1 Cumberland Place for guidance in a foreign land.

Although Gore lacked close friends among the English, he had several well-placed acquaintances. Most upper-class Englishmen welcomed foreigners who carried properly accredited introductions. Through the efforts of Rufus King, Gore was entertained by the Duke of Bedford at his sheep shearing at Woburn Abbey and by Thomas Coke of Holkham Hall in Norfolk. In searching for ways to improve the yield of his land in Massachusetts, Gore was attracted by Coke's experiments to increase the productivity of agriculture in England.[55] Also, he probably had some exchange with the Barings in London; before he left Boston he received a letter of introduction from Alexander Baring addressed to his father, Sir Francis Baring of the English banking house. The younger Baring had come to the United States to speculate in land, and while in Boston had formed a high opinion of Christopher Gore, whom he judged to be "as respectable a character as any in this country—a very good specimen of the New England Yankee & a good lawyer." Because of Gore's membership on the seizure commission and his knowledge of Maine lands, the younger Baring recommended him to Sir Francis as a useful acquaintance.

"He is a very leading man of Boston—generally known, & a civil reception of him will have a good effect."[56]

Gore and King were together in London when they heard the dismal news of the American election of 1800: the Republican party had captured the presidency of the United States and both houses of Congress. This sweeping shift of power had come to pass in spite of Federalist prophecies of anarchy should the Republicans ever win control of the national government, but in the early days of the new administration reports reached Gore that some prominent Federalists found President Jefferson less dangerous than they had anticipated. George Cabot wrote that the President's inaugural address was better liked by "our own party than his own," and that a majority of Federalists were in happier spirits than they would have been "with a Reelection."[57] In England neither Gore nor King felt well disposed toward the new administration, and King concluded that as a representative of the United States government his usefulness had ended.

When King resigned his office and sailed for home in the spring of 1803, he appointed no substitute because he expected that his successor would soon arrive. A year earlier during a vacation on the Continent, he had left Gore as chargé in London, but now that he had resigned as Minister he doubted Jefferson's approval should he choose a replacement for even a month. After King's departure Gore received several letters from Secretary of State Madison addressed to Rufus King or in his absence to Christopher Gore.

Although he had no illusions of the probable attitude of Jefferson's administration toward him, he realized, as England prepared to renew its war against France, that his government needed a high-ranking representative in London. He inferred from Madison's communications that the Administration had expected King to name a substitute, and he observed from the estimate of expenses that the government sent to him that several months might elapse before the new minister's arrival. After explaining his deductions to Secretary Madison, he informed him and Lord Hawkesbury that until the arrival of the American minister, he would assume the responsibilities of Chargé d'Affaires.[58]

Aware of the delicacy of his position, Gore was not surprised to learn that George Erving, American Consul in London, had expected the President to put the affairs of the legation in his hands; Gore even heard that Erving, if King should name Gore Chargé d'Affaires, had prepared a protest against "such unwarrantable assumption." William

Pinkney, a friend of Erving and an avowed supporter of Jefferson, approved Gore's conduct. He attributed the strange action of Jefferson and Madison to their promise, either expressed or strongly implied, to name Erving chargé in London on the departure of Rufus King, "which on more mature consideration, they had thought proper to abandon," and, having put themselves in a dilemma, hoped to save face by assuming that King had appointed Gore to fill his place temporarily.[59]

Gore confided to King that his sense of duty directed him to the course he had taken, which he did not believe either the government or his friends would censure. "If they do, I feel justified myself, and that is a consolation to be secured at all events."[60] President Jefferson, however, never showed Gore the courtesy of an official appointment as Chargé d'Affaires. The English government, probably on the recommendation of Lord Hawkesbury, accepted Gore in these unusual circumstances; he was received by the King and Queen and given diplomatic immunities even though his pretensions were never confirmed by the government of the United States. King wrote to Gore that if "Mr. Jefferson would do as he ought, he would appoint you as my successor."[61]

During the two months between King's departure and the arrival in July 1803 of the new Minister, James Monroe, Gore directed the business of the American legation in London. He reported to Washington the progress of minor negotiations, and to Secretary Madison he sent several dispatches telling of Napoleon's efforts to exclude English trade from the continent of Europe and describing England's extensive military preparations for war against France. At no time, however, did he receive a single word from any officer in Jefferson's administration.

After King and his family returned to New York, the Gores found London a dull, lonely city. A few hours after their separation Rebecca Gore wrote to Mrs. King of her despair:

> . . . we had as you may suppose a trist dinner, after which, we walked around the garden, where like every other place I shall miss your society, indeed this is only the commencement, and sample of many gloomy days which I shall pass before we leave this uninteresting scene, where after my husband, there is not a single object who for half a moment would know whether I breathed or ceased to breath.[62]

Several weeks later Gore wrote that he and his wife missed the Kings more each day. "We are in many respects alone—I can truly say that in many things and on many topics I have none to communicate with, for though with these that are here I agree in part, yet not in all, and for a free communication . . . this is necessary."[63] Two or three evenings a week the Gores visited with the Pinkneys and occasionally with the Higginsons, but the Monroes they seldom met socially. Walking and reading and buying books occupied most of Gore's time. While delays continued to postpone the date of departure, the rising cost of living required an ever larger outlay. Gore was heartily weary of London. He wrote to Samuel Cabot that in no part of his time abroad had he more earnestly desired to leave England.[64] Eager to replace the present with the future, he turned his mind toward Boston to consider the life he would make there after an absence of eight years.

Should he reopen his law office or should he retire to Waltham? He put the question to Fisher Ames, who replied unequivocally in favor of the law. In spite of eight years away from Boston, Gore should attract the more important cases paying the larger fees and earn perhaps $2,000 a year. "Your time of life, your reputation, property, and moderation as to the passion for gain, will be assigned as reasons . . . for your declining the toil of promiscuous business." Ames urged Gore to continue his style of living by practicing law rather than to change it for an idle life of less elegance. Should future political office appear desirable to Gore, an active profession in Boston would keep him in sight and readiness.[65] Even though George Cabot concurred with Ames's advice, Gore accepted it with misgivings. "The length of time I have been absent, and my devotion to other Studies, and different habits, all lead me to mistrust myself," he wrote to King.[66] During the last months of his residence in London, he attended court and read law to prepare for his practice in Boston.

On February 23, 1804, the board established by the seventh article of Jay's Treaty completed its business, and Gore was free at last to return to the United States. "Our commission closed with perfect Harmony," he wrote to King. "I can only say that personally I have been treated by Lord Hawkesbury and Hammond with great kindness and attention."[67] To British claimants against the United States the Board awarded almost $110,000; to American merchants and shipowners the commissioners required the British government to pay, in addition to the £60,000 that had been awarded in earlier settlements, the unexpectedly large sum of almost $6,000,000.[68] Gore had done well for the commercial interests of Massachusetts.

The experience of the seizure commission proved that arbitration could settle disputes if participating governments used their constructive influence to mediate the conflicts. In large part the London Board owed its success to the very reasonableness of the British government that Gore had vigorously defended in his support of Jay's Treaty. Although he suffered pettiness, delay, and condescension from Britain's commissioners, England's good faith in the large matters of policy sustained his confidence in its government. Grenville, alert to any danger signals in the Board's proceedings, smoothed difficulties that threatened to strain Anglo-American friendship; on two occasions the Lord Chancellor overruled the English members of the Board in favor of the opinions of Pinkney and Gore; and the British government accepted without protest and paid with promptness the large sum charged against it. This peak of pleasant relations between England and the United States in a long period of conflict depended primarily upon enlightened diplomacy.

On the American side Rufus King as Minister to the Court of St. James and Pinkney and Gore as claims commissioners provided the essential ingredients. King applied his talents to develop and sustain Anglo-American harmony, particularly in solving the problems of the London Board that arose from the difficulties of the debt commission in Philadelphia, and Gore and Pinkney brought to the deliberations of the claims board a knowledge of the controversial field of maritime law that surely equaled that of their English counterparts. The inability of the two governments to agree on a definite standard of judging the cases increased the complexity of the Board's work and underlines the wisdom and patience of the five commissioners who carried the proceedings to a conclusion that satisfied both Great Britain and the United States. Fisher Ames sent Gore an appropriate tribute: "The brilliant success of your Commission ought to . . . wreathe very green honors about your head, my friend. . . . Your own mind and your friends will bestow the due praise."[69]

Having completed his mission in London, Gore lost no time in arranging his voyage to Boston. "Our goods are on board the *Minerva*," he wrote to King, "and we shall probably be there ourselves within a fortnight."[70] Early in March the Gores boarded their ship at Gravesend and thirty days later arrived in Boston as spring was coming to New England. Gore reported that their friends received them with kindness, "and we are more happy than for a long time past."[71]

Boston's grateful merchants and shipowners arranged a distinguished welcome. The *Centinel* reported that 180 "of the most respectable citizens of Boston" gave a "very sumptuous and elegant PUBLIC DINNER" at Concert Hall for Christopher Gore as a testimony of "the high sense they entertained of his eminent services as Commissioner, under the British Treaty, and as expressive of the congratulations on his return to his native country." Although the party lasted until a late hour and thirty-eight toasts were drunk, the *Centinel* assured its readers that the entertainment was conducted "with the greatest order and decorum." To the Republican *Independent Chronicle*, however, the Federalists' gay evening was "A Fresh Attempt to Scandalize the Constituted Authorities." Toasts were drunk to Rufus King, Governor Strong, and to ex-President Adams; to Jay's mission to England, "dictated by enlightened policy, and executed with good faith"; and to John Trumbull and William Pinkney for their "talents, integrity and eminent services." After the guests had drunk seventeen toasts, Christopher Gore proposed: "The American Flag: May it continue to mark honorable enterprize, and prosperous commerce—may it ensure protection, and extend the Nation's glory." When Gore withdrew, Benjamin Lincoln, the presiding officer, gave in his honor: "Christopher Gore Esqu.—May the public gratitude for his able and successful services, be as ardent and sincere, as the zeal that performed them."[72]

For the immediate future Gore planned to practice law while he purchased a town house in Boston and built a country residence at Waltham. He professed a lofty disdain for politics as long as the Republicans should control the government. Shortly before he left England he expressed his sentiments to Rufus King:

> It is unnecessary for me to say that nothing would tempt me to engage in public life, under those who now rule our country, for nothing is more certain than that they would not employ me. Yet I may be permitted to remark, that so different are all their notions and conduct from what I conceive wise and honest, that were their dispositions toward me exactly the reverse of what I know them to be, mine could not change. . . .[73]

Three months after his return to Boston Gore wrote to Trumbull that he enjoyed more "Happiness and Tranquility" than he had known for eight years.[74]

VI
Distinguished Bostonian

WHEN Gore returned to Boston from London, he was forty-five years of age, handsome, urbane, distinguished. During the next decade he reached the fullest development of his potentialities and reputation; not only did his political career come to its full flower, but in Boston's artistic, legal, economic, and intellectual endeavors he participated with conspicuous excellence. Prominent cultural and scientific societies requested his membership, and Harvard University elected him to its governing boards. His capital investments placed him among the leaders of Boston's economic expansion, and his political and professional distinction brought him to the famous Selfridge murder case as counsel for the defense. Soon after his return from England he built a country house that stands as one of America's finest examples of Federalist architecture.

When the Gores realized the extent of the damage by fire to their property in Waltham, they began during their residence in England to plan their new country house. They collected ideas from estates they visited and from books of architectural plans and illustrations that landed gentry frequently used in designing their country places. The affinity between the south side of Gore's new house and the garden fronts of Chilton in Berkshire and Saxlingham Rectory in Norfolk, both designed by John Soane, suggests that the Gores may have studied these country houses in Soane's *Sketches in Architecture*, published in 1793, and in his *Plans, Elevations, and Sections of Buildings* of 1788. The new house at Waltham reflects ideas that were current in the architecture of France and England during the Gores' residence in those countries. The five-part structure, with a projecting central block and wings of lower elevation connecting the terminal pavilions appeared frequently in England, permitting an easy arrangement of spacious rooms for formal entertainment and smaller ones for the more intimate life of the family. French and English architects, by not extending the front hall to the rear of the house, frequently designed an unbroken line of rooms across the southern, or garden exposure; they added corner pilasters to their buildings; and they brought the oval room into such popularity that even the Gores' plan of one elliptical room against another was not unusual.[1]

When Gore and his wife lived in Paris in 1801, they gave particular attention to the city's new buildings. Under the influence of Etienne-

Louis Boullée and Claude-Nicolas Ledoux, France had become a center of innovation in architecture. Although Jacques-Guillaume Legrand had considerably less distinction than Boullée and Ledoux in France and abroad, he rated high among Parisian architects, and his work attracted the Gores. Like his two more famous colleagues, Legrand found appeal in geometric figures and in contrasting shapes and materials to make distinctive surface patterns, and in reaction against the richness of the Baroque he emphasized designs of more simple composition and sought to derive his effect from the whole rather than from details. On the top of the Halle aux Draps (1786) in the Place des Innocents he and Jacques Molinos, Legrand's frequent collaborator, placed a barrel roof that won praise for its elegant simplicity. A drawing of their Amphithéâtre du Jardin des Plantes shows a building of classical line with ornamentation limited to small columns and a *bas relief* at the main entrance. In designing the semicylindrical front of the Théâtre Feydeau (1790), the two architects attempted to achieve an original surface pattern by placing seven small arches above the three larger ones of the vestibule, and their repetition of the convex outline of this façade in the semicircle of the auditorium was, Legrand thought, a noteworthy innovation.[2]

The Gores undoubtedly saw in Paris two residences designed by Legrand, the Hôtel Gallifet (1775) on the Rue Grenelle and the Hôtel Jarnac (1787) on the Rue Monsieur. Both houses are rectangular in shape, two stories high, constructed of stone, and distinguished by their Ionic columns rising full height. The Hôtel Jarnac, the smaller, plainer, more imaginative and beautiful of the two, contains large windows on its similar front and back façades.[3] In June 1801 through the introduction of a Captain Izzard, the Gores met Legrand, who delighted them. "He has been useful and obliging," Gore reported to King. "I do not mean to deprecate the character of French, English, or American, but such kind of man is not to be found in the two latter."[4] Early in July Gore wrote to King, "Mrs. G. is now with Monsieur LeGrand in the adjoining parlour building houses. . . ."[5]

Back in London after six months on the Continent, Rebecca Gore sketched plans of the house she wanted to build in Waltham, and when she had finally achieved a satisfactory expression of her ideas, she sent the draft to Legrand. On October 20, 1802, Gore put the following details in a letter to Rufus King, who was then in Paris:

> Mrs. G. has sent the plan of our intended house, with a wish that you should explain it to LeGrand, & request him to make a

> compleat & perfect plan according to our sketch—we do not mean to be more than three feet out of ground—See the oval room, the chimney to be in the place where the centre window was in. I fear that the smoke cannot be well conveyed away, if we have a window over the fireplace, which Mrs. G. wishes—and so likewise in the chamber above. On this pray converse with him, and if it cannot be effected, we must have a stack of chimneys run up in that place, according to the old way—If we can rid ourselves of the smoke conveniently & surely, then I should prefer to have the window over the fireplace.[6]

Twelve days later Gore wrote to King, "I shall be much obliged, if you will attend to my plan with LeGrand. We have in idea built our house, and mean, *si la guerre ne defend pas*, to go the next summer to Paris to purchase some drawing room & bed room furniture, for its ornament, & our comfort."[7] Today's tourist may see in Napoleon's library at Malmaison the distinctive arrangement of a window above a fireplace. Although when the Gores visited France Napoleon lived and worked at Malmaison and the house was not open to American sightseers, they could have seen the design elsewhere in Paris and its vicinity.[8]

No source has come to light that names with certainty the architect of Gore Place. Gore's letter to King, the only documents on the authorship of the house, suggest that Legrand drew the plan based on Mrs. Gore's sketch, but since the house was built 3,000 miles from Paris, his plan was undoubtedly modified to make it suitable to the skills of local workmen and to the materials available in the area.

The Gores' house displays certain features that might have come from the hand of Legrand. His love of geometric forms could have prompted the arrangement of the oval room on the garden side opposite the room on the entrance front that has an inner wall of elliptical shape. Legrand used lunettes to achieve contrasting patterns on the main front of the Théâtre Feydeau; at Gore Place the lunettes above the rectangular windows on the north side of the wings and pavilions present a pleasing surface pattern that is repeated on the south side. The design of an entresol in each of the wings that connect the central block to the terminal pavilions might have come from France; in one of the two rooms of the east entresol the ceiling is an elliptical arch, in the other it is in the form of a barrel arch. Legrand, who often used skylights, may have been responsible for the geometric one atop the central unit of the Gore house. The north front with its two identical front doors, one at each end of the central block,

GORE PLACE, WALTHAM, MASSACHUSETTS
Wood engraving by Rudolph Ruzicka, 1938, of the south facade

GORE PLACE, WALTHAM, MASSACHUSETTS
THE SOUTH FAÇADE

GORE PLACE, WALTHAM, MASSACHUSETTS
THE NORTH FACADE

PORTRAIT OF CHRISTOPHER GORE BY JOHN TRUMBULL

GORE PLACE, WALTHAM, MASSACHUSETTS
THE SPIRAL STAIRCASE

GORE PLACE, WALTHAM, MASSACHUSETTS
THE STATE HALL WITH TABLE OWNED BY CHRISTOPHER GORE

GORE PLACE, WALTHAM, MASSACHUSETTS
THE OVAL DINING ROOM

JOHN TRUMBULL'S "PRIAM RECEIVING THE BODY OF HECTOR"
Bequeathed by Mrs. Christopher Gore to the Boston Athenæum in 1834; deposited at the Museum of Fine Arts in 1876; since 1963 lent to Gore Place

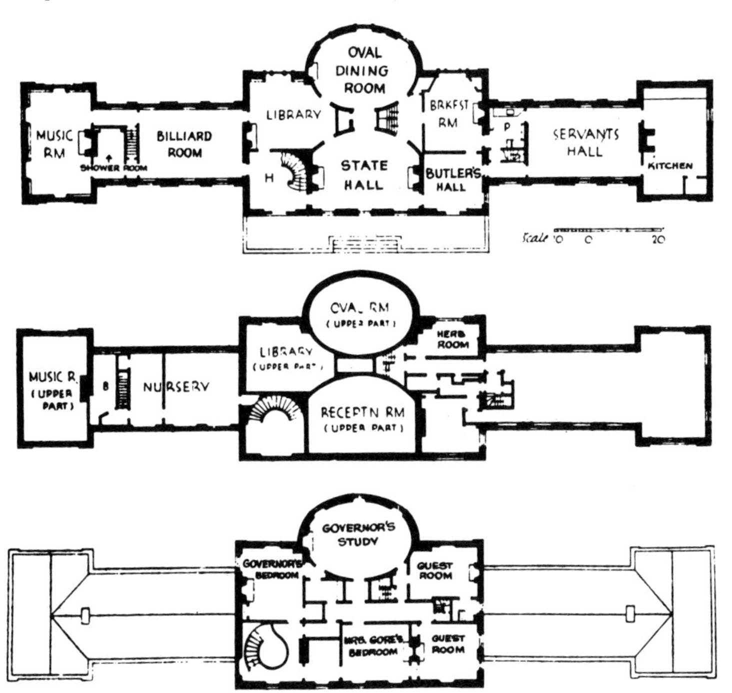

GORE PLACE, WALTHAM, MASSACHUSETTS
PLANS OF THE THREE FLOORS

THOMAS AMORY HOUSE, BEACON AND PARK STREETS, BOSTON
THE BOSTON RESIDENCE OF CHRISTOPHER GORE, 1809-1816

GORE HALL, HARVARD COLLEGE, CAMBRIDGE
THE COLLEGE LIBRARY, 1841-1912, BEGUN IN 1838 WITH A LEGACY FROM CHRISTOPHER GORE

presents an uncommon design. The east front of Legrand's Hôtel Gallifet with a door at the right and a porte cochere at the left may have inspired the arrangement.[9]

Gore told King that the interior of his house would have "perfect freedom from ornamentation." Even though the newer houses on the eastern seaboard showed increasingly less decoration, the Gore house, lacking cornices, ornamental ceilings, and enriched strings for the staircase, achieved unusual simplicity. The fireplace mantels, set in Connecticut sandstone rather than in the imported marble that Gore wished but found too expensive, provided the principal ornamentation, and the figures and garlands in the decoration may have been reproduced from molds made in Europe and widely used in the United States.[10]

The Gores, having recently built a country house at Waltham, must have known quite accurately, as they discussed their plans with Legrand, the available building materials and the capabilities of the local workmen. In place of stone, widely used for construction in France, they chose brick, which was easily acquired in Massachusetts, but they may have painted it a light color to give it the appearance of stone. By the time the Gores built their house certain designs that had originated in Europe had become popular in Boston and presented no problem to local builders. Oval rooms came well within their competence, and many doorways in New England boasted sidelights and elliptical, segmental fanlights. Although the lunette windows are used distinctively in the design of the Gore house, their construction was common enough in Boston. The Gores may have brought from France the idea for their casement sash or French windows, although at least one house in Boston had this type. The dramatic, circular staircase with no wall below the strings, appears to be self-supporting; the style is unusual, but it was not unique in the Boston area.[11]

Three months after Gore arrived from England, he began to assemble materials to build his house. Lumber came by raft on the Charles River to Watertown, and from there Gore's own teams hauled it to Waltham. During the winter he collected the lime, the bricks, the clear boards, and in March 1805 he broke ground for the construction of the house. The Gores lived at Waltham the following summer, as they had the preceding one, probably in the wing of the house that survived the fire of 1799.[12]

They spared no expense to make their new home a place of comfort and convenience. Brass rollers assured the smooth gliding of drawers in the pantry and bedroom cupboards, specially designed hinges raised the doors to clear the carpets. The louvre boards in the door of Gore's bed chamber provided good ventilation, and in the entrance hall a layer of goat hair under the floor lessened the chill of the marble squares. The plumbing facilities included a water closet and a "bathing tub," with a hole in the ceiling above the tub to improvise a shower. In the cost of the house labor accounted for a comparatively small item; glass and stone, however, required a substantial outlay, and nails and hardware amounted to more than 20 per cent of all the expenditures. When construction was nearly completed, Gore reported to King that the great objection to his house was its dimensions, which were too large for the size of his family, and though built with economy the house had cost more than he would have wished and would keep him longer at the bar than would suit his "love of indulgence." Gore, having listed in detail in his Account Book the expenditures for the construction of his house, calculated the total cost to be $23,608.14. The fee to an architect is singularly absent; perhaps Gore paid that item in Europe several years before he began the entries in his book.[13]

Gore enhanced the beauty of his house by the landscaping of the grounds. He ran a mile walk or bridle path around the home lot, divided the enclosed area into quarters, each of which he belted with rows of trees, and in the northwest section he laid out a kitchen garden and deer park. He placed his house on a slight eminence far back from the road and concealed it with trees; from its south elevation an expanse of lawn carried the eye to a distant stone wall and a pond beyond.[14] Gore had a liking for English gardeners and when he had been in London only a few months, he drew up a contract with William Hay, a Scot, who promised to work on the Waltham farm with "sobriety, honesty, faithfulness, industry, and skill" for twenty-five guineas a year.[15] Gore brought from England not only a knowledge of better ways to grow field crops but a collection of seeds and plants for experimental cultivation. Throughout the Boston area Gore Place won fame for the English character of its landscape, its magnificent forest trees, for the abundance and variety of its fruits and vegetables and flowers, and for the elegant simplicity of its country house. Here for almost twenty-five years the Gores spent at least half of every year.

In Boston they found no place of continuing satisfaction for their winter residence. After they returned from England in 1804, they delayed until 1809 the purchase of a town house. The first winter they rented property on Tremont Street, and during the next year they leased a large, three-story house, formerly occupied by Josiah Quincy, that sat in spacious grounds at the corner of Pearl and High streets and offered an unobstructed view of Boston's harbor. After the construction of the new State House on Beacon Street, the city of Boston moved its almshouse, workhouse, and granary from Park Street to the remote area of Barton's Point and opened for sale to private owners the property facing the Common. At the corner of Park and Beacon streets opposite the State House, Thomas Amory, a cousin of Mrs. Gore, built a square, brick mansion designed by Bulfinch, and when it was later enlarged and divided into several houses, Samuel Dexter purchased the one facing Beacon Street and the Gores bought the house next door on Park Street. Until they sold the property in 1816, this was their residence each year from December to May. Although Gore complained that his town house had cost him over $27,000, it with his country place at Waltham enabled him to live in style and comfort.[16]

His expenses required a substantial income, and he sought part of it in profits from capital investments. Although he told King in 1805 that he might hazard "some adventure abroad," Gore put most of his money into Boston enterprises—insurance, transportation, real estate, and the manufacture of textiles. Two kinds of insurance interested him. Underwriting marine insurance in Boston had made his father-in-law rich, and the continued prosperity of this business prompted Gore to invest $1,000 in the recently organized New England Marine Insurance Company. In 1815 he subscribed to the Massachusetts Mutual Fire Insurance Company, Boston's first successful effort to protect property owners against loss from the town's frequent and disastrous fires.[17] A much larger part of his capital, however, he committed to the development of Boston's transportation facilities. When he died in 1827, the inventory of his estate listed $61,000 invested in bridges, locks, and canals.[18]

A quarter of this sum represented his holdings in the stock of the Middlesex Canal Company, which a group of wealthy commercial and political leaders organized in 1793 to tie Boston to New Hampshire by building a canal from the Mystic River through Middlesex County to the Merrimack River. Of the company's 800 shares of stock, 524 were held by sixteen men; James Barrell, a merchant and the largest stockholder, owned eighty shares, Gore had seventy, and Craigie fifty-one. In projecting a canal through which New Hampshire could ship to Boston its stone, iron ore, lumber, and agricultural products and Boston could send to New Hampshire groceries, lime, fish, and English imports, the stockholders envisioned a happy combination of profits for themselves and cheap, efficient transportation for the public. Construction, which began in 1794 and ended nine years later, included the dredging of a channel twenty-seven miles long and the building of numerous bridges and aqueducts. Unlike most canals in the United States, the Middlesex was developed entirely with private capital, but like many other ventures in transportation, it was a financial failure throughout its fifty-year history. Burdened by large assessments during construction, the stockholders hoped that later profits would repay them. From 1803 to 1819, however, the receipts from tolls went into the business instead of the stockholders' pockets; the first dividend, declared in 1819, amounted only to three-fourths of one per cent; and when later receipts promised higher dividends, expenditures for new parts absorbed the profits. Although the Middlesex Canal brought financial loss to the stockholders, its technical contribution to canal building and its economic effect on the area were substantial gains. Contemporary experts said the canal offered the best artificial navigation in the country and quickened the development of the Merrimack Valley, a benefit that later accrued to the railroads.[19]

Two years after the Middlesex Canal had been in operation, Gore and eighteen other Boston businessmen organized the Canal Bridge Corporation to build a bridge across the Charles River from Lechmere Point in Cambridge to Barton's Point in Boston. In requesting permission for their project from the state legislature, the petitioners argued that the proposed bridge would connect the Middlesex Canal more closely to the Boston markets, increase the value of property in East Cambridge, and provide a shorter, cheaper route to Boston from the area north of Cambridge than that over the West Boston Bridge. Although the proprietors of the West Boston Bridge and the adjacent land in Cambridgeport opposed the building of another toll bridge that would decrease their property values and toll receipts, Gore and his associates won permission to span the Charles River from Lechmere Point to Boston. Their bridge, known as the Craigie or Canal Bridge, opened for traffic on August 30, 1809, and continued for almost one hundred years until the Charles River Dam covered its site.[20]

As soon as the Canal Bridge was completed, its proprietors organized the Lechmere Point Corporation to develop the land around the Cambridge end of their bridge. Andrew Craigie, previous owner of the property, held 800 shares; Gore followed with 200, Harrison Gray Otis and Israel Thorndike each had sixty, and four other Bostonians, one of them Gore's brother-in-law, William Payne, each owned twenty shares. Although Gore frequently bought and profitably sold parcels of land in the older sections of Boston, the Lechmere Point venture marked his largest speculation in real estate and his only one in a development. The stockholders planned to open the area "for settling, managing, improving, or dividing said common lands" and to build a dam from Prison Point to Charlestown to provide power for their proposed sawmill. Although most of their ideas never progressed beyond the planning stage, they did construct roads, lay out streets, one of which was Gore Street, and survey building lots; they built a "brew house," a tavern, a brick store, and two small houses; and they reached the peak of their success when they persuaded the authorities of Middlesex County to locate the courthouse and jail at Lechmere Point. In spite of their energetic promotion and an expenditure of funds that forced Craigie into impoverished retirement, the developers attracted few settlers and those only to the main street, where their buildings "stood like lonely sentinels." The speculation failed because the Lechmere Point Corporation tried to make East Cambridge a center of trade forty years too soon.[21]

Gore timed more shrewdly his investment in the Boston Manufacturing Company. In 1817 he bought ten shares in this new cotton textile corporation, established at Waltham by Francis Cabot Lowell, a rich merchant of Boston, with assistance from two other merchants, Nathan Appleton and Patrick Tracy Jackson. These men organized their company not to perpetuate the craftsman's making of cotton cloth but to make money for themselves, and the methods they adopted to this end proved revolutionary in the history of textile manufacturing in the United States. Making full use of the newly invented power loom and of their own executive abilities, they departed from the usual organization of cotton textile production in many small, specialized, independent shops to integrate under one roof and under one management all the processes of manufacture from raw material to finished product; they found their labor supply among young women in rural areas who worked in the factory a few years before marriage and lived in the respectable boardinghouses that the company provided. In organizing for large-scale production and in separating the executive function from the actual making of cloth, Lowell and Jackson made the Boston Manufacturing Company not only the prototype of the modern industrial corporation but also a highly profitable venture.

The proprietors, with large financial resources and a protected domestic market, moved rapidly ahead. In 1817, two years after the Boston

Manufacturing Company had opened for business, it paid its first dividend, $170 a share, a return of 17 per cent. Three years later Gore bought forty more shares of stock at $1,000 a share. Between 1815 and 1822 the sales of cotton cloth rose from $412 to $260,658, and the accumulated dividends for the period totaled 105½ per cent. The time had come to expand the company's production.[22]

In 1822 with a group of business friends, the stockholders of the Boston Manufacturing Company organized the Merrimack Company, another cotton textile enterprise, and laid the economic foundations of the city of Lowell. Three years later other merchants joined the proprietors of the Merrimack Company to form the Hamilton Company, and in 1827 more investors helped to establish the Appleton Company. Gore bought fifty-four shares in the Merrimack Company, valued five years later at $57,210, and when Jackson and Lowell bought control of their own water power he invested $34,000 in stock of the Merrimack Locks and Canals Corporation.[23]

The phenomenal expansion of cotton textile manufacturing in Massachusetts proved to Gore that the livelihood of the Commonwealth no longer depended primarily upon navigation and foreign trade. In the last decade of his life he invested most of his capital in the production of textiles. Although he did not participate as a director nor, because of crippling rheumatism, attend the stockholders' meetings, he found in the mass production of cotton cloth the rapidly growing, highly profitable investment he had failed to find in the development of real estate and transportation.

Prominent societies in Boston, seeking rich and distinguished members with a respect for intellectual endeavor, requested Gore's participation. In 1798 while living in London he was elected to the Massachusetts Historical Society, and four years later he was asked to join the American Academy of Arts and Sciences. The Academy, founded in Boston in 1780, invited to its membership citizens of Massachusetts who had contributed with distinction to politics, literature, or science, and it also elected honorary members from other parts of the United States and from Europe.[24] Although Gore held no office in the Academy, for more than a decade he helped to direct the affairs of the Massachusetts Historical Society.

Founded during President Washington's first term by Jeremy Belknap, clergyman and historian, the Massachusetts Historical Society was the first organization of its kind in the United States. Its original members came together to establish a central depository for historical books and manuscripts and to publish rare documents. In limiting the membership to sixty, they gave their new organization the social likeness of a club. During the years of Gore's association, the Society occupied an upper room in the central pavilion of Charles Bulfinch's Tontine Crescent. Republican James Sullivan, the first president, held office until 1806, when the Society elected Federalist Christopher Gore to succeed him. "Paltry conduct," the *Independent Chronicle* called the vote against Sullivan, and William Bentley of Salem, attributing the change of officers to political rancor at the preceding gubernatorial election, refused to attend further meetings. By the time Gore left the presidency in 1818, however, party politics exerted no influence on the affairs of the Society.[25]

Having neither an official editor nor a paid librarian, the Society depended heavily upon the guidance and recommendations of its officers. The years of Gore's presidency saw continuing progress in its steady acquisition of published and manuscript materials and in the publication of its volumes of *Collections*. Before the study of history had achieved professional status, the gentlemen-scholars who wrote of past events relied heavily upon the holdings of the Massachusetts Historical Society.

Christopher Gore was a builder of libraries. Throughout his life he regularly purchased books for his enjoyment and enlightenment, and from his own library he bequeathed a large collection to the Massachusetts Historical Society. In 1804 when legal treatises were still few and difficult to obtain, Gore, as a proprietor and trustee, assisted in the founding and development of the Social Law Library. Although it was established primarily to serve the lawyers of Suffolk County, the proprietors extended its use to all lawyers, judges, and legislators in the state.[26]

Few alumni could equal Gore's devotion to Harvard College. Not only did he leave it the largest bequest it had yet received, but he served on its governing boards for twenty years, first as an Overseer (1810-15) and then as a Fellow of the Corporation (1812-21). Several years before Gore joined the Board of Overseers, Harvard underwent a fundamental change of emphasis. The Unitarians, in an effort to free the College from the grip of fixed Calvinist dogma, won control of the theological department and the presidency. From this time on in an atmosphere of inquiry and of receptivity to new ideas, Harvard moved forward in the development of its liberal tradition.[27]

Gore became an Overseer after a Federalist victory in the state election of 1809 brought about a new composition of the Board. Heretofore that body had included the governor, the lieutenant governor, the members of the council, the state senate, and the ministers of the Congregational churches in six of the surrounding towns. In 1805 an incident occurred that precipitated a change. The students of Harvard staged a walk-out to protest what they believed to be bad food, and, when the college authorities demanded an immediate return to classes and a withdrawal of complaints, the students refused to submit. A committee of the Overseers, led by Republican Lieutenant Governor Levi Lincoln, investigated the situation and reported in favor of reforming the commons and pardoning the offenders. A prolonged debate ensued between the Federalists and Republicans on the Board. Gore, although not yet a member, supported the Federalists' insistence on upholding authority, which prompted the *Independent Chronicle* to comment: "Messrs. Gore and Otis, we hear, have strongly recommended to the students of Harvard college a submission to its government. It would be well if these honorable characters should practice the same respect for the National Government. . . ."[28]

By a narrow margin Harvard's Overseers rejected Lincoln's request for leniency, and the students yielded. But the possibility that a Republican Board of Overseers might sometime prevail over a Federalist Corporation so alarmed the Fellows of Harvard that when Gore was governor of the state and the Federalist party controlled the General Court, the legislature rushed through a law that eliminated the members of the Senate from the Board, prescribed a definite number of clerical members, and provided for the election of fifteen laymen by the Board itself. The first lay members, all Federalists congenial to the Fellows of the Corporation, included Christopher Gore.[29]

In 1812 he succeeded Theophilus Parsons as a Fellow of the Harvard Corporation. Since the Fellows were busy men with faith in the wisdom of President John Thornton Kirkland, a beloved scholar and gentleman, a Unitarian and a Federalist, they granted him large powers and left the direction and operation of the University to him and the faculty. Like Gore, the other members of the Corporation were Federalists and Unitarians, conservative in politics and liberal in religion, and in governing Harvard they gave their first concern to the promotion of scholarship and learning. During the years of Kirkland's presidency (1810-28) Harvard established the Law and Theological schools, founded fifteen new professorships, appointed to the faculty its first European-trained scholars, and reformed its undergraduate curriculum.[30] Some alumni opposed the broader course of study. Rufus King deplored to Gore in 1820 that his son's senior year at Harvard included no subjects in the classics, that instead young men spent their time on "Chemistry, & Philosophy, and Eloquence" and preferred "modern Poetry and History . . . to the fine Models of both Greek & Roman Masters." King declared that he would not accept "the pretension that we are all to become Chemists; few, very few, of the Great Statesmen of old or mod. times were even Mathematicians."[31] Gore replied that he also opposed the trend toward a smattering of knowledge that was implied in the "disposition to learn a little science and neglect the Languages." He informed King that he had tried to prevent the addition to Harvard's curriculum of chemistry and mineralogy, the latter with success, and that he had urged President Kirkland to appoint "a profound Latin Scholar from Germany as a Tutor & Professor" to counteract the popularity of science.[32]

When Gore opened his law office on the third floor of Scollay's Building on Tremont Street after his return from England, he attracted important cases with large fees. The need to engage in petty bickering at the bar no longer plagued him, and the income from his legal practice rose higher than Fisher Ames had anticipated. Andrew Craigie, for example, paid him $600 for arguing before the General Court in support of building the bridge between Lechmere Point and Boston. In addition to handling particular cases that came to him because of his increased prestige, he conducted a continuing, profitable business in the settlement of estates.[33] ". . . I literally pass all my Hours in the Courts of Law or preparing for them," he wrote to King in 1807.[34] Gore's office attracted young men in pursuit of a lawyer's training.

In the summer of 1804 Daniel Webster, a gangling youth from New Hampshire, arrived without credentials to ask permission to become an apprentice. Interested by the forthright approach, Gore took him in. Webster later wrote that he "was conscious of making a good stride onward," that because of Gore's reputation and the large cases that came to him he preferred that office to any in town.[35] The two men grew fond of each other. Gore invited young Webster to his home and sent him away with bottles of Madeira; Webster admired Gore's tact and courtesy, his learning and easy communication; "I could not possibly be better situated," he wrote. Before Webster completed his training, he was offered the clerkship of the Court of Common Pleas for Hillsborough County, New Hampshire, where his father was a judge. Elated at the prospect of a salary and the beginning of his career, Webster prepared to accept the appointment, when Gore, fearing the position would lead nowhere, dissuaded him. "Go on and finish your studies," Webster reported him as saying. "You are poor enough, but there are greater evils than poverty; ... pursue your profession; make yourself useful to your friends, and a little formidable to your enemies, and you have nothing to fear."[36] In March 1805 on Gore's recommendation the Suffolk County Bar admitted Webster to the practice of law.

During the early years of the nineteenth century the Federalists in Massachusetts held a firm grip on the state's legal profession that limited its development and influence and on occasion injected political strife into the courts. When a more democratic interpretation of society and government became popular after the Republicans won control of the national government in 1800, the law in Maryland, Pennsylvania, and Virginia, showing diversity of opinion and independence of thought, moved ahead to meet the needs of an expanding country. The conservative bar of Massachusetts, however, clung to the narrow traditions of the common law, and its most distinguished members carried little influence outside New England.[37] The Republican party in Massachusetts claimed allegiance from only a few of the state's lawyers and from none of the judges, a situation that the Federalists gladly perpetuated. "No Republican has a seat on your bench or is admitted to a participation in your judicial consultations," wrote "Amicus Curiae" in the *Independent Chronicle*;[38] nor did the Republicans succeed in their attempt to penetrate the closed Federalist judiciary through an elective system of judges.

Partisan strife, aggravated by the political exclusiveness of Boston's bar, dominated the criminal case of Thomas O. Selfridge, a Federalist lawyer accused of killing Charles Austin, son of the Republican leader, Benjamin Austin. At the trial Isaac Parker presided as judge, and Samuel Dexter and Christopher Gore represented the defendant; all were prominent Federalists. James Sullivan, said to be the richest, ablest, and most powerful Republican in Massachusetts, spoke for the state.

On August 4, 1805, the readers of Boston's newspapers learned that bad feeling existed between Selfridge and Benjamin Austin, for in the public prints Selfridge had called Austin a scoundrel and a liar, and Austin had let it be known that "someone" would take Selfridge "in hand." When Selfridge left his office in the Old State House at noon on August 4 to walk to the branch of the United States Bank, he put a pistol in his pocket. The trouble between him and young Austin had begun at a Republican dinner on Copps' Hill on the fourth of July. When the Republicans refused to pay the bill of $630, which they considered exorbitant, the owner of the tavern asked Selfridge to begin proceedings to collect the debt. Although Selfridge advised the creditor to move cautiously, Benjamin Austin circulated a story that Selfridge incited him to bring suit. When Austin refused to retract this damaging accusation, Selfridge printed a provocative statement in the local newspapers. The strained relations between the two men came to a climax as Selfridge walked down State Street that August noon and met Austin's son carrying a heavy club. Before passersby were aware of the drama in their midst, Selfridge had been seriously beaten, and Charles Austin lay dead with a bullet through his chest.[39]

On the following day Gore reported to King that Ben Austin had undoubtedly sent his son to beat Selfridge, who was too feeble to defend himself and no "Match at cudgelling." Gore believed, however, that efforts to make the incident a party affair would soon subside, "for Ben Austin's conduct was base and mean in the extreme. . . ."[40] Although the coroner's jury gave a verdict of murder against Selfridge, the grand inquest changed it to manslaughter, prompted, the Republicans declared, by Federalist Judge Theophilus Parson's prejudiced charge to the jury.[41] Prosecution Attorney Sullivan had planned to try Selfridge for murder, and, failing this, he hoped to emphasize the defendant's malice, but in the trial the counsel for the defense so weakened his attempt that he built his case instead around the dangers of permitting a man to take the law into his own hands.

When the trial opened on December 24, 1806, Gore spoke first and asked the question that concerned the court for the next three days: had the shooting been committed in self-defense or to vindicate a previous malice? Gore maintained that the killing would be excusable if the circumstances of Austin's attack justified a reasonable apprehension of harm that Selfridge would have a right to prevent. Dexter argued for the necessity of self-defense, that if a man's life were in jeopardy, he might properly defend it. Sullivan countered that each citizen must seek his safety only in the laws of his country.[42]

Both Gore and Dexter maintained that Selfridge had killed Charles Austin to protect his own life. They stressed the older man's feebleness and his difficulty in walking, his serious skull injuries from Austin's heavy club, and the use of his pistol only after Austin's attack. Witnesses for the defendant testified that Selfridge justifiably believed that Austin held a felonious intent towards him; evidence showed that Selfridge, guilty of no obvious premeditated malice, had been going about his professional business in State Street when Austin struck him, that, anticipating such an attack and being unable to fight, he had armed himself for protection. Before a jury that included both Federalists and Republicans, Gore and Dexter built a convincing argument for justifiable homicide. Judge Isaac Parker instructed the jury to consider whether, according to the facts presented by the prosecution or by the defense, any reasonable, legal justification for the killing had been proved. After deliberating for fifteen minutes, the jury announced its verdict of not guilty.[43]

The Selfridge case intensified political strife in Boston. Before the trial began, Benjamin Austin announced his candidacy for Congress, and Gore reported to King that "Sullivan and Austin are endeavouring to avail themselves of the Death of the Son to blacken the Federalists. . . ."[44] Even the patriotism of Paul Revere, the jury's foreman, came under malicious attack from the Republicans, and Benjamin Austin presented to the state legislature a memorial condemning an acquittal that was more political than judicious. Although the Federalist press refrained from sensational statements, for a year after the shooting the *Independent Chronicle* assailed the Federalists for their miscarriage of justice.[45] In 1807 when Christopher Gore campaigned for the governorship of Massachusetts, a Federalist pamphleteer, defending him against Republican slander, admitted that Selfridge had committed "a most flagrant and outrageous murder," and he explained Gore's participation in the trial on the grounds of professional duty once the defendant had requested his counsel.[46]

VII

His Excellency the Governor of Massachusetts

WITHIN the five years after Gore's return from England, the Federalist party in Massachusetts moved from weakness that portended its early extinction to a burst of strength that won it control of the state legislature and carried Gore into the governorship. Federalism owed its revival to the crisis in American affairs that developed out of the war between France and England; in President Jefferson's solution to the problems arising from that conflict, the Federalists found a compelling, popular cause. Until this turn of events, however, they looked out upon a dismal prospect.

In the national administration in Washington and even in the state governments of New England the Republican party advanced triumphantly. The elections of 1807 gave it supremacy in every New England state save Connecticut, and in Massachusetts for the first time since the retirement of Governor Samuel Adams in 1797, the party of "demogogues, democrats, and disorganizers" won control of every branch of the government, a concentration of power that prompted Gore to declare that the affairs of state would be "as bad as Vice & Folly can make them." Gore held only contempt for Governor James Sullivan, whom he described as "always whiffling about," and he vowed never to make "the smallest advance towards conciliating such a Wretch. . . ."[1] In the presidential election of 1804 Jefferson carried the entire country, excepting only Delaware and the New England states of Connecticut, Massachusetts, and New Hampshire. Jefferson's victory baffled Gore, who, with justifiable pride in the Federalists' achievement of having established a new government and equipping it with sound finances, adequate defense, and the respect of foreign nations, failed to understand why the voters shunned them to favor a president who talked vaguely about the virtues of agriculture and the rights of man and presented no concrete diplomatic, economic, or military proposals of his own.

High-principled Federalists like Gore refused to compete with skillful Republican organizers who praised the wisdom of the ordinary voter and sought to attract the economic-social group to which he belonged. They lagged well behind the Republicans in building statewide political organizations that could reward the hard working, punish the unfaithful, compromise disputes, nominate candidates, dispense patronage, and bring the voters to the polls. Indeed they lost their positions of command as their representation in Congress dwindled and, more significantly, as Jeffersonians replaced their holders of appointive offices. To Gore who believed that Federalists were superbly equipped to rule, this was the cruelest blow of all, and it explains some of his acute bitterness toward Republican administrations. When Washington, Hamilton, and Adams retired from politics, the party's leadership passed to Pinckney and King, who, although sincere and conscientious statesmen, lacked the breadth of view, the imagination, prestige, and personality to extend their influence on a national scale and pull their party together. Having neither leaders of commanding stature nor a constructive program of wide appeal and refusing to flatter the ordinary voter whose opinions they distrusted, the Federalists shrank to a minority and admitted their inability "to conquer the vast body that keeps the field."

Nor, as Gore read the future, could he discern any promise of political resurgence, for in his opinion the vast Louisiana territory, purchased from France at the direction of President Jefferson, had forever destroyed the nation's regional balance of power. He observed to King: "Everything that the present administration wishes to effect may be done through the Western States, now fast bound by the ties of gratitude. The wealth of the Southern and Western States will soon leave us far in the rear on that score, as we already are on that of population."[2] Agriculture would henceforth dominate over commerce, and, although the Federalists had always drawn support from farmers of the coastal areas, Gore surmised that the expanding frontier would find little attraction in a leadership of the rich and wellborn from the eastern seaboard.

Even though he was discouraged by Federalist prospects when he returned to Boston, Gore did not retire in waspish despair. Continuing Federalist defeats convinced him that he must join the younger Federalists who, challenged by the successful techniques of local and state Jeffersonian organizations, had demanded the creation of a Federalist party. By 1804 the Federalists of Massachusetts were beginning to function as a statewide group. Gore worked to persuade his reluctant contemporaries of the wisdom of taking an active part in Federalist organizations in towns, in counties, and in the state, and he served regularly as a member of the state Central Committee.[3] The fascination of political office irresistibly drew him back to the Massachusetts State House in spite of his earlier disavowal of interest while Republicans should rule the national government. On April 7, 1806, Suffolk County elected him a senator with more votes than it gave to any other senatorial candidate, and for the next three years he sat in the General Court, two years in the Senate and one in the House of Representatives. Having often prophesied disaster should the Republicans win political control of the state and nation, Gore rationalized to Rufus King his reentry into politics: "It appeared to me that we ought not by deserting our Friends and Country in the Hour of peril, to surrender when our Advice and Experience may be of use to them and ourselves. . . ."[4]

At the opening of the first session of the legislature in 1806 Gore fought to defeat the chicanery of the Republican majority. Caleb Strong, a Federalist from Northampton, had won the governorship by 176 votes, but the legislative committee, customarily appointed to give the official report of the votes for governor and lieutenant governor, contrived to turn Strong's slim victory into a defeat. Composed of five Republicans and two Federalists, the committee adopted the arbitrary rule that in all cases of misspelling the candidates' names, the votes would stand if the spelling conformed to the sound of the name. Accordingly they threw out all votes for "Stron," "Stoon," or "Stong," but retained those for "Sullivin" or "Sullivon," and declared James Sullivan the new governor. Gore, with several other Federalists, drew up a protest against this "ridiculous construction" and denounced the committee's attempt to "reduce the Chief Magistrate to a humiliating dependence on the legislature." In the Senate he tried without success to amend the committee's report by moving that votes for Strong be taken from the column entitled "scattering" and be credited to the Federalist candidate. The Republicans stood firm, and both the House and the Senate adopted the report. They failed, however, to anticipate the public's outrage, and subsequently several Republican legislators joined the Federalists in regrouping enough votes to give Caleb Strong a majority of forty. Christopher Gore represented the Senate on the joint committee that called upon the new governor to inform him of his election.[5]

Unable to loosen the Republicans' grip on the legislature, Gore could only protest their action. Since he believed that Jefferson's administration had determined to destroy the commerce of Massachusetts and had inadequately prepared the country to repel even the smallest aggression from abroad, he particularly opposed any official sanction by the General Court. In January 1807 Gore became a member of a joint committee, heavily weighted with Republicans, to prepare "a respectful address to the President of the United States." The "homage of confidence and esteem" that emerged from the committee demonstrated Gore's meager influence. The address approved Jefferson's frugality, the preservation of national interest and honor in dealing with Europe, the extension of territorial limits, and the thriving commerce in spite of seizures of ships and cargoes by the French and English; it carried to the President an assurance of continued confidence and a promise that the people of Massachusetts would support the requisitions of their government. When the address reached the Senate for debate, Gore attacked it as an unnecessary expression in the "existing state of the country's affairs"; he declared that the legislature's action exceeded its duty and that he found the address erroneous in many principles. The Republicans with a majority of votes carried it through the General Court and sent it to a grateful Jefferson.[6]

Although Gore denounced the Republicans' use of political power, until 1807 he had no valid complaints on economic grounds. From 1803, when England declared war against France, until the *Essex* decision of 1805, American neutral ships almost monopolized the transatlantic carrying trade. France normally restricted direct trade with its West Indian colonies to its own merchant marine, but to prevent starvation on the islands during the war, it admitted ships flying the stars and stripes. American trade with England, always larger than with France, grew more extensive during the war owing to expanded exports of cotton and, more particularly, to the reshipment from American ports of English West Indian produce, the value of which between 1800 and 1805 increased by $20 million. Before the Franco-British war, American exports and imports never totaled more than $30 million; by 1807 exports reached $108 million and imports $138.5 million.[7] Of all the American carriers in foreign trade, the largest number came from Massachusetts, and under cover of neutrality they earned tremendous profits for their owners. The ephemeral nature of this prosperity, however, injected a hint of anxiety. Gore wrote to King on March 10, 1805, "We have been somewhat alarmed here the last week at the Possibility of a Peace. Our Merchants are very anxious that Great Britain should not impair her Dignity, or hazard her security, by any pacific negotiations for the present."[8]

Not peace but the demands of British merchants limited America's commerce. Almost as intent upon preventing American domination of their rich West Indian trade as in defeating Napoleon, Britain's commercial interests called for restrictions against their Yankee competitors.[9] Their government responded in the summer of 1805 when the British Court of Appeals handed down a verdict on the seizure of the American ship *Essex;* the court ruled that the movement of a cargo from the West Indies to the United States and from there transshipped to Europe could not be called a continuous voyage and was therefore contrary to the Rule of 1756, a decree laid down by the British courts that prohibited in wartime any trade that was forbidden during peace. The decision broke the Anglo-American rapprochement and proclaimed England's new hostility toward American neutral commerce.

In spite of this attack on America's $50 million reexport trade, throughout 1806 the shipowners of Massachusetts continued to win handsome profits from their hazardous voyages. Gore reported to King that the shipments of West Indian produce in American bottoms netted Boston merchants between 25 and 50 per cent, "notwithstanding many Losses and Embarrassments."[10] By the end of the summer the soaring profits moved Gore to write: "Our Merchants are now trembling at the Expectation of a General Peace, which would greatly derange their Plans and Enterprizes, as these are founded on the Basis of a countinued War in Europe for several years."[11]

War did continue in Europe, but when the struggle between England and France reached a stalemate, it forced Boston's ships to cope with even greater risks. Nelson's victory at Trafalgar gave England domination of the Atlantic, and after the battle of Austerlitz, France soon controlled most of Europe. English Orders in Council alternated with Napoleonic decrees, each more extensive and uncompromising, until by 1807 the Anglo-French efforts to strangle each other swept from the Atlantic most of America's carrying trade.

England's search of American ships for deserters from the British Navy worried the ordinary American citizen more than it did Christopher Gore, who, like the merchants of Massachusetts, valued ships and cargoes more than the individuals who comprised the crews. When the British ship *Leopard* fired on the American frigate *Chesapeake* and removed four sailors, one a British subject and the other three, Americans who had escaped from the Royal Navy, the American people demanded retribution for this insult to their national honor. At a meeting in Boston called by a group of moderate Federalists, 2,000 Federalists and Republicans united to protest Britain's high-handed conduct. Ultra-conservative Federalists, however, refused to attend; much as they chafed under British humiliations and restrictions of trade they wanted no part in any protest that might worsen the conflict between the United States and England. By smuggling and subterfuge as well as by legal trade, Boston merchants still gathered profits that war against England would surely end. The moderate Federalists chose Gore to serve on a bipartisan committee to draft a statement of Boston's opinion, but in 1808 during Gore's campaign for the governorship, his opponents denounced his failure to attend the town's meeting and to serve on the committee to which he was appointed, an absence that foreshadowed his alliance with the ultra-conservative Federalists.[12]

Gore speculated on the course the Republicans would pursue towards England's attack on the *Chesapeake.* He believed that although the President would like to excite the public mind against the British, his administration would be fearful of "encouraging this Temper lest it should go beyond their Views, and carry them into scenes, to which their Talents and pecuniary resources . . . should prove incompetent. . . ."[13] Jefferson replied with a plan for peaceful coercion. To win Anglo-French recognition of American neutral rights and thereby protect American ships and seamen from seizure and impressment, Congress passed the Embargo Act, which, from December 22, 1807, to March 1, 1809, prohibited American vessels from leaving American harbors for foreign ports and placed coastal and fishing vessels under stringent regulations not to land their cargoes outside the United States; at the same time the Congress enacted the Embargo, it put into effect the Non-importation Act of 1806 to prevent the importation of specified British manufactures. Although the Embargo applied to both belligerents, Jefferson directed his experiment primarily toward England, and although he failed to force England's acceptance of America's neutral rights, he nearly destroyed the commerce of Massachusetts.[14]

Gore knew the Commonwealth had much to lose. In 1807 it owned more ships than any other American state. It ranked first in the country in registered tonnage, and it held four-fifths of the nation's fishing fleet. The restrictions imposed by France and England caused only temporary concern among Yankee traders, who soon found that their profits more than compensated for the nuisance of British inspection and the cost of licenses to cross the blockade to French ports. Even when England and France intensified their struggle, seizing an ever larger percentage of neutral vessels and cargoes, the shipowners of Massachusetts asked no protection; the greater the risks the larger the profits. Their returns far surpassed the value of the ships that earned them. Yet Congress ordered these men to forego their tremendous earnings that their vessels might be safe from capture. To Gore Jefferson's senseless policy was a deliberate attack upon Federalist wealth and power. In spite of Yankee violation and evasion of regulations and in spite of the brisk coastal trade, the Embargo more severely curtailed the commerce of Massachusetts than did the governments of France and England.[15]

Economic distress invaded every part of the Commonwealth. Deprived of their usual income from exports, the farmers sank deeper into debt, and without the West Indian market, the fishing fleet found its catch excessive for domestic consumption. Of all the areas of the state, the port towns suffered most from the Embargo. Employees in maritime industries lost their jobs; workers in the codfish industry, men concerned with the construction and maintenance of vessels, the sailmakers, stevedores, and laborers at the wharves soonest and most severely felt the pinch of Jefferson's coercion. During the winter of 1809 coastal towns enacted measures for relief of the unemployed and organized kitchens to feed the hungry.[16] In Boston, where before the Embargo unoccupied houses and shops rarely appeared for rent, in 1809 there were 500 to let. "Wharves where immense bustle were visible before, are in a manner departed."[17] Gore wrote to King in early December that all those in Suffolk County who had lived by navigation and especially by the fisheries were "obliged to depend on charity for food and fuel."[18]

The economic realities of Jefferson's experiment revived the Federalist party in Massachusetts. In February 1808 from the United States Senate Timothy Pickering opened a campaign in his home state to reestablish the position of Federalism through opposition to Jefferson's administration and its Embargo. His initial blast was an open letter to Governor James Sullivan. After a violent denunciation of the judgment and motives of President Jefferson, whom he sincerely believed to be directly influenced by Napoleon, Pickering called upon the government of Massachusetts to take action against the Embargo, a plea that suggested nullification, and he proposed that a convention of commercial states organize an impressive, united attack against Republican foreign policy.[19] Gore hoped that Pickering's letter would "arouse our People from their sleep, which really appears like the sleep of death. . . ."[20] Republican Governor Sullivan, however, refused to present the letter to the legislature and returned it to the writer. The zealous Pickering had also sent a copy to George Cabot who, before the spring election of 1808, ordered its distribution to all parts of the state. Pickering's letter helped the Federalists to win a majority in the legislature, but it failed to unseat the governor. For the gubernatorial race in 1808 the party chose Christopher Gore. He lost the election by only a thin margin to the incumbent Sullivan, reputedly the most powerful Republican in Federalist territory. When Gore failed to win the governorship, Suffolk County elected him to the House of Representatives for what proved to be a significant term in the state's relations with the federal government.[21]

The newly elected legislature convened in Boston in May 1808 and chose as an early item of business the expulsion of John Quincy Adams from the Federalist party by choosing his successor to the United States Senate nine months before the end of his senatorial term. Adams had voted in favor of the Embargo to protect American property, and he had countered Pickering's explosive statements with a plea for moderation and national unity.[22] His defense of Jefferson's administration proved him a Federalist deserter, who, Gore declared, had "conspired to produce much of the evil we now experience in the State of our Affairs."[23] Gore reported to King that to select a candidate "that cannot be objected to by the friends of Mr. Adams seems the great Difficulty." Many urged Gore to be the next senator, "believing that such a Choice would prevent all chance of a Division," but Gore considered absence from Boston a greater sacrifice than he should then be required to make.[24] The legislature elected James Lloyd, a merchant of Boston, whose political and economic orthodoxy the Federalists trusted. To make certain that during the remainder of his term Adams would follow the wishes of Massachusetts' conservative leadership, the legislature presented him with instructions to guide his voting in the Senate. This was the final humiliation; Adams resigned his seat and joined the Republican party.[25] "He walks into State Street at the usual Hour of Exchange," Gore reported to King, "but seems totally unknown. . . ."[26]

In the House of Representatives Gore acted upon Pickering's advice to inform Congress of the true sentiments of the people of Massachusetts toward the Embargo. He drafted resolutions, introduced by Leban Wheaton of Norton, that vigorously denounced the Administration's commercial policy, and when they came to the House for debate, he led the fight for their adoption. Gore set forth the Federalists' anxiety and alarm at "the operation of an Embargo of . . . unlimited duration, by which not only foreign commerce is annihilated, but the most grievous restraints and embarrassments imposed upon the intercourse between the different States. . . ." He pronounced the Embargo unconstitutional because Congress could not repeal it without consent of the President, he assailed the Act as a "novel and dangerous experiment" that discouraged individual effort by destroying its rewards, and he condemned the power it gave to state governors to issue licenses in interstate commerce because the system would promote monopolies. Ending in a burst of defiance, Gore advised citizens to support the national government only when it provided for their common defense and general welfare.[27] Republican legislators attacked the resolutions as unrepresentative of the true opinion of the state. Joseph Story from Essex County argued for two hours in favor of the Embargo because it prevented both war and submission, but he could not command enough votes to thwart the Federalist majority. In a vote of 248 to 219 the General Court adopted the resolutions and sent them to Senator Pickering to advance the campaign of Jefferson's critics.[28]

Years later when Story was a Justice of the United States Supreme Court, he recalled his association with Gore in the House of Representatives. "From my earliest acquaintance with him, when I was a young man in the Massachusetts Legislature, he always treated me with the greatest kindness and with no common share of distinction. Such kindness was to me rare and valuable at that period, amidst political contentions, and I have never forgotten it."[29]

Although the Republicans lost the battle over Gore's resolutions, they continued their fight by drawing up a protest to enter in the House Journal. They declared their opposition because the resolutions insinuated "that the Embargo is the cause of present difficulties whereas the cause is conflicting ordinances of the belligerent nations in Europe;" they condemned the resolutions because they inferred that the Jefferson administration had neglected to foster the interests of the United States and particularly Massachusetts, whereas commerce, navigation, and fisheries had greatly prospered under the present rulers. To send this statement to Congress, the protest concluded, would excite distrust, weaken the "public arm," and "add new vigor to belligerents abroad."[30]

Gore, having won the legislature's approval of his denunciation of Jefferson's Embargo, urged his party to exert itself at the national level. A Republican defeat in the presidential election of 1808 would most certainly end the Embargo, and the Federalist leaders in Massachusetts set out to organize a victory for their party's candidate. Their first step, Gore realized, must be to insure the choice of Federalist electors from their own state. Since they anticipated Sullivan's rejection of their candidates, the majority leaders conceived a plan to depart from the usual procedure of submitting the legislature's choice to the governor and determined instead to name the electors by a majority vote of both houses. Gore reported to

King that some members hesitated because the manner of selection did not conform with the practice in the rest of the country, "but I trust they will accede to our wishes."[31] Believing that opposition to the Embargo would be stronger in the autumn than in June and that desire for a change of rulers in Washington would be correspondingly greater, the Federalists postponed the announcement of their plan until the autumn session of the General Court.[32]

When the Republicans learned of the Federalist intent to bypass the governor in the choice of presidential electors, they cried "unconstitutional" and demanded approval from all "three branches of the legislature." In a speech to the House Gore defended election by legislative order. Admitting that in Massachusetts a resolve must be submitted to the governor, he argued that the federal Constitution left the manner of selection to the discretion of the state legislatures and that the General Court could therefore make the choice by an order. Gore maintained, furthermore, that the Constitution of Massachusetts did not include the governor as a part of the legislature. In a vote that adhered to party lines, the Federalists carried their proposal.[33]

In their second step to win the presidential election of 1808, the Federalist leaders in Massachusetts drafted a plan to test the party's strength in other states of the northeast. A legislative caucus appointed a committee of twenty, which chose a small working group composed of Harrison Gray Otis, President of the Senate; Timothy Bigelow, Speaker of the House; James Lloyd, George Cabot, and Christopher Gore to correspond with Federalists in other states on the selection of candidates for the next presidential election. They began by sounding out New England; Otis went off to Rhode Island, Bigelow to New Hampshire, and Lloyd to Vermont, each to discuss prospects with party leaders. They returned to Boston reporting widespread economic discontent and a determination to unseat the Republicans.[34] Gore exulted to King, "I think the Federalists were never more united or more encouraged than at present. The embargo is producing real and extensive distress."[35] Spurred on by their findings in New England and their desire to prevent the election of Madison to the presidency, Gore's committee proposed that a meeting of Federalists "from as many states as could reasonably be notified" should be held in New York to choose the party's candidates for the national election.[36] From Gore's letter to King the Federalists of New York learned of the plan for a convention, and they appointed a committee to enlist the cooperation of Federalists in New Jersey, Connecticut, and Maryland.

Gore informed King that the Federalist leadership in Massachusetts wished to support "a federal Candidate and that from New York" rather than from South Carolina if there were the least probability of success. If this should not be the case, Gore continued, "I think they have a leaning to Clinton, under the Idea, that he wou'd support and cherish Commerce, and further that they could make a Bargain with which he would comply, as to the principal measures and officers of the Government."[37] The proposal that the Federalists support the Republican George Clinton of New York as a coalition candidate for the presidency gathered support. Rumors circulated that Clinton opposed the Embargo and the French influence in the national government, and word reached Gore that Republicans dissatisfied with the choice of Madison were bidding for Federalist endorsement of Clinton. To many Federalists the coalition offered a tempting prospect.

In the third week of August 1808, the Federalist convention met in New York. Delegates arrived from New Hampshire, Vermont, Massachusetts, Connecticut, New York, Pennsylvania, Maryland, and South Carolina; Otis, Lloyd, and Gore represented the Federalists of Massachusetts. So deep was the secrecy around the proceedings that not one newspaper even mentioned the convention's existence. The delegates nominated Charles Cotesworth Pinckney of South Carolina and Rufus King of New York to be their candidates for president and vice-president, giving Pinckney the top position because they wished to attract voters outside the northeast. The chief support for the coalition behind Clinton came from Boston, with Otis and Cabot, two of the more realistic Federalist politicians, most strongly in favor. The majority of delegates, however, preferred an independent ticket that would preserve the party's identity. Gore voted with the majority.[38]

In spite of their careful preparations in 1808 for the nomination of their candidates, the Federalists badly neglected them during the campaign. Boston's *Columbian Centinel*, always alert for Federalist news, ignored the nomination. King attributed the general lack of enthusiasm to the desire of some Federalists to swing their support to Clinton at the last minute. When the electoral college met to cast their votes for the president and vice-president, the opportunity for a maneuver toward Clinton never developed; they gave 122 votes to Madison and forty-seven to Pinckney. Although the Federalists carried all of New England except Vermont; outside that area they won only Delaware and a few minority votes in Maryland and North Carolina.[39]

Having failed to unseat the Republican administration, the Federalists of Massachusetts, propelled by their legislative majority, turned the General Court into an instrument of protest against the Embargo. In the House of Representatives Christopher Gore sought guidance from Senator Pickering in Washington. Both men detested Jefferson and his foreign policy; both believed that Napoleon dictated the President's moves and that the United States would soon be at war against England unless the Federalists prevented it. Being so convinced, they searched for a sure-fire method to force the Administration to end the Embargo, having always in mind the tantalizing possibility that the voters might soon denounce their oppressors and demand a change of rulers.

On December 20, 1808, before the convening of the winter session of the General Court, Gore wrote to Pickering that in Massachusetts opposition to the Embargo grew more daring and that the Federalist leaders would have no easy task to temper the zeal of the legislators. "They see nothing but destruction of their property, and slavery of their persons, in the present course, and indeed he must be a man of strong view who can discern a ray of light whereby we can extricate ourselves from this labyrinth." He then asked Pickering to determine by conversation with congressional representatives what measure of cooperation Massachusetts might expect from other states. "The opposition, to be effectual of any change in our rulers," Gore continued, "should comprehend all New England. . . . Unless, therefore, we can unite both as to the manner as to the end, it may be doubtful whether, if we can, we ought not to prevent the State taking any further steps this winter. . . ." He doubted, however, that they would be able "to oppose successfully, for any length of time, the display of such hostility as will shake our Union to the centre. . . ."[40]

Pickering replied to Gore that a convention of New England states seemed "proper and necessary" to unite that section for effective action, and he urged that Federalist leaders in the General Court immediately draw up a "strong and solemn address" setting forth the evils of the Republican administration as demonstrated by its acts, that the document be laid before the legislature and "sent forth by their authority to the people." More vigorous protests, however, should be postponed "until the very crisis of our affairs." He referred Gore to the tenth amendment: "How are the powers reserved to the States respectively, or to the people, to be sustained, but by the respective States judging for themselves and putting their negative on the usurpations of the general government."[41]

The ideas embodied in the letters of Gore and Pickering reflected a widespread discussion that began in the early days of the commercial restrictions and gained momentum as hardships mounted. Less than three months after the Embargo went into effect, Gore had written to Rufus King that the question was frequently asked in Boston whether the states to the east of the Delaware might not combine for the purpose of preventing a war against Great Britain. Gore asked King whether Republicans in New York who suffered from the Embargo might be willing to join in the fight to repeal it.[42] By December 1808 even the moderate Federalists in Massachusetts favored the same united action that Gore proposed from the party's conservative right. Harrison Gray Otis had swung to the side of Gore and Pickering when he wrote to Congressman Josiah Quincy favoring a convention of northeastern states to decide upon some "mode of relief" from the Embargo.[43] Republican leaders like Governor Sullivan and Congressman Joseph Story had no doubt that the right wing leadership of the Federalist party had formally approved withdrawal.[44] Even President Jefferson feared that the real object of the Massachusetts Federalists was "to take advantage of the first war with England to separate New England from the union."[45] The party, however, did not propose secession. Although its leaders recommended united action of the northeastern states to express their opposition to Jefferson's policy of commercial restrictions, they expected to make their protest as members of the Union.

Gore admitted that the Federalists of Massachusetts aroused more opposition to the Embargo in their own state than in any other. He wrote to King at the end of December 1808: "The other N. England States are probably not so ardent as Masstts. To run counter to them would destroy our own Majority and occasion a dreadful Revulsion."[46] Gore thought violence a possibility, but he believed that if any outbursts occurred, they would take place in the rural areas rather than in Boston "where the Merchants are too rich to hazard much on uncertain projects and in Defiance of Law." Pickering had advised Gore to hold the people in check until the "very crisis of our affairs." That summit of discontent loomed dangerously close when Congress in January 1809 passed the Force Act that permitted federal officers to seize without warrant goods suspected of foreign destination, forbade the loading of ships without official permission, and even authorized the use of militia to enforce its provisions. Shipowners, expecting relief from Congress, had filled their vessels with American produce and were ready to sail. The new legislation required them to unload or present exorbitant bonds, and many of them, their patience exhausted, defiantly ordered their ships to sea. All along the coast the Force Act provoked a simultaneous resistance that exceeded the violations under the Embargo.[47]

When news of the federal government's latest coercion reached Boston, ships in the harbor changed their colors to black and hoisted them to half-mast, and more than 4,000 angry citizens converged on Faneuil Hall for the "Second Rocking of the Cradle of American Independence." Declaring that "no resource remains to us but the protection of our State Legislature" and praying for that body's interposition "to save the people's liberties and property," they presented resolutions to the General Court that surpassed in resistance to the national government any other measures that came from Boston during the crisis over the Embargo. The town meeting assailed the Administration's attempt to raise the military above the civil authority, and it commended General Lincoln and others who resigned offices through which the national government intended to impose its arbitrary edicts. The citizens of Boston resolved that they would not voluntarily aid or assist the enforcement of the Embargo and that anyone who gave help would be considered an enemy of the Constitution.[48]

Two days after Boston's determined stand against the Force Act, the General Court assembled in regular session. In the House of Representatives Gore went to work to defeat two resolves presented by Benjamin Crowninshield, Jr. Unlike most shipowners in Massachusetts, the Crowninshields of Salem blamed Great Britain rather then President Jefferson for the loss of their foreign trade, and they supported the Administration's policy of retaliation. Crowninshield proposed, first, that the Massachusetts legislators should denounce Britain's Order in Council of November 1807 as a violation of neutral rights that demanded their resistance, and, second, that the people of Massachusetts should "rally round the standard of their own nation and its government and . . . afford them their utmost support. . . ."[49]

Gore wrote and presented the House committee's report to deny approval. Refusing to be trapped by Crowninshield's implied sanction of war against England, he declared that Massachusetts had no constitutional authority to involve itself with a foreign government. In reply to Crowninshield's second proposal, Gore maintained that since the Republicans had produced only wretchedness at home and loss of prestige abroad, the legislature would be unmindful of its responsibility to the people of Massachusetts if it voted to approve in advance any measure the national government might adopt. The nation's foreign affairs would improve, Gore advised, if the United States would direct its retaliation toward France.

"To this end let Congress repeal the embargo, annul the convention with France, forbid all commercial intercourse with the French dominions, arm our public and private ships, and unfurl the republican banner against the imperial standard." John Adams called Gore's report a declaration of war against France, and the Federalist majority in the House, convinced that England defended freedom for all the world, enthusiastically endorsed his arguments against the Crowninshield Resolves.[50]

At the climax of its hostility towards Jefferson's foreign policy, the General Court dispatched a "Memorial and Remonstrance" to Congress and an "Address to the People" of Massachusetts. The Remonstrance condemned the Force Act because it was neither defined nor secured by standing laws and because its enforcement subjected the rights of the individual to the "arbitrary will of an Executive officer." It declared that France, contemptuous and hostile, offered the Administration no likelihood of accommodation, while Great Britain "manifested a strong desire" to adjust the claims of the two nations, and it urged Congress to choose the side of England "in that glorious struggle now carried on in Europe against the tyranny of France."[51]

In a speech to the House Gore declared his complete agreement with the "Address to the People." Here the Federalist legislators made no attempt to disguise their hatred for those who had destroyed New England's influence and forced its people into poverty. For these disasters they blamed the landowners of the South who had persuaded the Administration to support legislation that penalized commerce and who had "wheedled the New England farmer into a belief that he had no greater interest in the success of navigation than a Virginia planter." Their more bitter attack they directed against the Jefferson administration: in failing "to estimate properly the danger and state of our foreign relations" it had opposed all defensive measures against France and had preserved the national animosity toward Britain by a ruinous Embargo; in contrast to its rising government revenues, the Administration's expenditure for national defense appeared "truly contemptible." Among Gore's irritations the loss of public office rankled most, and he applauded when the "Address to the People" lashed out against Jefferson, who had "originated the idea of driving from the National Councils men who are the natural Representatives of your true interests" and replacing them with those who flatter the ruling party and implement its policies.

The General Court proposed that to equalize New England's position in Congress with that of the South, a constitutional amendment should abolish representation for slaves and another should safeguard Massachusetts' economy from a repetition of "destructive and insidious theories." To achieve a more perfect Union, the South must patronize commerce and navigation, and New England must exclude from its councils those who had advocated the present destructive system. Only then would there appear in Congress a temper of mutual accommodation that would restore to the eastern states their rightful share of wealth and influence. The Massachusetts House of Representatives approved the "Address to the People" by a vote of 133 to seventy-four.[52]

In the second winter of grueling depression, a number of Massachusetts townships, representing one-third of the taxable property of the state, sent petitions to the General Court for relief from the Embargo and the Force Act. The quantity and urgency of the appeals gratified Gore who looked upon the legislature as the protector of the people against the tyranny of the national government. On February 15, 1809, the General Court responded with a "Report and Resolutions," which declared that the Force Act was "unjust, oppressive, and unconstitutional" and not legally binding on the citizens of Massachusetts, but it counseled the people to abstain from forcible resistance and to "apply for their remedy in a peaceable manner to the law of the Commonwealth." Still believing that its surest and quickest relief lay in the united opposition of the New England states, the General Court sent copies of its resolutions to Rhode Island and Connecticut to sound their attitudes toward cooperation.[53] Before Massachusetts had time to summon a convention, relief came from another quarter.

On March 1, 1809, three days before Jefferson retired from the presidency, he signed a bill to repeal the Embargo and the Force Act. His cherished experiment in foreign policy had failed. Although it postponed war, it did not prevent one. In its almost exclusive application to England it contributed to the false charge of French influence in the Administration, and in failing to coerce either or both belligerents to recognize America's neutral rights, the Embargo did not even fulfill the immediate purpose of its creation. Jefferson's policy brought incalculable loss to his own people. It pitted one American against another, the violator of the law against its enforcer. No benefits justified the exorbitant cost of economic dislocation and human misery; no compensations offset the weakened moral fiber as lawbreakers won prestige, and courts in Massachusetts refused to convict the guilty. In alienating the commercial northeast Jefferson created a climate of hate that destroyed national unity. Massachusetts could take major credit for ending the Embargo; it had protested, threatened, defied, and aroused, until the resistance of New England townships shook the foundations of the national government.[54]

Not the least of Jefferson's misfortunes from the Embargo was the revival of Federalism in New England. Although the party in Massachusetts could hardly be blamed for fighting a policy that seriously disrupted the region's economy or for using that calamity to win political power, the Federalists raised partisan animosity dangerously high. In their hatred of Jefferson's administration they made the Republican party an enemy more to be feared than any foreign power, and their arrogant preachments of New England's superiority to the South seriously divided the country when its approaching war against England demanded unity. In the General Court of Massachusetts no man had more strongly protested the Embargo than Christopher Gore. In the winter of 1809 a grateful party nominated him for governor.

Boston's newspapers waged a spirited gubernatorial campaign between Gore and Levi Lincoln, the Republican incumbent who had come to office at the death of Governor Sullivan. The *Columbian Centinel* promised Gore's protection of the peoples' liberties and property and took as its slogan "Gore, Liberty, Free Trade, Union, and the Constitution."[55] The *Boston Gazette* printed a sketch of Gore's life in which it described the Federalist candidate as a remarkable prosecutor in court, a polished gentleman, an accomplished scholar, and a practical farmer beloved by his tenants.[56] It reprinted an editorial from the *Northampton Gazette* that declared that Gore, if elected, would closely follow the "example of Washington," while Levi Lincoln, ignoring the high principles of the first President, had governed Massachusetts "with low cunning and artifice in place of wisdom."[57] In a battle of adjectives, the *Boston Gazette* contrasted the "mild, affable, gentle, and unassuming" Gore with the "haughty, reserved, vindictive, and overbearing" Lincoln, and for the climax of its last issue before the election, the *Gazette* carried an endorsement of Gore written by the moderate and esteemed Federalist, Caleb Strong. The former governor assured the voters of Massachusetts that having known Christopher Gore for more than twenty years he could attest to his Christianity, his correct morals, amiable manners, superior talents, and his unblemished honor and integrity.[58]

Between Gore's nomination in February 1809 and his election in April, the *Independent Chronicle* assailed him in every issue. The newspaper maintained that his record in the legislature proved him to be a dangerous puppet of the Essex Junto, that he sought to dissolve the Union, and that his support of Britain against France and his father's Toryism during the Revolution strengthened the charge of disloyalty; Gore's wealth implied dishonesty and his defense of Thomas Selfridge, immorality.[59] "Kitty Gore," the *Chronicle* called him and inquired, "Whose carriage is that, that rolls so majestically thro the street, decked in scarlet and gold? One might as well elect the Duke of York."[60] To alienate moderate Federalists from the conservative Gore, the *Chronicle* deplored the party's shabby treatment of Harrison Gray Otis, who had been "a kind of dray horse for the federalists for many years," while the name of Gore had "risen like a comet."[61]

At least one important Federalist expressed misgivings about Gore's candidacy. John T. Kirkland, soon to become President of Harvard, wrote to Congressman Josiah Quincy that although the friends of Otis would support Gore, the nomination was not the best that could have been made, and he judged Gore's running mate, David Cobb of Taunton, too jolly to carry the responsibilities of the lieutenant governor. Kirkland declared that Otis attended church more regularly than Gore and that good Congregationalists would not concede that Federalism would be safe "under the superintendance of a Governor, who belongs to the Chapel Church, avowed Unitarian." He expected, however, that Gore would be elected because he represented the "party of five-sixths of the mind, wealth, and character of the State."[62]

On the first Monday in April 1809, 93,322 adult males went to the polls in Massachusetts and by a majority of 1,255 votes elected Christopher Gore to be their governor. The impetus of the Embargo and the Force Act enabled Gore to carry seven counties and to win by a slender margin.[63] Two months later loyal Federalists from miles around came to Boston to attend the inauguration of their successful candidate, whose distinguished appearance was quite as impressive as his service to the party. With black eyes, powdered hair, and round, florid face, Gore stood tall, "of full person" and erect carriage, elegantly dressed in a suit of plum-colored silk, decorated with embroidery and lace.[64]

Governor Gore's inaugural address to the Senate and House of Representatives forecast the character of his administration. Toward the national government he showed conciliation, for although Congress had followed the Embargo with the Non-intercourse Act, the new legislation permitted a relatively free and profitable flow of trade. To safeguard commerce in the future, however, Gore recommended that Massachusetts propose a constitutional amendment to limit the duration of commercial restrictions to thirty days. He commended the citizens of the state for their fortitude during their recent privations, and he praised and defended the preceding legislature, "which did what duty rendered indispensable, and it surely did no more." Reminding his listeners of their obligation to promote the Protestant religion, he cautioned them to commit no offense toward Christians of any denomination because of their nonconformity. He requested the legislature's concern for agriculture and manufacturing and its attention to literature and science, especially in the University at Cambridge. He recommended the appointment of a comptroller to act as a check on the state's treasurer, and, to maintain an able and independent judiciary, he asked for an increase in the salaries of the justices. Gore assailed the "principle" that attachment to a party should be the only criterion for office and that political appointment should reward those who promoted a man to power. Deploring the recent "violence and animosity of party spirit," he urged the legislature, in its concern for the public welfare, to set an example of tolerance.[65]

The Federalist-dominated legislature quickly responded to Gore's major recommendations. It drafted an amendment to the Constitution to safeguard commerce against indefinite restriction, but of the other states only Connecticut approved it.[66] The threatened resignation of Theophilus Parsons as Chief Justice of the Supreme Judicial Court so that he could improve his income by private practice dramatized the need for higher salaries for the justices. The Republicans, having no representatives among them, opposed an increase until Joseph Story convinced them of its necessity in order to maintain the high quality of the state's judiciary. In a bipartisan vote the legislature gave $600 more to each associate justice and added $1,000 to the salary of the chief justice.[67]

Governor Gore made one striking political innovation in Massachusetts; during late summer and early autumn he traveled through northern and western counties to visit his constituents. Since neither fondness nor admiration for the average citizen could have prompted him to embark on a tour among the voters, his compelling desire to win the next election must have motivated him to choose this way of competing against the Republicans. The towns in which he stopped responded with parades and artillery salutes, and the local dignitaries feasted and toasted the Governor and his wife. On his return from the district of Maine, Gore stopped at Beverly, where an escort of Essex Hussars conducted him to the house of Israel Thorndike, the town's most substantial citizen, while ships at

Beverly Bridge fired salutes; reports from Salem told of a reception at Sun Tavern where "all classes of citizens" filed by to greet their chief executive.[68] Gore wrote to King that "excepting more Bustle than was agreeable, our Tour was very pleasant."[69] Only Pittsfield made an unfriendly impression; during Gore's visit the editor of the *Pittsfield Sun* and his Republican friends hanged the Governor in effigy on the village common.[70]

While Gore and his party progressed from one town to another, anti-Federalist newspapers carried a running commentary on the Governor's elegant style, "like that of an English prince or noble, dashing down among his tenants before an election."[71] All who lined the roads to watch the Governor and his party drive by found the spectacle worth their effort. The Gores sat in an open carriage upholstered in red hammer cloth and pulled by four long-tailed bays; the coachman and outriders wore bright livery, and the Governor's aides formed a mounted escort.[72] To Gore's political supporters in Boston the Governor's accouterments appeared proper for a rich man of social distinction who had recently lived in a sophisticated European capital and now held the highest office in the Commonwealth. To many voters in the hinterland, however, Gore's entourage appeared pretentious. His tour may have dazzled, but it did not endear him to his constitutents, and some prophesied that it would cost him the next election.

In 1810 and 1811 the Federalists could find no cause of sufficiently popular appeal to reelect Gore. Although the *Boston Gazette* declared that an election of the Federalist candidates would save the nation from a ruinous war against England and prevent Massachusetts from falling back into "degradation and democracy," the revival of trade gave little support to threats of disaster. On the repeal of the Embargo American merchantmen swarmed out to foreign ports in the Orient, the Baltic, the Mediterranean, and the West Indies. In mid-April 1809, when the British minister in Washington and the American secretary of state agreed to abandon both the Orders in Council and the Non-intercourse Act, American trade boomed until the British government repudiated the agreement and Madison revived non-intercourse. Since the President's order could not be immediately effective, during the autumn of 1809 American ships returned to their home ports laden with British goods. A few months later Congress permitted non-intercourse to lapse but threatened to revive it against either belligerent who did not follow the others in revoking its decrees or orders against American neutral ships.[73]

Gore tried without success to make the government's restrictions serve his political advantage. When he declared that the voters of Massachusetts "unless restrained by the actual power of Bonaparte" would rise against the Non-intercourse Act and some Federalists even threatened nullification if Congress did not repeal the act, few voters showed any concern; their privations, so mild and brief in comparison with the effects of the Embargo and Force Act, aroused no support for Gore's militant recommendations against the Administration. In 1810 and 1811 the Republican Elbridge Gerry, sixty-five years of age and no admirer of the common man, won the governor's race over Christopher Gore. Kirkland wrote to Josiah Quincy that "to have such a chief magistrate as Mr. Gore" for another year would have been delightful and beneficial, "but it cannot be expected, nor is it essential." Kirkland believed that in ordinary times Massachusetts could get along well enough with men like Governor Elbridge Gerry and Lieutenant Governor William Gray, and in extraordinary times "we shall probably do as we have done, make a successful counteraction and even secure the helm."[74]

The following year Gore declined the Federalist nomination. He explained to King that during the last twelve months "such an apathy was apparent among the Federalists that there was no Prospect of Success, and I told the Committee that They and I must be convinced of this Truth."[75] When he heard that some Boston Federalists believed that Caleb Strong would win more votes, he requested the withdrawal of his name. Caleb Strong, resident in an agricultural county and unencumbered by wealth, Unitarianism, and anglicism, regained the governorship for the Federalist party as war against England was about to start.

Only in 1809 when the Republican administration in Washington appeared determined to destroy Massachusetts' commercial economy did a majority of the state's voters follow Gore's conservative, antinational leadership. When the crisis passed, they gave their allegiance and votes to the Republicans. Gore governed the Commonwealth with efficiency, intelligence, and impeccable conduct; no enemy ever assailed him for the misuse of his wealth for political advantage or the betrayal of his office for the cheap satisfactions of demagoguery. To every office he held he brought a deep concern for the welfare of Massachusetts. But the election returns showed that his administrative virtues, high principles, and unflagging devotion failed to outweigh his aristocratic manner, his Unitarianism, his English bias, his display of wealth, his antinationalism. Gore admirably fits Harrison Gray Otis' description of the Essex Junto: "There is not one of those sworn brothers who is or ever was, a politician, or who ever had what old John Adams calls the tact of the feelings and passions of mankind; but they are men of probity, of talent, of influence, and the Federal party may say of them, *Non passum vivere sine te nec sum te!*"[76]

VIII
The Honorable Senator from Massachusetts

IN spite of Gore's failure after 1809 to win another gubernatorial election, he continued to hold an important place in the Federalist party in Massachusetts. His immediate and forthright opposition to the United States' declaration of war against England on June 18, 1812, placed him in high favor with the commercial interests of Massachusetts and won him a seat in the United States Senate. Gore had warned that Madison's bungling foreign policy would lead to war, but when it actually brought the United States into Europe's conflict with American hostility directed toward the wrong belligerent, incredulous Federalists marveled that such catastrophe could spring from unimportant causes.

The President declared that America fought England to win freedom of trade and sailors' rights, and indeed the difficulties arising from the Orders in Council, aggravated by impressment of American seamen, finally moved the Administration and Congress to action. Yankee shipowners, however, wanted no war to protect their interests, which, they contended, were well enough served by the vessels that escaped capture. Although the Administration learned soon after the war began that England had repealed its offensive Orders in Council and would end its blockades, Madison continued to fight because England continued to impress American seamen. To Christopher Gore impressment constituted no cause for war. He based his contention on a report issued by a Massachusetts legislative committee in 1813 that fifty-one of the leading shipowners of the state who had employed 1,500 sailors in the last twelve years, had lost only a dozen men, and the committee estimated that no more than a total of 100 Americans had been impressed. A more accurate figure would have approached 6,000. John Quincy Adams asserted that no nation could be independent if it permitted its citizens to be stolen by another power, but the Federalists no longer listened to him. Beyond the immediate reasons for declaring war, Madison sought to develop a more complete independence from England, a quest that appeared to Gore as visionary as it was undesirable.[1]

Gore hoped that the Republicans' outrageous war would bring victory to the Federalists in the national elections of 1812. Rufus King wrote that he had heard that Gore approved the coalition candidate, to which Gore replied, "It is more than can be warranted by my Conduct, or Conversation, to say that I was for co-operation of the Federalists in the Election of Mr. Clinton."[2] Although the candidate from New York carried every northern state except Pennsylvania and Vermont, Madison won in the electoral college by nineteen votes. Unable to end the war by victory at the polls, the Massachusetts Federalists set out to limit the ability of the Madison administration to wage it.

A month after the fighting began, the lower house of the General Court issued an "Address to the People of Massachusetts" urging them to oppose the war without fear, to organize a peace party, and to send no volunteers to the army except for defense of the national domain. The state showed little enthusiasm for privateering; against fifty-eight vessels equipped in Baltimore, Boston fitted out only thirty-one. In its conflict with Massachusetts over the control of the state's militia, the Madison administration was caught in a bind of Yankee obstructionism. Three times Governor Strong refused to release a detachment of militia to the federal government to augment the national army, maintaining that since Massachusetts was neither invaded nor in immediate danger of invasion, the President of the United States held no jurisdiction over the militia. When the commander of the national forces in Massachusetts then marched his men out of the state toward Canada, the General Court appropriated $100,000 for the purchase of firearms, cannon, and gun powder and authorized the Governor to appoint three commissioners to organize the defense of the coast. By February 1813 the Commonwealth had built its own fighting force of almost 70,000 soldiers, and in the spring election of that year the voters went to the polls to back those candidates who opposed the Administration's war against England. The Federalist party carried all New England.[3]

In this critical state of affairs Christopher Gore entered the national government as spokesman for the people of his state who believed that their welfare depended upon friendship with England. ". . . we may do good," Senator Rufus King wrote to Gore, "we may encourage & soothe the Govt. to restore peace—and shd. we contribute to this very important purpose, it shd. not fail to produce very satisfactory reflections at a future day. . . ."[4]

In the spring of 1813 Governor Strong appointed Gore to the United States Senate to fill the vacancy created by the resignation of James Lloyd. Rufus King had persuaded Gore to allow his name to be considered for the office. ". . . pray think of it—" he wrote, "I know of nothing which would sweeten the future years which may be allotted to me more than again renewing that intercourse and friendship which subsisted between us in a foreign Country. Our wives would fully participate in our happiness. . . ."[5] In his recommendation to Governor Strong, King wrote of the "prudence & integrity" that Gore would bring to the Senate and of the cooperation he would give to King in promoting "the public welfare." Strong replied that he was already convinced of the wisdom of nominating Gore, and if "both Houses are federal, as there is much reason to expect, there is no doubt but that they will elect Mr. Gore, if he is appointed by the Executive."[6] The election proceded as Governor Strong had anticipated. Gore received 357 votes from a total of 459, and on May 28, 1813, he began his term as United States Senator from Massachusetts.[7] Since the Thirteenth Congress had assembled in extra session four days earlier, he set out at once on the long, uncomfortable journey to the national capital.

In 1813 Washington offered neither elegance nor comfort to members of Congress. Although the north and south wings of the capital were in use, the space between them, intended to bear the dome, was covered with rough boards and served as an improvised passageway. The government lacked funds to bring reality to L'Enfant's plans for a monumental city, and along Pennsylvania Avenue "the President's Palace," completed in 1809, was conspicuously the only building of any merit. A few trees planted during Jefferson's administration added some beauty to the street, but the ugly shanties that lined its sides made a stronger impression.

Most congressmen lived in boarding houses and paid about $15 a week for service, wood, candles, food, and brandy. Gore found nearby Georgetown a more pleasant environment than Washington, and, although his quarters fell short of his style of living in Boston and Waltham, he maintained as much formality as he could. Years later Daniel Webster recalled the large, white house that had been the Federalist headquarters when he entered Congress, where Gore, King, and Marshall were fellow-boarders and from which "Governor Gore used to drive out . . . in a coach drawn by four horses, attended by servants in livery."[8] Senator Jeremiah Mason wrote to his wife in Portsmouth, New Hampshire, that "Messrs. King and Gore and their wives are the best people I have found here. I see them pretty frequently, and the more I see of them the better I like them. Mr. King is a very great man; Mr. Gore great enough."[9] The presence of the British in Chesapeake Bay and the fear of their attack on Washington dulled the gaiety of the capital's social life. Politics, however, moved at a brisk pace.

Through the Thirteenth Congress the Republicans controlled both houses, and when the extra session opened they counted twenty-seven members in the Senate to the Federalists' nine; of the latter, Mason, Gore, and King carried the most influence. The senior senator from Massachusetts was a Republican, Joseph Varnum, whom Gore had first met as an opponent more than twenty years earlier at the federal constitutional ratifying convention; Vice-President Elbridge Gerry, who had defeated Gore in the gubernatorial campaigns of 1810 and 1811, presided in the Senate.

Gore took to Washington three fixed ideas that determined every speech he delivered and every vote he cast: the economy of Massachusetts depended primarily upon commerce and demanded good relations with England; the upheaval that Republican foreign and domestic policies inflicted upon the nation stemmed from the Administration's devotion to France and hatred of England and from the political domination of the agrarian South and West; to prevent the dissolution of the United States as a sovereign nation the Madison administration must be so discredited that the Federalists would win control of the government. Gore interpreted the national crisis as part of a continuing conflict between New England and the federal government in which the Republican party, led by the slaveholding South, tried to destroy the northeast's commercial economy, had reduced its political power through the acquisition of new territory, and in the disastrous war against England had left the coast of Massachusetts undefended.

Gore had scarcely taken his seat in the Senate when the General Court, never slow to make its opinions known, instructed him and Joseph Varnum to exert their utmost endeavor to repeal the unconstitutional act that admitted Louisiana to statehood. It sent a "Remonstrance" to Congress, which Gore presented to the Senate, that protested the war against England as improper and impolitic when France more justly deserved America's enmity; it deplored the high taxes collected from Massachusetts, which were "beyond all proportion to her political weight in the union;" and it complained of the South's swollen political power that derived from its slave population and aimed to destroy New England's commerce. Lest Congress labor under a false impression that everyone in Massachusetts agreed with the Federalists, the Republican minority of the General Court sent a protest against the legislature's "Remonstrance," which Varnum presented to the Senate. This group asserted its high regard for the Administration's annexation of territory and for its conduct of a "just and necessary" war.[10]

In the Senate Gore took as his chief antagonist the President of the United States, and he made his first attack when Madison tried to eliminate New England's legal and illegal profits from the importation and sale of spirits and of wool and cotton cloth. To close the last loophole through which English goods still entered the United States, disguised as the products of another country, Madison proposed to prohibit the entrance of these articles from whatever country they originated. When this bill to strengthen the Non-importation Act came before the Senate, Gore proposed that textiles be omitted from its provision. He saw no wisdom in accepting the measure simply because the President had requested it. Was it not in such manner that Congress had approved Madison's recommendation of December 9, 1813, that, since Britain's blockade of the coast south of Rhode Island caused "invidious discrimination" among American ports, the United States should, in effect, extend Britain's blockade northward by laying an embargo against the coastal and foreign traffic of American ships? Although laws were already in force that prohibited trade with the enemy, Congress had quickly complied with the President's request and closed the ports of Boston, Newport, and Salem.[11] While Gore was speaking to the Senate, Madison's embargo, rigorously enforced, had locked New England's ships in their harbors. Few senators, however, sympathized with New England's plight, for the northeast had been the only section of the country to make substantial profits from the war. Until the enactment of Madison's embargo, Britain's blockade south of Rhode Island gave Boston a monopoly of America's importing business, permitted fishing near the coast, allowed a thriving trade with Halifax, and offered favorable opportunities for smuggling.[12]

Having discounted to the Senate the value of the President's past judgment, Gore turned to Madison's present request for the prohibition of imports of wool and cotton cloth. He reminded his audience that laws were already in force to shut out British imports and that experience had shown that such pressure had no effect upon the enemy. Jefferson's Embargo had failed to wring England's recognition of America's neutral rights, and shutting out British imports had won no concessions for Napoleon. Did the Senate believe that England would be frightened into submission by Madison's most recent proposal? "She attempts to capture our ships, to destroy our trade, and prevent us from receiving supplies from abroad. We co-operate most manfully in this work of ruin; nay, we do more to this end, in a few short days, than she could do in many years. We annihilate our ships, destroy our produce, imprison all our citizens, suffer not one to escape from the United States, doom whole States to sloth and famine, allow no man, woman, or child, to cross a river or bay without permission from the President . . . brake down all the barriers heretofore thought necessary to the support of public and individual liberty, disregard the provisions of our Constitution, and subject ourselves and property to martial law. When our vindictive foe has obtained so efficient an ally, in bringing destruction on the people of this country, he may cheerfully sustain the loss which will be incurred by retaining at home, or selling at a reduced price, a few blankets that might be smuggled into the United States by some crafty foreigner from a neutral port."[13]

Gore scorned Madison's attempt to make non-importation palatable through the encouragement it would give to American manufacturers, a promise that ill became a government that had most unfeelingly destroyed those manufactures that sprang from, and were supported by, navigation and commerce. "Instead of promoting these hardy employments, you offer the loom and the shuttle. You huddle together men, women, and children, in one contaminated . . . mess, and you render your men more effeminate than your women." By giving a monopoly to favored manufacturers, Madison would destroy whatever remained of American commerce. Gore warned that in spite of government aid, textile factories in the United States would never succeed because of their high labor costs and because capital investments in foreign trade brought higher returns than money lent to the producers of factory-made cloth. Four years later Gore changed his mind about the losses and miseries involved in textile manufacturing in Massachusetts and joined the movement of capital from sea to factory, but in 1813 he believed that Madison's plan to strengthen the country's war effort was designed instead to persecute New England. In concluding his speech Gore urged the Senate to reject the President's request to persist in a policy so devoid of reason.[14]

Daniel Webster praised Gore's speech, but some Federalists, who earlier might have acclaimed it, now condemned it. These entrepreneurs, finding their usual channels of commercial activity closed by war and restrictive laws, turned to the manufacture of those articles made scarce by nonimportation and sought by legislation to protect and expand their ventures. Elisha R. Potter, a Federalist of Rhode Island, where a spate of little factories grew, declared that Gore's proposal would continue the importation of textiles, which "we do not want, and can well do without." A majority of senators agreed, and they voted down Gore's motion to exclude wool and cotton cloth from Madison's list of prohibited imports.[15]

The President failed in his attempt by legislation to shorten the war, and except briefly, to bring New England to heel. Although the bill that would exclude wool and cotton cloth passed the House and Senate, it later died in committee, and three months after the embargo went into force the President asked Congress to repeal it and the Non-importation Act. Since these measures had had little effect upon England at war, they could hardly be expected to impress after that nation had defeated Napoleon. On April 14, 1814, Congress accepted the President's recommendation to abandon the system of commercial restrictions around which both he and Jefferson had built their foreign policy.

The immediate effect of the repeal brought little relief to New England because Britain then extended its blockade north to New Brunswick, and few vessels were able to slip through it. Not all Yankee traders were undone, however; some shipped their goods overland in wagons, even beyond the northern boundary, and in September 1814 the British provided a way out when, having captured Castine in the district of Maine, they declared it a free port. Gore reported to King that cartloads of specie moved from Massachusetts to Canada and that an uninterrupted trade ran between them in bills of the British government.[16]

Gore's next attack on the President challenged Madison's use of the executive power of appointment. At the end of February 1814 Gore entered a motion that in the opinion of the Senate the President of the United States had no authority during the recess of the Senate to appoint John Quincy Adams, James A. Bayard, and Albert Gallatin to be envoys extraordinary with the rank of minister to negotiate a treaty of peace with Great Britain. When the motion came before the Senate for consideration, Gore made clear that the object of his attack on the President was to preserve the powers granted to the Senate in the Constitution. He argued that since the power of appointment was vested in both the Executive and the Senate, the only time the President could make an appointment without the latter's advice and consent was to fill a vacancy that occurred when the Senate was not in session. Madison could not lawfully commission Adams, Bayard, and Gallatin to fill vacancies because these offices had not previously existed; therefore, the President had deliberately usurped the power of the Senate.[17]

In a well-reasoned rebuttal, Senator William Bibb, Republican of Georgia, maintained that since Russia offered its mediation to establish peace between England and the United States during recess of the Senate, creating then a new and necessarily vacant office, the President filled it in the exercise of his constitutional power with no disregard of the rights of that body. As precedents for Madison's action, Bibb enumerated similar appointments of Washington and Adams, and he declared that the Constitution gave the Senate no power to censure the Executive. Bibb asked Gore why, when the President submitted the nominations for the Senate's approval at its next meeting, had he voted for Adams and Bayard and thereby sanctioned the very act that he later denounced as unconstitutional.[18]

Senator Outerbridge Horsey, a Federalist from Delaware, opposed Gore's motion because it implied censure of the President, a measure without precedent, for an act that appeared to many senators to be completely constitutional. Since the need for the appointments arose during the recess of the Senate, the President was within his constitutional rights to meet it, and in acting with dispatch to secure peace if possible, he fulfilled the intent of the Constitution.[19]

On April 2 Gore replied to his critics that their arguments stemmed from expediency, necessity, and advantages resulting from prompt action and the supreme power of the President, while the issue in question pertained only to the Constitution. Gore had approved the nomination of Adams and Bayard because the question then before the Senate was the fitness of the men for office, not the right of the President to appoint them during the Senate's recess. Since the Senate and Executive were coordinate branches in the power of appointment, either had the right to judge whether or not the other infringed upon its privileges. The sequence of events leading to the appointments denied the necessity of Madison's precipitous action. Russia offered mediation on March 8, 1813, Madison appointed the envoys on April 17, the Senators would convene on May 25, and had the President wished their advice and consent he could have summoned them earlier. Gore closed his defense with a statement written by James Madison when he was in the Virginia legislature in which he warned against the surrender of power to those who administer it. The Senate majority, believing Gore's motion to be petty and factious in time of crisis, postponed consideration of it and later discarded the proposal by failing to refer it to a committee or even to resume discussion of it.[20]

When Gore returned to Massachusetts during recesses of Congress, he found increasing opposition to the war. He reported to King that some Bostonians discussed the advisability of declaring "that the Union is dissolved and that Massachusetts is willing to be at peace with G. B., and that her ports shall be open to all Nations." Others proposed that Massachusetts should ask permission of Congress to make an armistice with the enemy. "What may arise from Discontent and Distress that are daily augmenting, it is impossible to tell."[21]

When England and its allies won victories, the Federalists in Boston demonstrated their enthusiasm. They celebrated Russia's defeat of Napoleon with prayers of thanksgiving at King's Chapel and a banquet at the Exchange Coffee House. They drank to the health of Alexander the Great and to the Russian nation and armies; but to "Our National Rulers," the Federalists proposed: "May the people see in them now what history may say of them hereafter." Gore, unable to attend, sent a letter of gratification that the Russians had driven back "the invaders of their homes and firesides."[22] Two years later, when news of England's victory at Waterloo reached Boston, the happy Federalists set a day for public acclaim. "The Hon. Mr. Gore" made an impressive speech, recounting events "which have delivered a great portion of Europe from the most ironhanded Despotism," and he presented resolutions to congratulate the head of the House of Bourbon on "his restoration from exile to the throne of his ancestors. . . ." Festivities continued into the night as 2,000 lamps illuminated the State House, and a band played in the colonnade.[23]

In all of Massachusetts probably no more than a third of the population favored the war. The South wholly supported the Republicans, and the Middle States divided their allegiance between the two parties. Federalist predictions of Republican incompetence proved true in the government's financial embarrassment and military disgrace, but contrary to the Federalists' expectations, the country did not ask them to take control of the government. Instead, the threat of defeat produced a strong undercurrent in support of the war that the Union might be preserved. "War is the law of the land," one writer declared, "and the Kings, the Gores, and the Websters should refrain as a minority from trying to coerce Madison to retire from office."[24] In the elections of 1814 the Federalists made sharp advances in the Middle States, and in New England they intensified their assault upon the Republicans; Newburyport, Massachusetts, gave no votes at all to its Republican candidate for Congress.[25] Jefferson wrote to Elbridge Gerry that the Federalists preferred colonial status under the British Empire to an independent government in which they could have only a proportional share in the direction of its affairs. "But I trust," he continued, "that such perverseness will not be that of the honest and well-meaning mass of the federalists of Massachusetts; and that when the questions of separation and rebellion shall be nakedly proposed to them, the Gores and Pickerings will find their levees crowded with silk stocking gentry but no yeomanry; an army of officers without soldiers."[26] Jefferson exaggerated the charge against Gore, who, although allied with the conservative faction of Boston's Federalists, had never joined the extremists in advocating separation from the Union.

In Washington the Federalist congressional minority met in October 1814 to consider the party's legislative action during the national crisis. Gore was called to chair the meeting, and a committee that included Pickering, King, and Gore was appointed to determine how much support the Federalists in Congress should give to the Administration's war effort. In its report the committee declared that the Federalists would be the last to give up the "rights of Soil and Sovereignty belonging to the Nation," and, although the party believed the war to be unnecessary and inexpedient, the committee urged all Federalists to unite in adopting vigorous measures to repel the nation's invaders and to protect its rights and honor. To this end Congress should grant supplies of both men and money. The committee proposed that Federalists should support the recommendations of the Committee of Ways and Means for raising money by indirect taxes. Since commerce, "heretofore, the only and abundant source of revenue, has by the folly of our Rulers, and the power of the Enemy, been entirely destroyed," Congress must lay a direct tax, but the report specified that it should be apportioned among the states according to the ability of each to pay. Although the committee did not expect the party's unanimity in the choice of objects to be taxed nor did it believe that public credit and peace could be restored without changes in the heads of executive departments, it urged agreement on the general principle that supplies be granted for the nation's defense. On one point it refused support: it would not approve any plan to enlarge the army by means of conscription. The Federalists in Congress accepted the report and applied its recommendations almost immediately to their consideration of the Administration's bill to authorize the President of the United States to raise a national force of 80,000 militiamen.[27]

Secretary of War Monroe admitted the failure of the government's recruiting a wartime army and explained that most of the available men preferred to join the state militias as substitutes in order to obtain the high bounties offered for such enlistments. This situation forced the Administration to rely upon the militias for its main fighting strength, a dependence that frightened both Federalists and Republicans. As a military force the militia had proved incompetent in repulsing the British in Maine, in defending Baltimore and Washington, and in giving effective service at Norfolk, Niagara, and Plattsburg; as a political force it threatened the national government with the formation of state armies and the transfer of sovereignty to the states. Massachusetts, tense with revived rumors of disunion, had the largest militia, equipped and trained at the expense of the state and under the command of officers appointed by Governor Strong. On all but a few occasions the Governor had withheld this force from the national government. Having failed to enlarge the regular army, the Administration hoped to make the state militias a more impressive instrument of war by increasing their time in the armed forces from six months to two years, by placing them under the command of officers of the regular army, and by assuring their service through conscription. When the bill came before the Senate, both Federalists and Republicans attacked it as unconstitutional and a threat to individual freedom.[28]

Gore spoke at length in opposition. He contended that no power of the individual states was "so positively and emphatically reserved" to them as their control over their militias, and upon this force the states depended for their protection in time of peril. The Constitution authorized the federal government to call out the militia only for a brief emergency, not to serve for two years to defend the national frontiers in a major war. Through the Constitution the several states had granted to the United States power to raise armies and to provide for the common defense, but the Madison administration had done neither, and through this bill it attempted to take from the states that force which they had reserved to themselves for their own needs and apply it to uses for which the United States was committed to provide by other means. Gore declared the provision to class the militia into divisions and take from each an individual by compulsion was "the first step on the odious ground of conscription," and "never will and never ought to be submitted to by this country, while it retains one idea of civil freedom. . . ."[29]

Although no members spoke in favor of the militia bill, the Senators approved it in November 1814 by a vote of 19 to 12. Later they refused to accept a change proposed by the House of Representatives that the length of service be cut to one year; and when compromise failed, Rufus King moved that consideration of the measure be postponed. The Senate accepted his motion and in effect destroyed the bill to give the President power to raise 80,000 militiamen.[30]

President Madison could more easily withstand Gore's denunciations than the withering effect of Boston's financial policy. In the panic that started by England's sack of Washington on August 24, 1814, the banks of Philadelphia and Baltimore suspended specie payment, those in New York soon followed suit, and by September every bank from New Orleans to Albany paid its obligations in discounted notes; only the banks of New England maintained specie payment. From all over the country money flowed to Boston to pay for imports and domestic manufactures. Federalists calculated that New England's banks drew half a million dollars a month from the South, and John Lowell complained that Boston bankers were at their wits' ends to dispose of their capital. Since Boston held the nation's supply of hard money, the Federalists who controlled the city's banks, save one, set the standard of exchange for the United States by discounting from 25 to 30 per cent the notes of all banks outside New England, including those of the United States Treasury. Most of the federal government's bank credits, deposited in the South and West, had shrunk appreciably, and the Treasury received in revenue only depreciated bills with which to pay its debts. Even the states of New England paid their taxes, customs, and loans in discounted notes instead of the specie they alone possessed because they preferred to save their money in coin for more profitable endeavors. The Federalist bankers of Boston had no interest in helping a bankrupt Republican administration wage war against England. On July 28, 1814, Gore told King that since the first of June two banks in Boston had shipped $1,800,000 to Canada, and he warned that should "any application be made to these Banks for a Coalition with those to the South of them, it will not succeed."[31]

Nor did Madison's administration get any substantial help from New England through the sale of war bonds. Boston took only $75,300 of the 1813 government loan of $16 million and less than $500,000 of the 1814 loan of $25 million.[32] No money of Gore's supported the Republicans' war against England. The Federalists exerted so much pressure of disapproval against those who bought government securities that not many individuals had the courage to defy them. The *Independent Chronicle* on April 14, 1815, carried an advertisement of brokers who promised that the names of all subscribers who purchased bonds through them would be kept secret, and on the same day the *Boston Gazette* asked, ". . . if [moneyed] men withhold their aid, and so force the government into a peace, will not their capital be better employed, [than] if engaged in trade?" Some Federalists purchased British treasury notes, and by the end of the war New England may well have lent more money to the

British government than to its own. During the summer of 1814 Gore informed King that the federal government had asked the Massachusetts Bank for a loan of $200,000 in "unquestionable Security." The Bank's reply was prompt: ". . . that if the Security was Satisfactory the amount cou'd be had. The Pledge offered was any Quantity of the last Loan, and the Reply as prompt as the other, that they shou'd not consider themselves secured for one thousand Dollars, by a deposit of the whole Loan."[33]

In the Senate Gore was as determined as the bankers in Boston to keep the wealth of Massachusetts from the grasp of the national government. The Secretary of the Treasury had calculated that in addition to the government's present resources he would need $52 million to carry on the government and the war during 1815 as they had been conducted during the preceding year, and he would require a larger sum to win the war.[34] Raising money through loans had proved impracticable because few people would lend; issuing Treasury notes brought little benefit because only the most needy creditors would accept them. To find money to continue the war, Congress enacted two bills: one for the issue of interest-bearing Treasury notes to the value of $10 million and the other for increasing the direct taxes by $6 million for the next year. Gore, with six other senators, opposed the second bill. He knew that the states outside New England would escape the full impact of their obligations by paying their taxes in depreciated bank notes and that the New England states alone would have to supply the government with any sound money it might obtain. He knew, also, that since Massachusetts was already spending more than the other states on its own defense, its burden would be particularly heavy, and this additional war levy would raise its expenditures disproportionately high.

On January 5, 1815, the day of the Senate's roll call, Gore explained and defended his opposition to the tax bill. After reviewing the gross mismanagement of the war, he abandoned all hope that the Administration would wisely apply any congressional grants of men or money for the country's protection. He declared that although he approved the power of the federal government to tax the nation's land and buildings as the bill required, he would vote against it because the national government had placed the state he represented outside the protection of the United States and determined "that while it shall bear the full proportion of the taxes, none of the fruits shall redound to her relief." Gore reminded the Senate that when the states surrendered to the federal government the principal sources of their revenue to provide for their own defense, they received from it the solemn promise of protection. But in the present war, which had been of the Madison administration's own choosing, Massachusetts had been entirely abandoned. Troops raised there for the regular army had been marched out of the state, and even the militia would have been led off to Canada or Rhode Island if Governor Strong had not refused to comply with the government's order. When the Administration failed to repel invasion of the Maine coast, Governor Strong had been forced to call out numerous detachments of the militia to defend the Commonwealth, and when the national government had refused to pay them, Massachusetts had met the obligation from its limited resources. "The present year the Commonwealth has expended more than $700,000 for her own defence. She is now called on by this bill for $632,041 to defend other parts of the territory of the United States; and her citizens, more exposed than any other, are left to provide for their own defence."[35]

Rufus King, in accordance with the Federalists' decision to approve supplies of men and money during the country's emergency, supported the tax bill. He declared that although the conflict with England was "unnecessary, improvident, and contrary to every maxim of prudence," the country was nevertheless at war and in danger, and he would vote for those supplies of men and money without which the United States could not defend itself.[36] In putting the grievance of Massachusetts above the immediate need of the nation, Gore believed that he supported the best interests of the United States, for if bankruptcy could drive Madison from the presidency and return the Federalists to power to end the war, the national welfare would indeed be served.

Gore approved the calling of the Hartford Convention, an appeal by Massachusetts to other legislatures in New England to meet at Hartford on December 15, 1814, to recommend measures for their common defense and for the security of their political and economic future. Frustrated Federalists in Massachusetts could tolerate no longer the continuing persecutions by the federal government. For fourteen years the Republican administrations had demeaned them in order to favor the agrarian interests of the South and West, had reduced their national influence through the acquisition of new territory, had cut them off from positions of executive power, destroyed their maritime prosperity, and of most immediate concern, had led them into a disastrous, unnecessary war and then left them defenseless before the invader. What could be more natural and effective than a meeting of the New England states to air their regional grievances and formulate demands for their salvation? Gore had suggested this procedure during Jefferson's Embargo, and it had been revived in later crises, but heretofore relief had appeared before the call for united action had been issued. The Hartford Convention marked the climax of New England Federalism's concern for its regional security. Although both Federalists and Republicans widely assumed that the delegates would plot secession and join forces with the British, the convention proceeded with moderation.[37]

When its report reached Gore in Washington, he read it with enthusiasm and announced that the delegates had executed their difficult task "with wisdom and discretion." He wrote to Governor Strong: "The result of the Hartford Convention is here and affords satisfaction to most, if not to all—to some, because they see not the point nor the consequence of the recommendation as relates to taxes."[38] The legislatures of Rhode Island and New Hampshire took no action on the Convention's proposed Constitutional amendments to protect New England's minority interests and bring that section closer to its original position of influence within the Union; Vermont and eight other states passed resolutions that condemned them. Only Massachusetts and Connecticut approved them all and accepted the recommendation to raise state armies and retain a part of the national taxes collected within their boundaries.[39]

Massachusetts had already organized an army of 10,000 men, and six other states, finding the federal government unable to provide defense, had taken similar action. New York raised 20,000 troops, and Maryland, Kentucky, Virginia, South Carolina, and Pennsylvania each established its own force.[40] After months of failure to recruit an adequate army, Congress could not resist the use of the state armies as a means of getting soldiers. On January 22, 1815, Gore informed Governor Strong that the bill "authorizing the raising of State troops by the States, and at the expense of the United States . . . has passed both Houses. . . ." To many Federalists this legislation to enlarge the national armed service by admitting state forces up to 40,000 men answered the demand of the Hartford Convention that the states be allowed to assume their own defense. While the bill awaited President Madison's approval, Gore, who had voted against it, marveled to Governor Strong that the federal government would permit the states "to raise and keep in pay, at the expense of the United States, troops which may be used for purposes hostile to, or not conformable with, the views of the paymaster." That the Madison administration would accede to the principle of state armies proved its extreme helplessness. "Spasms of a dying government," Gore called it, and although he did not express outright the consequences that he believed would follow this weakening of the national sovereignty, the less cautious Timothy Pickering in a letter to John Lowell anticipated a dissolution of the Union.[41]

News of the successful peace negotiations between the United States and Great Britain stopped the rumors of secession. On February 16, 1815, the Senate approved the Treaty of Ghent without one dissenting vote, but, except for the provisions to settle boundary and fishing disputes, its only achievement was the ending of hostilities. Herein lay the cause of Gore's anger. Having been forced into a war he did not want, to win rights he did not seek, and having suffered the destruction of his state's commerce and the invasion of its territory, he expected the Treaty of Ghent to fulfill at least a part of the aims for which the Republicans had led the nation to war against England. He vented his feelings to Governor Strong that the treaty "must be deemed disgraceful to the government who made the war and the peace, and will be so adjudged by all, after the first effusions of joy and relief have subsided."[42] Gore's attack on the treaty reflected his political frustration that the widespread dissatisfaction with the Republicans' conduct of the war had won the Federalists no positions of executive power.

Back in Boston two months later, Gore found that the people in Massachusetts had so desired peace that had it not come when it did they would have been willing to secure it even at a sacrifice of some of their state's territory. He also found that in retrospect the delegates to the Hartford Convention felt a little silly. George Cabot came to see Gore, laughing "very heartily at his going to Hartford," and explaining that he had been prevailed upon to take the journey to "allay the ferment and prevent a crisis." On the constructive side, Cabot stressed the importance of the Convention as an organized body that could quickly reconvene "to provide for the exigencies of the moment" should the federal government lose its power through capture or disintegration.[43] It was Gore's judgment, based on his conversations with delegates from Boston, that the "great desideratum" of the Hartford Convention had been to obtain peace on any terms, and he thought it not unlikely, had the war continued, that "some rash and unadvisable step would have been taken."[44]

How effective was the Federalist resistance in Massachusetts to the War of 1812? The state subscribed only niggardly sums to supply the federal government's financial needs, it withheld specie that could have strengthened the nation's credit, and it usually refused to assign its militia to the national service; extremists like Timothy Pickering advocated secession, Governor Strong secretly dispatched an agent to Canada to learn Britain's attitude toward a separate peace with New England, and a number of Federalists openly anticipated the collapse of the Union. Massachusetts contributed the least of all the states in moral support. In terms of men and money, however, the national government found the Federalist resistance to the war less of a handicap than the languid assistance of its friends. Virginia maintained complete loyalty to the Madison administration, and, since its population and property values surpassed those of Massachusetts, it should have contributed slightly more in men and money. This was not the fact. Massachusetts gave four times more financial support than Virginia and supplied more soldiers to the regular army than Virginia and the Carolinas combined.[45]

Although Gore's term of office ran until 1821, he remained in the United States Senate only a little more than a year after the war ended; the physical discomforts and the political futility of his life in Washington seemed more than he could bear. In April 1815 he wrote to King that if they could be accommodated "tolerably well" in Georgetown or Washington, he would attend one more session of Congress, but he did not wish to live in a mixed lodging house and make "a joint mess with the multitude."[46] Gore returned to the Senate, and in the first session of the new Congress he cast negative votes on two important issues. Reflecting the opinion of many Federalists in Massachusetts, he opposed the tariff bill of 1816 to raise the import duties, and he opposed any federal assistance for the construction of roads and canals that would encourage the development of the West.[47] In his inflexible devotion to the interests of Massachusetts Gore never permitted his imagination to see the future grandeur and power of his country. In June 1816 he resigned. "I have sent my Resignation, as Senator, to the Mass'ts Legislature," he wrote to King from Warm Springs, Virginia, where he had gone to try the baths for his swollen, rheumatic legs. "My health wou'd not admit of my attendance, if I were inclined, but if I had the Strength of Sampson I shou'd have no Inclination. . . ." He could see no benefits to the nation "from any further struggle of Federalists," and the presidential election of 1816 confirmed his weary pessimism.[48] Gore was a member of the electoral college when Rufus King, the Federalists' candidate for the presidency, carried only Massachusetts, Connecticut, and Delaware.

As Gore settled into the elegant serenity of Waltham, the party spirit that had dominated Congress during his tenure in the Senate had, according to Jeremiah Mason, almost disappeared. "It is possible some occasion may again call it up," he wrote. "But the distinctions between Federalists and Democrats will, I think, never again be felt as strongly as they have heretofore been."[49] Although the Federalist party dominated politics in Massachusetts until 1832, it ceased to be a national political force. In the United States Senate Gore's relentless opposition to President Madison and the war against England contributed to its demise. His overwhelming concern for the political and economic grievances of Massachusetts and his refusal to compromise with an expanding democracy removed him from the mainstream of American life and hastened the end of the very thing to which he had devoted a lifetime of service.

Gore's political career paralleled exactly the life of the Federalist party from its rise in exuberant nationalism to its end in sectional strife. In 1788 as a young attorney he had represented Boston at the Massachusetts convention that ratified the federal Constitution, and in 1816 when Monroe was about to usher in the "Era of Good Feelings," he departed from public service.

IX

Unreconstructed Federalist

CHRISTOPHER Gore returned to Waltham to face the most trying decade of his life. From his last year in the Senate until his death in 1827, he struggled with the progressively worsening pain and deformity of rheumatoid arthritis. The baths at Warm Springs, Virginia, gave him little relief and none of the cure he had hopefully anticipated, and in his last years his erect figure was bent almost double, and his weak legs could scarcely support his body. As long as he could find means of locomotion, however, he drove out to inspect his fields and to oversee the management of his farm. During the first years of his retirement he was able on fair days to ride seven or eight miles in a chair, and later, when rigid muscles demanded more concessions, Rufus King sent him a low-slung phaeton from England. Gore wanted to spend the remainder of his life in his country house, and to make it comfortable in winter he installed more stoves, laid woolen carpets, and hung double windows. For the next five years he and his devoted Rebecca lived the seasons round in Waltham, but as Gore grew more inactive, they found their rural environment too lonely in winter, and in 1822 they bought a house on Cambridge Street in Boston, where they lived from December to May near their families and friends.[1]

From the time Gore was a young attorney he had dreamed of leisure to devote himself to his farm and library and to observe the political scene without the stress of participation. Now that retirement had come he chafed at his "painful and useless Existence," writing to King that his disease benumbed "all those Faculties which either give or receive joy." In the next sentence, however, he reproved himself for complaining when he had all the relief that skill could provide and "every Alleviation that the most unbounded Affection and most assiduous Care can afford. Surely then I ought to bear with Patience what I can neither Cure nor avoid. . . ."[2] To the best of his ability he turned his attention to the pursuits he had envisioned for his later years.

Books had always been an important possession, and as Gore's leisure and isolation increased, they became indispensable. ". . . I do not repine"; he wrote to King about his illness, "for I have yet a Satisfaction from Books."[3] His sizable library held volumes of broad subject matter ranging from the classics, many in Latin, some in Greek, and all handsomely bound in leather, to the works of contemporary English and American authors. When Richard Henry Dana began the publication of his literary periodical, *Idle Man,* he sent Gore a copy of the first issue. Back came an immediate, discerning appraisal with an order for a year's subscription: "Many of the thoughts are new," Gore told Dana, "none trite, or vulgar. . . . The sentiments are distinctly and thoroughly expressed; and while the Style has all the Correctness of Swift, it has a mellowness and refinement not always found in his."[4]

Gore returned to Waltham to be a full-time farmer, and his frequent reports to Rufus King about his crops and experiments show his high enthusiasm. "We are in the full Labour of Haying and having abundant crops," he wrote in the late summer of 1816.[5] The grapery held 1,100 bunches of fruit, the potatoes looked uncommonly fine, and the wheat produced from King's seed had turned out better than the crop grown from seed that Gore had imported from England. The production figures at Gore Place were an annual concern, and in late 1817 Gore told King with justifiable pride that his harvest included: "Hay 106 Loads, Potatoes 1200 Bushels, Rye 102, Wheat 41, Corn 130, Cyder 48 Barrels. This is exclusive of what my market cart carries to market. The annual produce of that is about 1,799 Dollars."[6] Each spring and summer Heathcot, the gardener at Gore Place, regularly delivered to the Boston market the first fruits and vegetables of the season. In 1830 pears from the tree that Heathcot had raised from seed won first prize from the Massachusetts Horticultural Society.[7]

Gore's concern for improving agriculture throughout the Commonwealth made him an enthusiastic supporter of the Brighton Cattle Show, a project launched in 1816 by the Massachusetts Society for Promoting Agriculture, to which the public was invited to exhibit prize livestock and to buy and sell cattle and farm products. Immediately successful, the show expanded and became an annual event. Its popularity extended the Society's influence among "practical farmers" and gratified Gore and other members who seriously tried to fulfill their organization's aim of raising the quality of agriculture in Massachusetts. During its first twenty-five years the Society had distributed thousands of pages of information, for which, beginning in 1812 the legislature annually gave $1,000; it had promoted the formation of agricultural societies around the state; and had introduced new plants, better breeds of livestock, and improved techniques; but its chief beneficiaries continued to be its own gentleman-farmer members who, like Gore, had more interest in experimentation and production than the farmer who pushed his own plow. Privately the Society's members worried about its "circumscribed" usefulness and its failure to awaken a "livelier interest in improving agriculture," but publicly they explained that during the Society's first quarter century it had been ahead of its time, that knowledge comes "first from educated men to their less informed neighbors." Through the happy innovation of the Cattle Show the Society at last found a popular and effective way to arouse in "the great body of Massachusetts yeomanry" a desire for better farming.[8]

Confined to his own fields and furrows, Gore anxiously watched the Federalists of Massachusetts move toward the conservative wing of the Republican party, and, with a sharpness aggravated by the frustrations of an observer, he denounced the large numbers of his party who, cheered by President Monroe's congenial policies and motivated by the lure of government office, appeared willing to drop their political identity and join the opposition. When Monroe, eager to erase the bad feelings that survived the War of 1812, announced his plan to visit Boston, Gore reported to Jeremiah Mason, "It has been a question who should evince most devotion, the Federalist or Democrat. The former appears to have got the start in the race," and indeed the hospitable Federalists arranged elaborate receptions and invited the President to their homes.[9] Gore's "want of health" prevented him from going to Boston to pay his respects to the Chief of State, but he invited the distinguished visitor to stop at Gore Place. "The President is in Boston," Gore wrote to Jeremiah Mason on July 14, 1817, "he rides hard, visits everything, and in so rapid a manner that it is utterly impossible he should burden his mind with any superfluous knowledge. This day . . . he stopped at my house, ate a strawberry, bowed and shook hands cordially, returned to Boston to meet the Town oration, the Governor's collation, and the Cincinnati address and their dinner. . . ."[10] Most Bostonians thought the whirlwind visit an eminent success, and the *Centinel* printed some pleasant remarks about it under the caption "The Era of Good Feelings."[11] Five years later Gore still deplored those Federalists who smiled agreeably at the Republican administration. "It is curious to observe how everyone praises the present Chief, while no one has any Confidence either in his talents, or his Sincerity."[12] By that time even Gore conceded that "the Federal Party died long since by Suicide," and that it had continued in Massachusetts only because of the "great moderation & mediocrity" of the Federalist Governor, John Brooks.[13]

The uncritical behavior of Massachusetts Federalists toward Monroe's administration was closely tied to their desire to obtain from the federal government payment of their state's million dollar militia claim for defense of the Commonwealth during the War of 1812. From Washington King candidly wrote to Gore that although he thought "the policy and decisions of Massachusetts during the late war were unfortunate, if not incorrect," he was grieved to observe "the spirit of submission" in the conduct of its congressional representatives and "the arrogance and authority with which some of the other States are encouraged" to treat them.[14] Gore made no apologies for the Commonwealth's wartime action, and he informed King that he would "never cease demanding Reimbursement as a Right, in mild & decent Language, but I would not crouch for it; and, if refused for any length of time, I should think the Representatives of the State justified in opposing every appropriation of money to any other Purpose." He assailed those Federalists like Harrison Gray Otis who "have ever been desirous to barter anything for the Payment of the Massts.' Claim,"[15] and he denounced their futile policy of peace and harmony toward Republicans: "All our Plans & Projects are, at present, of the small and feeble cast, we court Democracy & Swear she is kind; at the moment she disregards all our Interests, & treats our Reputation & our Citizens with marked contumely & Neglect. And this nasty claim for Expenses, during the late war, is at the Bottom, & the Motive of many of our coaxers. . . ."[16] On May 31, 1830, after thirteen years of agitation Congress finally awarded to Massachusetts about one-half the amount of the claim and at the same time required from the state's governor and legislature a renunciation of those principles by which Massachusetts had defied the federal authority in the War of 1812.[17]

In Gore's opinion the obsession of some Massachusetts Federalists to conciliate the South in order to win high offices and payment of the militia claim explained the "vacillating and unaccountable" conduct of the state toward the extension of slavery in Missouri. At the beginning of the controversy over whether Missouri should enter the Union with or without slavery, citizens from all parts of the Commonwealth instructed their representatives in Congress to admit the new state only if slavery were excluded. To Gore's distress no mention of this widespread, antislavery sentiment appeared in the Boston newspapers because from Washington Senator Otis and in Boston legislators Josiah Quincy and William Sullivan "urged most vehemently a total Silence on the Subject," and for the same reason the state legislature issued no statement until too late to influence Congress.[18] "Massachusetts cowers under the arrogant Pretentions of Virginia," Gore wrote to King, "and without a Struggle submits to have the Chains, under which she groans, rivetted and increased."[19] He attributed the origin and motive of this "dreadful Policy" to the attempt "to conciliate all, who have the Disposal of Office & Distinction,"[20] and to Mason he wrote, "The people on the Missouri Question are a great way in advance of their leaders."[21]

Gore opposed the extension of slavery not primarily on moral grounds but because it would worsen the political and economic position of Massachusetts within the Union, and he drew his supportive arguments from the state's history between Jefferson's Embargo and the Treaty of Ghent. Rufus King held the same opinion as Gore, and in the Senate debates of 1819-20 he declared that since the Southern states already had twenty representatives in Congress and twenty electoral votes based on their slave population, further extension of slavery would be unfair to the Northern states and fatal to their interests; Congress should therefore prohibit slavery in a new state as well as in a territory.[22] Gore considered the Missouri Question to be "of greater importance to the character of the nation and the political power of New England than any before Congress."[23] When in March 1820 both the House and Senate passed the Compromise prohibiting slavery in the Louisiana territory north of thirty-six degrees thirty minutes but permitting it in the state of Missouri, he declared that Massachusetts had "much to take to her own Charge, on this Subject. Her Infirmity of Purpose, her vacillating & dilatory Conduct neither afforded support to her Friends nor deterred her Foes."[24]

Even without the problem of slavery, Gore worried about the admission of new states. He confessed to King in 1824 that he had "long distrusted the practicability of preserving the union of States, consisting of so many discordant Interests, and in such various stages of Civilization—with the constant addition of new and undisciplined Communities whose Wants and Passions are unrestrained by the Experience, which has evinced to the older, the necessity of Compromise, founded on the general Good."[25]

The Federalists' show of goodwill toward the Republican administration was the outward expression of their compelling drive for public office. "Nothing but the most fulsome and indiscriminate Praise has been lavished from all our Presses on the Measures and Officers of the Nation," Gore complained to King near the end of Monroe's second term, and the responsibility for this foolish policy he placed on Harrison Gray Otis.[26] Nor had the conciliation borne any fruit, Gore pointed out to King, for although Otis and his followers "are constantly eulogizing the National

Administration, . . . to be a Federalist . . . is a sufficient Reason for Exclusion from Office & Influence."[27] Contrary to some expectations in Massachusetts, Monroe appointed William Wirt of Virginia instead of Daniel Webster to be attorney general, an indication to Gore that Monroe's attachment to Federalism could be easily set aside.[28] He could have added that even if the President had wanted to invite a former political opponent to a high-ranking position in the government, the opposition of Republican leaders tied his hands. In 1824 Daniel Webster obtained a promise from John Quincy Adams that if elected President, Adams would appoint to office at least one Federalist and probably others. With Webster's help Adams won the election and promptly designated Rufus King to be the American Minister to the Court of St. James, but few other Federalists achieved appointment to valued offices until 1830, when the creation of new party groups brought them into positions of top leadership in the national government. By midterm in Adams' presidency the deep burn of his apostasy had healed in the breasts of most Massachusetts Federalists, and it was the administration of this Republican President from Massachusetts that finally reconciled Gore to the blending of the two parties. In April 1826 he wrote to King that Adams had "unquestionably risen in the Estimation of all good men here," and that the administration of the federal government "appears to have increased much in Popularity & especially among the old Federalists in Massachusetts."[29]

The slow pace of time at Gore Place quickened with the arrival of letters from Rufus King, "whom," Gore once noted, "I have longest known and the most intimately loved and esteemed."[30] With sympathetic understanding of the confinement imposed by Gore's disability, King wrote frequent and lengthy reports of his more swiftly moving life in Washington, and, for Mrs. Gore's entertainment, he spiced his politics with social gossip. Gore replied promptly with news of Boston and caustic comments on the schemes of its proscribed Federalists. This correspondence, so vital to Gore's morale, marked the finale of their long friendship, which in the opinion of John Lowell was "more confidential, and more affectionate" than any other he had known.[31] Uninterrupted for fifty years, it had begun at Harvard, flourished in London and Washington, and, when the two men were separated, had continued in an exchange of letters that was sometimes as frequent as twice a week. Their wives found pleasure in each other's company, and the childless Gores delighted in the sons of Rufus and Mary Alsop King. When the Kings returned to the United States from England in 1803, they entrusted their boys, who were attending Harrow, to the Gores' care. James later attended Harvard, where his Uncle and Aunt Gore watched over him and disbursed sums for his tuition and allowances.[32] During Gore's retirement at Waltham, Frederick, the youngest son, came to Harvard, and, with a flair for accumulating debts and reveling in Boston and Cambridge, distressed his father. Gore advised King that Frederick's conduct at college would improve if he "could be brought to . . . seek for Happiness in library Fame, instead of shining as a Leader of festive Parties. . . ."[33] In their later years when the two friends saw each other infrequently, Gore commissioned Gilbert Stuart to paint King's portrait, that his friend's likeness might be close at hand to "gladden my remaining Days."[34]

Before Gore moved to Boston for the winter of 1826-27, a few months before his death, he drew up his last will. To various nieces and nephews, to James Gore King the younger, to the Massachusetts Historical Society, and to the American Academy of Arts and Sciences he gave sums of $1,000 or more. All other property he left to his wife, Rebecca, with the proviso that whatever remained after her death should go to "the President and Fellows of Harvard College for the uses of the University of Cambridge, and for the promotion of virtue, science, and literature in said University."[35]

In his gift to Harvard, which amounted to $100,000 Gore's "bounty" exceeded "the munificence of any other benefactor."[36] The University set aside $38,000 of the bequest to pay the life annuities required by the will and applied the remainder to the construction of a fireproof library, the cornerstone of which was laid in 1838, eleven years after Gore's death. In 1841 Gore Hall, constructed of Quincy granite in Gothic style, received the college library and with the aid of two additional wings housed it until 1912, when Widener Library was constructed on the same site. To quiet criticism from those friends of the College who believed that Harvard had spent too large a part of Gore's bequest on a building, President Josiah Quincy raised more than $21,000 to purchase books for the new library.[37] Today Gore's memory continues at Harvard in the name of a dormitory that is part of Winthrop House; its student chairs carry the decorative stamp of his coat of arms, and above the fireplace in the common room hangs a copy of one of Trumbull's portraits of Gore, a gift to the College from William Payne.

In the spring of 1825 King wrote to tell Gore of President John Quincy Adams' proposal that he should become Minister to England. Since he was seventy years of age and had long thought of retirement, he asked

Gore to advise him "without fear or flattery."[38] Gore applauded Adams' judgment and urged King to accept the appointment, but he lamented his friend's departure.[39] "Find time, if possible and come hither and visit your Friend for the last time; for I cannot expect to live until your Return."[40] King replied that the approaching marriage of Frederick prevented his making the journey to Massachusetts. "I cannot withhold another circumstance which pressed upon my mind, that the interview would be clouded by the apprehension that it might be our last, the parting of old friends . . . constitutes a scene which we both must have desired to avoid."[41] A year later King resigned his mission in England and returned to New York, but the two men did not meet again. On March 1, 1827, Christopher Gore died in his home on Cambridge Street in Boston at the age of sixty-nine years,[42] and Rufus King lived only two months longer.

In a formal eulogy on the late Honorable Christopher Gore in King's Chapel eleven days after his death, the Reverend Francis W. P. Greenwood extolled the virtues of his distinguished parishoner's upright, Christian life, made more illustrious by an "uncommon personal beauty" and an "internal grace and polish externally manifested."[43] For the grieving Rebecca, her husband's death ended an exchange of affectionate devotion that spanned forty years. Of the Bostonians who paused briefly to consider the man who had died, many recalled only vaguely the rich and prominent personage whose name they had heard infrequently during the last decade; a few objectively appraised the able mind, the restricted imagination, the exceptional talents. But those in Boston who deeply mourned Gore's passing were the old Federalists, the nostalgic beneficiaries of his charm and hospitality, of his fidelity to principles and friends; in the courts and in the legislature, in Washington and in London, he had defended their interests and advanced their causes. At King's Chapel on that day in late winter the final tribute came from John Lowell:

> Such a man's death, in the fulness of life, would have been a public loss. Such a man's excellent example continued to the close of a long life, is a great gain—it is a gain to our human character—it cannot be too much cherished by those who witnessed it, or may hear of it. A republican government, of all others, is most benefited by good examples; for virtue is its only strength.[44]

Bibliographical Note

THE surviving letters of Christopher Gore are almost exclusively those that he himself wrote, and they are preserved in the correspondence of a number of his friends in libraries along the Atlantic seaboard. The largest and most valuable collection is in the Rufus King papers in the New-York Historical Society. Not only do these letters, written frequently over a period of more than forty years, make possible the reconstruction of Gore's political career, but they present details of Gore's life that, in the absence of family papers, carry special import. Letters from Gore to King that were written between 1796 and 1801 and are in the possession of James Gore King of New York contain the only known statements by Gore on the authorship of his country house at Waltham, Massachusetts.

Although the King papers touch almost every aspect of Gore's life, they give no information on how he made his fortune. The most important sources for his financial dealings between the early 1780's and the 1790's are the collection of Andrew Craigie papers in the American Antiquarian Society and the volumes of the Massachusetts Old Loans in the National Archives. The Dreer, Etting, and Gratz collections in the Historical Society of Pennsylvania tell the most that is known about Gore's ownership of stock in the Bank of the United States, and the papers of the Massachusetts Bank, the Boston Manufacturing Company, and the Lechmere Point Corporation, all in the Harvard Business School Library, record his participation in Boston enterprises. Gore's Account Book, also in the Harvard Business School Library, shows the commercial character of his legal practice and lists some of his fees.

Scattered letters from Gore, concerned primarily with politics, are among the Timothy Pickering manuscripts in the Essex Institute, the Theodore Sedgwick, Timothy Pickering, Henry Knox, Robert Treat Paine, and Ellen Morton Washburn collections at the Massachusetts Historical Society, and in the Manuscript Division of the Library of Congress. The papers of the Department of State relative to the Commission under Article VII of Jay's Treaty, deposited in the National Archives, give an almost complete account of the work of the Commission, lacking only some of the opinions filed by its members and a summary of its expenses. Documents relating to the Commission and the opinions filed by the commissioners are in John Bassett Moore, *International Adjudications, Modern*

Series (New York, 1931), IV. Gore gave to Harvard College Library two manuscript volumes of the commissioners' opinions on cases that came before them from 1798 through 1799.

The most complete and valuable collection of published Gore letters is in Charles King, *The Life and Correspondence of Rufus King* (New York, 1894-1900), 6 vols. Many of these printed letters are inaccurately reproduced and should be checked against the originals, most of which are in the New-York Historical Society, and they omit the personal details of Gore's life. Letters written to Gore by George Cabot and published in Henry Cabot Lodge, *Life and Letters of George Cabot* (Boston, 1878), cover the years of Gore's residency in London. Letters written by and to Gore and printed in Henry Adams, ed., *Documents Relating to New-England Federalism, 1800-15* (Boston, 1877), contribute to an understanding of Gore's vigorous participation in the opposition of Massachusetts to Jefferson's Embargo. Gore's correspondence with Jeremiah Mason after his retirement, printed in George S. Hillard, ed., *Memoir and Correspondence of Jeremiah Mason* (Cambridge, 1873), gives his articulate opinions of Massachusetts Federalists who tried to win position in national politics during the administration of James Monroe.

The letters from Fisher Ames to Gore, printed in the first volume of Seth Ames, ed., *Works of Fisher Ames with a Selection from His Speeches and Correspondence* (Boston, 1854), 2 vols., contain information about Gore as a lawyer and politician. Comments about Gore in *The Writings and Speeches of Daniel Webster* (National ed.; Boston, 1903), 18 vols., and in Worthington C. Ford, ed., *The Writings of John Quincy Adams* (New York, 1913-16), 6 vols., are the most important sources for Gore's reputation as a lawyer.

Chapter Notes

The following abbreviations are used in the chapter notes:

American Antiquarian Society	AAS
Harvard Business School Library	HBSL
Harvard University Library	HUL
Library of Congress	LC
Massachusetts Historical Society	MHS
National Archives	NA
New-York Historical Society	NYHS

Notes to Chapter I

1. *New-England Palladium* (Boston), June 6, 9, 1809; Justin H. Smith, ed., *The Historie Booke . . . of the Honourable Artillery Company of London and the Ancient and Honorable Artillery Company of Massachusetts* . . . (Boston, 1903), p. 116.
2. Theodore W. Gore, "The Gore Family" (unpublished manuscript), New England Historic and Genealogical Society, Book I, pp. 6-19; "A Roll of Arms Registered by the Committee on Heraldry of the New England Historic and Genealogical Society," *New England Historic and Genealogical Register*, LXXXII (April 1928), 151; Thomas Fuller, *The History of the Worthies of England* (new ed.; London, 1840), II, 63, 162; Henry James Fowle Swayne, ed., *Churchwarden's Accounts, 1443-1702, County of Wilts* (Salisbury, England, 1896), pp. 245, 346-48.
3. William H. Whitmore, ed., *Genealogy of the Families of Payne and Gore* (Boston, 1875), p. 29. John Gore's sign belongs to the Bostonian Society and hangs at Gore Place, Waltham, Massachusetts. Whitmore, "The Gore Roll of Arms," *The Heraldic Journal*, I (August 1865), 113-40; Suffolk County Registry of Deeds, Index of Grantees, 1637-1799, Suffolk County Court House, VI.
4. Whitmore, *Genealogy*, pp. 28-30; Edmund M. Wheelwright, "Letters of an American Loyalist and His Wife," Colonial Society of Massachusetts *Publications*, III (February 1897), 384, 395-96. An early canvas of John Singleton Copley, painted around 1758 and now hanging at the H. F. duPont Winterthur Museum, Winterthur, Delaware, is of four Gore children, probably John, Sarah, Suzanna, and Rebecca.—James Thomas Flexner, *John Singleton Copley* (Cambridge, 1948), pp. 24, 129. At Gore Place hang portraits of Christopher Gore's father and mother, probably painted by John Johnston.
5. Gore, "The Gore Family," New England Historic and Genealogical Society, p. 19; "List of Freemen," *New England Historic and Genealogical Register*, III (January 1849), 95; "The Reverend John Eliot's Record of Church Members," *New England Historic and Genealogical Register*, XXXV (July 1881), 246-47.

6. "Agreement of Inhabitants of Roxbury for Forming a School," Charles M. Ellis, *The History of Roxbury Town* (Boston, 1847), p. 35.
7. Cotton Mather, *Magnalia Christi Americana: or The Ecclesiastical History of New England* . . . (translation by Lucius F. Robinson) (Hartford, 1853), I, 551.
8. City of Boston, *Report of the Record Commissioners, Containing the Roxbury Land and Church Records* (Boston, 1881), VI, 17, 18, 176; Suffolk County Probate Records, Suffolk County Court House, III, 81-83.
9. Francis S. Drake, *Town of Roxbury: Its Memorable Persons and Places* (Roxbury, 1878), p. 108.
10. Gore, "A Short History of the Gore Family," (unpublished manuscript), New England Historic and Genealogical Society, pp. 1-9.
11. *Laws and Liberties of Massachusetts* (1648 ed.; reprint Boston, 1929), p. 47.
12. Pauline Holmes, *A Tercentenary History of the Boston Public Latin School, 1635-1935* (Cambridge, 1935), pp. 165-66; Robert Francis Seybolt, *The Public Schools of Colonial Boston, 1635-1775* (Cambridge, 1935), pp. 67-76; Henry F. Jenks, *The Boston Public Latin School, 1635-1880* (Cambridge, 1881), pp. 10-12.
13. Jenks, *Catalogue of the Boston Public Latin School* . . . (Boston, 1886), pp. 87, 92.
14. *Proceedings and Addresses of the Boston Latin School Tercentenary, 1635-1935* (Boston, 1937), p. 49.
15. Thomas Hutchinson, *The History of the Colony and Province of Massachusetts Bay*, Lawrence Shaw Mayo, ed. (Cambridge, 1936), III, 188; Harvard College Board of Overseers' Records, HUL, II, 91; Samuel Eliot Morison, *Three Centuries of Harvard, 1636-1936* (Cambridge, 1936), pp. 135-36.
16. Albert Goodhue, Jr., "The Reading of Harvard Students, 1770-1781, as Shown by the Records of the Speaking Club," Essex Institute *Historical Collections*, LXXIII (April 1938), 107; Morison, *Three Centuries of Harvard*, pp. 138-45.
17. Harvard College Speaking Club Records, HUL, I, 96; Harvard College Library Charging List, 1762-1897, HUL, Senior Class 1776.
18. Samuel Chandler, Diary and Account Book, 1773-1775, HUL, p. 101.
19. Harvard College Faculty Records, HUL, III, 4-5.
20. Harvard College Faculty Records, HUL, IV, 14, 16, 20, 30; Percy W. Brown, "The Sojourn of Harvard College in Concord," *Harvard Graduates' Magazine*, XXVII (June 1919), 497-509; Board of Overseers' Records, HUL, III, 90; Harvard College Records, September 1750-April 1778, HUL, II, 439; College Book, HUL, VII, June 24, 1776.
21. Harvard College Quarter-Bill Book, 1770-1784, HUL, *passim*; Library Charging List, 1762-1897, HUL, Senior Class 1776; Samuel Chandler, Diary, HUL, *passim*.
22. John Trumbull, *Autobiography, Reminiscenses and Letters . . . from 1756 to 1841* (New Haven, 1841), p. 13.
23. "An Alphabetical List of the Sons of Liberty Who Dined at Liberty Tree, Dorchester, August 14, 1769," Massachusetts Historical Society *Proceedings*, XI (August 1869), 141.

24. "Address of Merchants and Others, of Boston, to Governour Hutchinson," *American Archives . . .* , Peter Force, ed. (Washington, 1837), 4th ser., I, 362.
25. Seybolt, *The Town Officials of Colonial Boston, 1634-1775* (Cambridge, 1939), pp. 234 ff.; Lewis Einstein, *Divided Loyalties; Americans in England during the War of Independence* (London, 1933), pp. 190-204; William H. Nelson, *The American Tory* (Oxford, 1961), pp. 86-97, 100, 101.
26. "List of Protestors Against the Solemn League and Covenant," Massachusetts Historical Society *Proceedings*, XI (October 1870), 394-95; John C. Miller, *Sam Adams, Pioneer in Propaganda* (Boston, 1936), pp. 301-06; Lorenzo Sabine, *The American Loyalists* (Boston, 1847), p. 330; Thomas Oliver to Dr. Henry Caner, Col. Jonathan Snelling, Major Adino Paddock, Capt. John Gore, Capt. Martin Gay, February 24, 1776, Colonial Society of Massachusetts *Publications*, III (February 1897), 387.
27. Carl Bridenbaugh, *Cities in Revolt; Urban Life in America, 1743-1776* (New York, 1955), p. 350; Chandler, Diary, HUL, p. 85.
28. Samuel Adams Drake, *Old Landmarks and Historic Personages of Boston* (Boston, 1873), p. 72.
29. Ronald S. Longley, "Mob Activities in Revolutionary Massachusetts," *New England Quarterly*, VI (March 1933), 98-130; James H. Stark, *The Loyalists of Massachusetts* (Boston, 1910), pp. 54-67.
30. "List of the Inhabitants of Boston, Who on the Evacuation of the British in March 1776, Removed to Halifax with the Army," Massachusetts Historical Society *Proceedings*, XVIII (December 1880), 267; E. Alfred Jones, *The Loyalists of Massachusetts* (London, 1930), pp. 77-78; Henry Wilder Foote, *Annals of King's Chapel* (Boston, 1896), II, 347-48, 350.
31. Emily P. Weaver, "Nova Scotia during the Revolution," *American Historical Review*, X (October 1904), 67; Lawrence Shaw Mayo, "The Massachusetts Loyalists, 1775-1783," *Commonwealth History of Massachusetts*, Albert Bushnell Hart, ed. (New York, 1930), III, 251-76.
32. Jones, *Loyalists of Massachusetts*, pp. 150, 308-09; George A. Ward, ed., *The Journal and Letters of Samuel Curwen* (4th ed.; Boston, 1864), pp. 249-64; Nelson, *American Tory*, pp. 153-69.
33. *Acts and Resolves of the Province of Massachusetts Bay*, V, 913, 968-71; John T. Hassam, "List of Confiscated Estates in Boston at the Time of the Revolution," Massachusetts Historical Society *Proceedings*, 2d ser., X (May 1895), 162; Suffolk County Probate Records, Suffolk County Court House, LXXVIII, 675.
34. Petition of Christopher Gore to House of Representatives, July 2, 1779, *Acts and Resolves*, 1778-1779, p. 721; Suffolk County Probate Records, Suffolk County Court House, LXXX, 718-19; LXXXI, 683-86.
35. Petition of John Gore to the Massachusetts Legislature, June 23, 1787, Massachusetts Archives, State House; "An Act for Naturalizing John Gore, Esquire," read and concurred by both House and Senate, June 2, 1787, Massachusetts Archives, State House.
36. Christopher Gore to Theodore Sedgwick, March 31, 1796, Theodore Sedgwick Papers, MHS.

37. Suffolk County Probate Records, Suffolk County Court House, XCIV, 182-83, 250-51.
38. *Massachusetts Soldiers and Sailors of the Revolutionary War* (Boston, 1899), VI, 640.
39. Trumbull, *Autobiography*, p. 50.
40. Thomas Coffin Amory, *The Life of James Sullivan* (Boston, 1859), II, 3-5; William T. Davis, *Bench and Bar of the Commonwealth of Massachusetts* (Boston, 1895), I, 225.
41. "Record-Book of the Suffolk Bar, July 21, 1778," Massachusetts Historical Society *Proceedings*, XIX (December 1881), 152-63; Hollis Russell Bailey, *Attorneys and Their Admission to the Bar in Massachusetts* (Boston, 1907), pp. 18-28; Nathaniel Dearborn, *Boston Notions* (Boston, 1848), p. 254; Davis, *Bench and Bar*, I, 323.

Notes to Chapter II

1. Robert A. East, *Business Enterprise in the American Revolutionary Era* (New York, 1938), pp. 3-38, 49-71; Merrill Jensen, *The New Nation; a History of the United States during the Confederation, 1781-1789* (New York, 1950), pp. 180-83, 214; Samuel Eliot Morison, *The Maritime History of Massachusetts, 1783-1860* (Boston, 1921), pp. 29-30; Gardner Weld Allen, "Massachusetts Privateers of the Revolution," Massachusetts Historical Society *Collections* (Cambridge, 1927), LXXVII, 53, 65-331.
2. Gore to Daniel Newcomb, July 16, 1780, Mellen Chamberlain Collection, Boston Public Library.
3. Christopher Gore, Account Book, HBSL, pp. 5-15; Dockets of the Court of Common Pleas, Suffolk County Court House, 1788, 1789, *passim*; James B. Hedges, *The Browns of Providence Plantations, Colonial Years* (Cambridge, 1952), pp. 258-59, 287-88.
4. Dockets of the Court of Common Pleas, Suffolk County Court House, 1780-1796, *passim*; Dockets of the Supreme Judicial Court, Suffolk County Court House, 1781-1790, *passim.*
5. Gore to King, August 22, 1789, Rufus King Papers, NYHS.
6. William H. Whitmore, ed., *Genealogy of the Families of Payne and Gore* (Boston, 1875), pp. 21, 23; Whitmore, "Boston Families in the Eighteenth Century," *Memorial History of Boston*, Justin Winsor, ed. (Boston, 1881), II, 549.
7. Worthington C. Ford, ed., *The Writings of John Quincy Adams* (New York, 1913), I, 58.
8. Alexander Baring to Francis Baring, May 5, 1796, Baring Brothers Papers microfilm, LC.

   Trumbull's portrait of Rebecca Gore is owned by Mrs. John M. Elliott of Boston.
9. Ford, *Writings of John Quincy Adams*, I, 37; Frank W. Grinnell, "The Constitutional History of the Supreme Judicial Court of Massachusetts from the Revolution to 1813," *Massachusetts Law Quarterly*, II (May 1917), 463-74;

Benjamin Austin ("Honestus," pseud.), *Observations on the Pernicious Practice of Law* (reprint; Boston, 1819), pp. 8, 9; Anson E. Morse, *The Federalist Party in Massachusetts to the Year 1800* (Princeton, 1909), pp. 25-39; Richard B. Morris, "Insurrection in Massachusetts," *America in Crisis*, Daniel Aaron, ed. (New York, 1952), pp. 23-26.

10. Morison, *Maritime History*, pp. 31-32, 38; Jensen, *New Nation*, pp. 191-93, 302-09; *Massachusetts Centinel* (Boston), April 20, 1785.
11. Oscar Handlin and Mary Flug Handlin, *Commonwealth; a Study of the Role of Government in the American Economy: Massachusetts, 1774-1861* (New York, 1947), pp. 40, 59; Robert A. East, "The Massachusetts Conservatives in the Critical Period," *The Era of the American Revolution*, Richard B. Morris, ed. (New York, 1939), pp. 349-62; Robert J. Taylor, *Western Massachusetts in the Revolution* (Providence, 1954), ch. 7; Massachusetts Old Loans Records, CCLIX, NA, 97.
12. Gore to King, November 26, 1786, King Papers, NYHS.
13. Gore to King, April 19, 1786, King Papers, NYHS.
14. Gore to King, June 25, 1786, King Papers, NYHS.
15. Gore to King, November 7, 1786, King Papers, NYHS.
16. Gore to King, November 26, 1786, King Papers, NYHS; Morris, "Insurrection in Massachusetts," *America in Crisis*, pp. 26-47.
17. Sidney Kaplan, "'Honestus' and the Annihilation of the Lawyers," *South Atlantic Quarterly*, XLVIII (July 1949), pp. 417-18; Taylor, *Western Massachusetts in the Revolution*, pp. 163-65.
18. Taylor, *Western Massachusetts in the Revolution*, pp. 166-67; East, "Massachusetts Conservatives," *Era of American Revolution*, pp. 363-66.
19. Gore to King, June 28, 1787, King Papers, NYHS.
20. Gore to King, June 28, 1787, King Papers, NYHS.
21. Gore to King, June 28, 1787, King Papers, NYHS.
22. Gore to King, October 7, 1787, King Papers, NYHS.
23. Gore to King, December 9, 23, 1787, King Papers, NYHS.
24. *Massachusetts Centinel*, December 8, 1787.
25. Gore to King, December 9, 1787, King Papers, NYHS. Delegates from Boston were: John Hancock, James Bowdoin, Thomas Dawes, Jr., William Phillips, Rev. Samuel Stillman, Charles Jarvis, John Winthrop, John Coffin Jones, Samuel Adams, Thomas Russell, Caleb Davis, and Christopher Gore.
26. Gore to King, December 23, 1787, King Papers, NYHS; John C. Miller, *Sam Adams; Pioneer in Propaganda* (Boston, 1936), pp. 377-85.
27. Gore to King, December 30, 1787, King Papers, NYHS.
28. Gore to King, January 6, 1788, King Papers, NYHS.
29. *Massachusetts Centinel*, January 9, 1788.
30. Gore to King, December 23, 1787, King Papers, NYHS.
31. Jeremy Belknap to Ebenezer Hazard, January 20, 1788, "Correspondence between Jeremy Belknap and Ebenezer Hazard," Massachusetts Historical Society *Collections* (Boston, 1877), 5th ser., III, 6; Samuel B. Harding, *The Contest over the Ratification of the Federal Constitution in the State of Massachusetts* (New York, 1896), pp. 46 ff.; Charles Warren, *Elbridge Gerry, James Warren*

and Mercy Warren and the Ratification of the Federal Constitution in Massachusetts (Boston, 1932), pp. 5-7; Oscar Handlin, "Radicals and Conservatives in Massachusetts after Independence," *New England Quarterly*, XVII (September 1944), 349-55.

32. Jonathan Elliot, *The Debates of the Several State Conventions on the Adoption of the Federal Constitution* . . . (2d ed.; Philadelphia, 1836), II, 13, 16-18.
33. Elliot, *Debates*, II, 64-67.
34. Elliot, *Debates*, II, 112-13.
35. Elliot, *Debates*, II, 102.
36. Thomas B. Waite to George Thatcher, November 22, 1787, "The Thatcher Papers," *The Historical Magazine*, 2d ser., VI (November 1869), 258; Cecelia M. Kenyon, "Men of Little Faith: the Anti-Federalists on the Notion of Representative Government," *William and Mary Quarterly*, 3d ser., XII (January 1955), 3-45.
37. Elliot, *Debates*, II, 174-78; Theophilus Parsons, *Memoir of Theophilus Parsons* (Boston, 1859), p. 78.
38. Gore to Thatcher, February 3, 1788, "The Thatcher Papers," *The Historical Magazine*, 2d ser., VI (November 1869), 269.
39. King to Knox, February 1, 1788, Charles R. King, *The Life and Correspondence of Rufus King* (New York, 1894), I, 319.
40. Elliot, *Debates*, II, 180-81; *Massachusetts Centinel*, February 9, 1788.
41. William Sullivan, *Familiar Letters on Public Characters and Public Events* (Boston, 1834), pp. 11-16; Forrest McDonald, *We the People; the Economic Origins of the Constitution* (Chicago, 1958), pp. 191-200.
42. Gore to Thatcher, February 3, 1788, "The Thatcher Papers," *The Historical Magazine*, 2d ser., VI (November 1869), 260.
43. Morse, *Federalist Party in Massachusetts*, pp. 58 note, 60 note; *Massachusetts Centinel*, May 31, 1788; Gore to King, March 2, April 9, 1788, King Papers, NYHS.
44. *Independent Chronicle* (Boston), October 9, 1788.
45. *Massachusetts Centinel*, November 5, 8, 12, 1788.
46. *Acts and Resolves*, 1788, p. 258.
47. *Acts and Resolves*, 1788, pp. 256-57. The districts were Suffolk; Essex; Middlesex; Hampshire and Berkshire; Plymouth and Barnstable; York, Cumberland, and Lincoln; Worcester; Bristol, Dukes, and Nantucket.
48. *Massachusetts Centinel*, November 8, 1788; Gore to King, August 10, November 26, 1788, King Papers, NYHS.
49. *Independent Chronicle*, November 20, 28, 1788; Journal of the Senate, Massachusetts Archives, State House, May 1788-February 1789, p. 29.
50. *Massachusetts Centinel*, November 26, 1788; Morse, *Federalist Party in Massachusetts*, p. 64 note; Gore to King, November 23, 26, 1788, King Papers, NYHS.
51. Gore to Sedgwick, August 17, 1788, Theodore Sedgwick Papers, MHS.
52. Gore to Sedgwick, August 31, 1788, Sedgwick Papers, MHS.
53. *Massachusetts Centinel*, November 15, 26, 1788.
54. *Massachusetts Centinel*, January 14, 17, 24, 1789; Morse, *Federalist Party in Massachusetts*, pp. 64-65, 214-15.

55. Gore to King, March 1, 22, 1789, King Papers, NYHS; *Massachusetts Centinel*, May 30, 1789.
56. *Independent Chronicle*, June 21, 28, 1790; Journal of the House of Representatives, Massachusetts Archives, State House, May 1789-March 1790, p. 183.
57. Gore to David Cobb, January 29, 1790, Massachusetts Archives, State House.

Notes to Chapter III

1. Robert A. East, *Business Enterprise in the American Revolutionary Era* (New York, 1938), pp. 114-22. Gore was not associated with Duer and Parker in army contracts as East has written on p. 120, using as his source a letter from Parker to Duer, November 25, 1782, William Duer Papers, NYHS. East misread "you" as "Gore."
2. Christopher Gore to Andrew Craigie, June 1783, Andrew Craigie Papers, AAS.
3. Parker gave Gore the power of attorney on July 1, 1784, Records of the Registry of Deeds, Middlesex County Court House, LXXXVI, 529.
4. Gore to Craigie, November 9, 1788, Craigie Papers, AAS.
5. Gore to Craigie, January 7, 1788, Craigie Papers, AAS.
6. Gore to Craigie, September 2, 1788, Craigie Papers, AAS.
7. Gore to Craigie, October 4, 1788, Craigie Papers, AAS. Nathaniel Appleton was Commissioner of Loans in Massachusetts.
8. Massachusetts Old Loans Records, NA, CCLXXXIV, 133-34.
9. Charles J. Bullock, "Historical Sketch of Finances and Financial Policies of Massachusetts from 1780 to 1905," American Economic Association *Publications*, 3d ser., VIII (May 1907), 273, note 9.
10. Gore to Craigie, January 7, 1788, Craigie Papers, AAS.
11. Gore to Craigie, August 12, 14, 1788, Craigie Papers, AAS.
12. Gore to Craigie, September 2, 1788, Craigie Papers, AAS.
13. Gore to Craigie, September 9, 1788, Craigie Papers, AAS.
14. Gore to Craigie, September 15, 1788, Craigie Papers, AAS.
15. Gore to Craigie, October 4, 1788, Craigie Papers, AAS.
16. Gore to Craigie, October 26, 1788, Craigie Papers, AAS.
17. Gore to Craigie, November 9, 19, 1788, Craigie Papers, AAS.
18. Gore to Craigie, November 23, 1788, Craigie Papers, AAS.
19. Gore to Craigie, November 16, 1788, Craigie Papers, AAS.
20. Gore to Craigie, November 19, 1788, Craigie Papers, AAS.
21. Gore to Craigie, March 1, 1789, Craigie Papers, AAS.
22. Gore to Craigie, March 22, 1789, Craigie Papers, AAS.
23. Gore to Craigie, March 1, 1789, Craigie Papers, AAS.
24. Gore to King, January 24, 1790, Rufus King Papers, NYHS.
25. Gore to King, May 6, 30, 1790, King Papers, NYHS.
26. Gore to King, July 11, 1790, King Papers, NYHS.
27. Paul Leicester Ford, ed., *The Writings of Thomas Jefferson* (New York, 1892), I, 285.

28. Gore to King, July 13, 1790, King Papers, NYHS; B. U. Ratchford, *American State Debts* (Durham, 1941), p. 56.
29. Joseph Stancliffe Davis, *Essays in the Earlier History of American Corporations* (Cambridge, 1917), I, 194-95.
30. Worthington C. Ford, ed., *The Writings of John Quincy Adams* (New York, 1913), I, 59; Massachusetts Old Loans Records, NA, CCLXIV, 3, 47, 60; CCLXX, 158; CCLXXXIV, 133-34; CCCXVII, 76; CCCXIX, 17; CCCXX, 19; CCCXXI, 20; Records of transfer of stock, CCXCIII, *passim*.
31. Rufus King Memorandum, December 21, 1788, Charles R. King, *The Life and Correspondence of Rufus King* (New York, 1894), I, 623-24; Davis, *Essays*, I, 151-73.
32. Craigie to Parker, July 27, 1788, Craigie Papers, AAS.
33. J. P. Brissot de Warville, *New Travels in the United States of America* (2d ed.; London, 1794), I, 95.
34. "Contract de Brissot avec Duer et Craigie," Claude Perroud, ed., *J. P. Brissot Correspondence et Papiers* (Paris, 1912), pp. 180-81.
35. Gore to Craigie, April 25, May 5, 1798, Craigie Papers, AAS.
36. Brissot to William Seton, January 30, 1789, Eloise Ellery, *Brissot de Warville* (Boston, 1915), p. 215; Craigie to Brissot, May 16, July 28, 1789, May 24, 1790, Scioto Papers, NYHS.
37. Davis, *Essays*, I, 163-73.
38. Gore to King and King's notation, May 22, 1792, King Papers, NYHS.
39. Craigie to Parker, no date, Craigie Papers, AAS; Davis, *Essays*, I, 254-59.
40. Craigie to Parker, April 6, 1788, Craigie Papers, AAS.
41. Gore to Craigie, April 13, 1788, Craigie Papers, AAS.
42. Papers of the Continental Congress, NA, no. 41, III, 560; *Journals of the Continental Congress, 1774-1778*, XXXIV, 193-94; Craigie to Parker, April 6, July 27, 1788, Craigie Papers, AAS; Samuel Osgood and Walker Livingston of the Board of Treasury to James Wilson and Jared Ingersoll of the Board of Treasury, June 5, 1788, Charles E. French Collection, MHS.
43. Gore to Craigie, November 16, 23, 1788, Craigie Papers, AAS.
44. Gore to Craigie, August 12, 14, 1788, Craigie Papers, AAS.
45. Craigie to Gore, August 10, 1789, Craigie Papers, AAS.
46. Gore to King, September 6, 1789, King Papers, NYHS.
47. Gore to King, September 27, 1789, King Papers, NYHS.
48. Davis, *Essays*, I, 130-41; Archer B. Hulbert, "Methods and Operations of the Scioto Groups of Speculators," *Mississippi Valley Historical Review*, I, II (March 1914, June 1915), 502-15, 56-73; Hulbert, "Andrew Craigie and the Scioto Associates," American Antiquarian Society *Proceedings*, new ser., XXIII (October 1913), 222-36.
49. Gore to Craigie, February 7, 1789, Craigie Papers, AAS.
50. Gore to Craigie, March 23, 1789, Craigie Papers, AAS.
51. Gore to Craigie, March 25, 1789, Craigie Papers, AAS.
52. Gore to Craigie, April 25, 1789, Craigie Papers, AAS.
53. N. S. B. Gras, *The Massachusetts-First National Bank of Boston, 1784-1934* (Cambridge, 1937), pp. 10-24, ch. III, *passim*.
54. Stock Journal, Massachusetts Bank, HBSL, XIV.

55. Stockholders' Records, Massachusetts Bank, HBSL, I, 15; Directors' Minutes, Massachusetts Bank, HBSL, II, 49-54; Gras, *Massachusetts-First National Bank*, pp. 45-63.
56. Journal, Massachusetts Bank, HBSL, no. 1, XXVI, *passim*; Discount Book, Massachusetts Bank, HBSL, I, II, III, *passim*.
57. Dividend List of the Massachusetts Bank, First National Bank of Boston, XIX, *passim*; Gras, *Massachusetts-First National Bank*, pp. 59-60.
58. Proceedings of the Stockholders of the Massachusetts Bank, First National Bank of Boston, I, 23; Stockholders' Journal of the Massachusetts Bank, First National Bank of Boston, XIV; *Gazette of the United States* (Philadelphia), January 18, 1792.
59. Gore to King, June 3, 1791, King Papers, NYHS; Gore to John Kean, no date, Dreer Collection, Historical Society of Pennsylvania; power of attorney from Gore to William Payne, September 12, 1795, Etting Collection; Historical Society of Pennsylvania, I, 26, 27; Gore wrote to John Trumbull on December 13, 1806, that he no longer owned any stock in the Bank of the United States—Trumbull Papers, Yale University Library; James O. Wettereau, "New Light on the First Bank of the United States," *Pennsylvania Magazine of History and Biography*, LXI (July 1937), 273; Bray Hammond, *Banks and Politics in America from the Revolution to the Civil War* (Princeton, 1957), pp. 122-27.
60. Gore to King, April 1, 1792, King Papers, NYHS.
61. Gore to King, August 7, 1791, King Papers, NYHS.
62. Joseph Barrell, Christopher Gore, Jonathan Mason to the President and Directors of the Bank of the United States, January 28, 1792, Gratz Collection, Historical Society of Pennsylvania.
63. James O. Wettereau, "Branches of the First Bank of the United States," *Journal of Economic History, Supplement* (December 1942), II, 74, 88-98.
64. Gore to King, December 25, 1791, February 1, 1792, King Papers, NYHS.
65. Gore to the President and Directors of the Bank of the United States, February 17, 1794, Miscellaneous Papers, New York Public Library.
66. James Parton, *Life of Thomas Jefferson* (Boston, 1874), p. 373.
67. *Boston Directory*, 1798; *Bounds and Valuations, 1798, Boston Town Records* (Boston, 1890), p. 262.
68. Gore to King, April 12, 1789, King Papers, NYHS.
69. Walter Muir Whitehill, *Boston, A Topographical History* (Cambridge, 1959), pp. 47-50.
70. Oscar Handlin, ed., *This Was America* (Cambridge, 1949), pp. 68-75.
71. Gore to Belknap, December 5, 1793, March 31, 1794, Jeremy Belknap Papers, MHS.
72. Henry Wilder Foote, *Annals of King's Chapel* (Boston, 1896), II, 476, 588.
73. Records of the Registry of Deeds, Middlesex County Court House, CI, 116; CXV, 342; CX, 399; CXIII, 112.
74. William Bentley, *Diary of William Bentley* (Salem, 1911), II, 60.
75. *Laws and Regulations of the Massachusetts Society for Promoting Agriculture* (Boston, 1793), pp. iii, iv.
76. *Massachusetts Agricultural Repository and Journal* (Boston, 1813), III, v; *Centennial Year of the Massachusetts Society for Promoting Agriculture* (Salem,

1892), pp. 5, 6, 16-19; *Transactions of the Massachusetts Society for Promoting Agriculture* (Boston, 1858), new ser., I, 9-34.

77. *Transactions of the Massachusetts Society for Promoting Agriculture,* I, 28; *Massachusetts Agricultural Repository* (Boston, 1798), I, 75.
78. Bentley, *Diary,* II, 60-61.
79. Gore to Craigie, September 2, 1789, Craigie Papers, AAS.

Notes to Chapter IV

1. Gore to King, August 22, 1789, Rufus King Papers, NYHS.
2. *Senate Executive Journal,* I, 29-30.
3. Charles D. Hazen, *Contemporary American Opinion on the French Revolution* (Baltimore, 1897), pp. 253-78; John C. Miller, *The Federalist Era, 1789-1801* (New York, 1960), pp. 126-28; William Nisbet Chambers, *Political Parties in a New Nation; the American Experience, 1776-1809* (New York, 1963), pp. 42-43, 76-77.
4. Charles Marion Thomas, *American Neutrality in 1793* (New York, 1931), pp. 13-62, 115-40; Miller, *Federalist Era,* pp. 128-30.
5. Gore to Lear, June 2, 1793, Christopher Gore MSS., LC.
6. Gore to Lear, July 28, 1793, Gore MSS., LC; *Columbian Centinel* (Boston), July 28, August, September, 1793, *passim.*
7. Gore to Lear, July 28, 1793, Gore MSS., LC; Gore to King, August 4, 8, 1793, King Papers, NYHS; Paul Lester Ford, *The Writings of Thomas Jefferson* (New York, 1895), VI, 364.
8. Gore to Lear, August 4, 6, 1793, Gore MSS., LC; Thomas, *American Neutrality,* pp. 126-35.
9. Gore to King, August 8, 1793, King Papers, NYHS.
10. Gore to King, August 4, 1793, King Papers, NYHS.
11. *American State Papers, Foreign Relations,* I, 179-82; *Columbian Centinel,* August 24, 28, 1793; Thomas Coffin Amory, *The Life and Writing of James Sullivan* (Boston, 1859), I, 286.
12. Ford, *Writings of Jefferson,* VI, 398-99; Jefferson to Gore, September 2, 1793, Ford, *Writings of Jefferson,* VI, 404-06; *Gore to Jefferson,* September 10, October 21, November 23, 1793, Miscellaneous Letters of the Department of State, NA; Gore to William Cushing, December 24, 1793, Robert Treat Paine Letters, MHS; Higginson to Hamilton, August 24, 1793, John C. Hamilton, ed., *The Works of Alexander Hamilton* (New York, 1851), V, 577-80; Thomas, *American Neutrality,* pp. 214-16.
13. Thomas, *American Neutrality,* pp. 109-17.
14. Gore to King, August 5, 1794, King Papers, NYHS.
15. Charlotte von Leyden Blennerhassett, *Talleyrand* (London, 1894), I, 233, 235, 244.
16. David Cobb to William Eustis, February 15, 1794, Frederick S. Allis, Jr., *William Bingham's Maine Lands, 1790-1820* (Boston, 1954), I, 469-70.
17. Gore to King, December 23, 24, 1793, King Papers, NYHS.

18. Gore to King, March 15, 1794, King Papers, NYHS.
19. Gore to King, March 15, 1794, King Papers, NYHS.
20. Samuel Flagg Bemis, *Jay's Treaty* (New York, 1923), pp. 186-91.
21. Gore to King, March 15, 1794, King Papers, NYHS.
22. Gore to King, March 3, 1794, King Papers, NYHS; Samuel Eliot Morison, *The Life and Letters of Harrison Gray Otis* (Boston, 1913), I, 53; *Columbian Centinel*, February 26, 1794.
23. Gore to King, March 15, 1794, King Papers, NYHS.
24. Bradford Perkins, *The First Rapprochement; England and the United States, 1795-1805* (Philadelphia, 1955), pp. 1-6, 14, 21-23.
25. Gore to King, May 15, 1790, King Papers, NYHS.
26. Irving Brant, *James Madison* (New York, 1950), III, 398; Joseph Charles, *The Origins of the American Party System* (Williamsburg, 1956), pp. 89-102.
27. Eugene Perry Link, *Democratic-Republican Societies, 1790-1800* (New York, 1942), pp. 13-73; Chambers, *Political Parties*, pp. 61-65; Noble E. Cunningham, Jr., *The Jeffersonian Republicans; the Formation of a Party Organization, 1789-1801* (Chapel Hill, 1957), pp. 63-65.
28. Gore to King, December 23, 1793, King Papers, NYHS.
29. Gore to Lear, September 3, 1794, Gore MSS., LC.
30. Articles by "Manlius" appeared in the *Columbian Centinel*, September 3, 6, 10, 13, 17, 19, 24, 27, 1794; Henry Knox to George Washington, September 2, 1795: "He [Gore] is author of Manlius sometime ago, and lately of the Federalist." Henry Knox Papers, MHS.
31. Ames to Gore, January 10, 1795, Fisher Ames Papers, Dedham Historical Society.
32. Ames to Gore, November 26, 1794, Ames Papers, Dedham Historical Society.
33. *Independent Chronicle* (Boston), September 11, October 9, 20, 27, 1794.
34. Chambers, *Political Parties*, p. 86; Alfred L. Burt, *The United States, Great Britain, and British North America from the Revolution to the Establishment of Peace after the War of 1812* (New Haven, 1940), pp. 141-58.
35. Gore to King, September 13, 1795, King Papers, NYHS.
36. Gore to Sedgwick, December 27, 1795, Theodore Sedgwick Papers, MHS.
37. *Columbian Centinel*, July 22, 25, 29, August 1, 1795.
38. Cabot to King, August 4, 1795, Henry Cabot Lodge, *Life and Letters of George Cabot* (Boston, 1878), p. 84.
39. Articles by "Constitutionalist" appeared in the *Independent Chronicle* on July 27, 30, August 6, 13, 17, 23, 1795.
40. Gore to King, August 7, 14, 1795, King Papers, NYHS.
41. Perkins, *First Rapprochement*, p. 5.
42. Perkins, *First Rapprochement*, pp. 13, 74-75.

Notes to Chapter V

1. Gore to King, December 22, 1795, Rufus King Papers, NYHS.
2. Gore to King, June 7, 1794, King Papers, NYHS.

3. Knox to Washington, September 2, 1795, Henry Knox Papers, MHS.
4. Gore to King, December 26, 1795, January 21, February 18, 1796, King Papers, NYHS.
5. Knox to Washington, February 21, 1796, Knox Papers, MHS.
6. *Journal of the Executive Proceedings of the Senate of the United States* (Washington, 1828), I, 204-05; John Bassett Moore, *International Adjudications, Modern Series* (New York, 1931), IV, 156; Bradford Perkins, *The First Rapprochement; England and the United States, 1795-1805* (Philadelphia, 1955), p. 54.
7. Gore to King, May 27, 1796, King Papers, NYHS.
8. Knox to Pinkney, May 24, 1796, Knox Papers, MHS.
9. Samuel Tyler, *Memoirs of Roger Brooke Taney* (Baltimore, 1876), p. 141.
10. Madison to Jefferson, May 9, 1796, James Madison, *Letters and Other Writings of James Madison* (Congressional ed.; Philadelphia, 1865), II, 100.
11. Gore to Theodore Sedgwick, March 31, 1796, Theodore Sedgwick Papers, MHS.
12. Gore to Sedgwick, January 28, 1796, Sedgwick Papers, MHS.
13. Gore and Pinkney to Timothy Pickering, August 27, 1796, Papers Relative to the Commission under Article VII of the Treaty of Amity, Commerce and Navigation between Great Britain and the United States, Department of State, NA.
14. Grenville to Jay, July 9, 1796, Henry P. Johnston, ed., *The Correspondence and Public Papers of John Jay* (New York, 1893), IV, 220.
15. Perkins, *First Rapprochement*, pp. 19-23, 54; Rufus King Memorandum, May 3, 1797, Charles R. King, *The Life and Correspondence of Rufus King* (New York, 1896), III, 545.
16. Gore to Stephen Higginson, July 4, 1796, Timothy Pickering Papers, MHS.
17. Hunter Miller, ed., *Treaties and other International Acts of the United States Government* (Washington, 1931), II, 252-53.
18. Genêt to Jefferson, September 14, 1793, *American State Papers, Foreign Relations*, I, 184-85; Hammond to Grenville, November 5, 1794, Moore, *International Adjudications*, IV, 27, note. Most of the documents relating to the commission under Article VII are presented in this volume.
19. Jefferson to Hammond, September 5, 1793, Moore, *International Adjudications*, IV, 6-8.
20. Moore, *International Adjudications*, IV, 143-45, 489-513; Gore and Pinkney to Pickering, December 4, 1797, Papers Relative to the Commission under Article VII, NA.
21. Moore, *International Adjudications*, IV, 81-88, 182-94.
22. Trumbull to Wolcott, May 2, 1797, John Trumbull, Letter Book, 1796-1802, LC.
23. Moore, *International Adjudications*, IV, 372.
24. Moore, *International Adjudications*, IV, 424-39.
25. Moore, *International Adjudications*, IV, 372-400.
26. Moore, *International Adjudications*, IV, 400-24.
27. Moore, *International Adjudications*, IV, 439-43; Perkins, *First Rapprochement*, p. 116.

28. Perkins, *First Rapprochement*, pp. 116-17; Trumbull to John Huntington, April 27, 1797, John Trumbull, Letter Book, 1796-1802, LC.
29. Moore, *International Adjudications*, IV, 474-81.
30. Perkins, *First Rapprochement*, p. 117.
31. Gore to George Cabot, December 8, 1798, Pickering Papers, MHS.
32. Gore to Pickering, July 1, 1799, Timothy Pickering MSS., Essex Institute.
33. King to Pickering, March 16, 1799, Pickering MSS., Essex Institute; Cabot to Wolcott, May 2, 1799, George Gibbs, ed., *Memoirs of the Administrations of Washington and John Adams* (New York, 1846), II, 239.
34. Moore, *International Adjudications*, IV, 102-04; Perkins, *First Rapprochement*, pp. 117-20; Grenville to Robert Liston, October 21, 1799, Instructions to the British Minister, 1791-1812 (unpublished transcript from the Public Record Office), LC.
35. Gore to Pickering, July 1, 1799, Pickering MSS., Essex Institute.
36. Miller, *Treaties*, II, 488-96.
37. Gore to King, March 7, 1800, typescripts of letters to Rufus King, originals in possession of James Gore King, hereafter cited as James Gore King Collection; Gore to President John Adams, no date, Sedgwick Papers, MHS.
38. Suffolk County Registry of Deeds, Suffolk County Court House, vol. 193, pp. 85, 86.
39. Gore to King, September 22, 1803, King Papers, NYHS.
40. Gore to King, May 5, 31, 1800, King Papers, NYHS.
41. Cabot to King, September 30, 1800, King, *Correspondence of King*, III, 311.
42. Cabot to King, October 16, 1799, King, *Correspondence of King*, III, 135.
43. Gore to King, May 12, 21, 1801, King Letters, James Gore King Collection.
44. Gore to King, September 10, 1801, King Letters, James Gore King Collection.
45. Gore to King, June 11, July 21, 1801, King Letters, James Gore King Collection; Gore to Trumbull, February 19, 1798, Ellen Morton Washburn Collection, MHS.
46. Gore to King, June 20, October 15, 1801, King Letters, James Gore King Collection.
47. Gore to King, August 11, September 10, 25, December 17, 1801, King Letters, James Gore King Collection.
48. Minutes of the Commission under Article VII, March 7, 1803, Papers Relative to the Commission under Article VII, NA; Moore, *International Adjudications*, IV, 109-19.
49. Gore to Pickering, July 4, 1803. Pickering Papers, MHS.
50. Gore to King, July 2, 1803, King Papers, NYHS.
51. King to Gore, October 24, 1803, King Papers, NYHS.
52. Gore to King, August 31, 1799, King Letters, James Gore King Collection; Gore to Trumbull, August 6, 1798, June 12, 1799, Washburn Collection, MHS.
53. Gore to King, August 31, September 7, 12, 1799, James Gore King Collection.
54. Gore to King, August 20, 1802, King Letters, James Gore King Collection.
55. Gore to King, July 2, 1803, King Papers, NYHS.
56. Alexander Baring to Francis Baring, May 5, 1796, Baring Papers microfilm, LC.

57. Cabot to King, March 20, 1801, King, *Correspondence of King*, III, 408; Robert Troup to King, March 23, 1801, King, *Correspondence of King*, III, 409.
58. Gore to Madison, June 4, 1803, Papers Relative to the Commission under Article VII, NA; Gore to King, June 5, 1803, King Papers, NYHS.
59. Gore to King, June 5, 1803, King Papers, NYHS.
60. Gore to King, June 5, 1803, King Papers, NYHS.
61. King to Gore, August 20, 1803, King Papers, NYHS.
62. Rebecca Gore to Mary Alsop King, May 19, 1803, King Papers, NYHS.
63. Gore to King, July 31, 1803, King Papers, NYHS.
64. Gore to Cabot, October 18, 1803, Samuel Cabot Papers, MHS.
65. Ames to Gore, October 5, 1802, Seth Ames, ed., *Works of Fisher Ames with a Selection from His Speeches and Correspondence* (Boston, 1851), I, 298-303.
66. Gore to King, November 1, 1803, King Papers, NYHS.
67. Gore to King, February 29, 1804, King Papers, NYHS.
68. Gore to Pickering, February 18, 1804, Pickering Papers, MHS; Perkins, *First Rapprochement*, pp. 142-43.
69. Ames to Gore, October 3, 1803, Ames, *Works of Fisher Ames*, I, 326.
70. Gore to King, February 11, 1804, King Papers, NYHS.
71. Gore to King, April 12, 1804, King Papers, NYHS.
72. *Columbian Centinel* (Boston), May 3, 1804; *Independent Chronicle* (Boston), April 30, May 3, 1804.
73. Gore to King, December 20, 1803, King Papers, NYHS.
74. Gore to Trumbull, July 7, 1804, Washburn Collection, MHS.

Notes to Chapter VI

1. Author's conversation with Miss Dorothy Stroud, Sir John Soane's Museum, London.
2. Emil Kaufmann, *Architecture in the Age of Reason* (Cambridge, 1955), ch. XII, *passim*, p. 158, fig. 141; Kaufmann, "Three Revolutionary Architects: Boullée, Ledoux and Lequeu," American Philosophical Society *Transactions*, new ser., vol. 42, pt. 3 (October 1952), 453-537. Unlike Boullée and Ledoux, whose writings set forth their creative ideas, Legrand described and analyzed buildings already constructed. In 1799 he published *Parallèle de l'Architecture Ancienne et Moderne* and in 1806, five years after the Gores visited Paris, he and Charles Paul Landon published *Description de Paris et de Ses Édifices* in two volumes.
3. Louis Hautecoeur, *Histoire de l'Architecture Classique en France* (Paris, 1952), IV, 126, 315, fig. 243.
4. Gore to King, June 20, 1801, typescripts of letters to Rufus King, originals in possession of James Gore King, hereafter cited as James Gore King Collection.
5. Gore to King, July 3, 1801, King Letters, James Gore King Collection.

6. Gore to King, October 20, 1802, King Letters, James Gore King Collection.
7. Gore to King, November 1, 1802, King Letters, James Gore King Collection.
8. Jean Bourguignon, *Collections & Souvenirs de Malmaison* (Paris, [1924]), p. 9, plate 19.
9. Research in archives in Paris and inquiries among French professors of architecture have not revealed any sketches or notes of Legrand.
10. Gore to King, November 24, 1804, Rufus King Papers, NYHS.
11. Fiske Kimball, *Domestic Architecture of the American Colonies and of the Early Republic* (New York, 1922), pp. 153, 209-55.
12. Christopher Gore, Account Book, HBSL, p. 16; Gore to King, March 10, 1805, King Papers, NYHS.
13. Gore to King, April 22, 1806, King Papers, NYHS; Gore, Account Book, HBSL, p. 64; Philip Dana Orcutt, "Gore Place, Waltham, Massachusetts," *American Architect*, CL (June 1937), 67-74. Gore Place is owned by the Gore Place Society, and the house is open to the public.
14. H. A. H. Berry, "Notes on Gore Place," Miscellaneous Papers, Gore Place Society.
15. Contract between Gore and William Hay, Henry Knox Papers, MHS.
16. *Boston Directory*, 1805, 1806; Samuel Adams Drake, *Old Landmarks and Historic Personages of Boston* (Boston, 1873), pp. 279, 353; Gore to King, April 22, 1805, King Papers, NYHS. Suffolk County Deeds, Suffolk County Court House, V, 33, 168, 226, 228, 232, 253; Walter Muir Whitehill, *Boston, A Topographical History* (Cambridge, 1959), pp. 55-65; 5 *Pickering's Reports*, 370.
17. Gore to King, May 8, 1806, King Papers, NYHS; *The Insurance Blue Book, 1874* (New York, 1874), pp. 51-53; Records of the Massachusetts Mutual Fire Insurance Company, HBSL, II, 19.
18. Middlesex County Probate Records, Middlesex County Court House, CLVII, 181.
19. Carter Goodrich, *Canals and American Economic Development* (New York, 1961), pp. 59, 67, 177; Christopher Roberts, *The Middlesex Canal, 1793-1860* (Cambridge, 1938), pp. 29-42, 159-82. At his death Gore owned stock worth $400 in the Piscataqua Canal Corporation and stock valued at $4,156 in the Amoskeag Canal Corporation.
20. Isaac Livermore, *An Account of Some of the Bridges over the Charles River* (Cambridge, 1858), pp. 22-23; Gore to Thomas Dwight, August 3, 1805, Dreer Collection, Historical Society of Pennsylvania.
21. Records of the Lechmere Point Corporation, HBSL; Lucius Robinson Paige, *History of Cambridge, Massachusetts* (Boston, 1877), pp. 203-09: John Holmes, "Andrew Craigie," Colonial Society of Massachusetts *Publications* (Boston, 1905), VII, 403-07.
22. Journal of the Boston Manufacturing Company, HBSL, I, 145 ff.; XI, 153, 169, 175-78; Joseph G. Martin, *Boston Stock Market, Eighty-Eight Years* (Boston, 1886), p. 90; Caroline F. Ware, *The Early New England Cotton Manufacture* (Boston, 1931), pp. 60-66. From 1815-1817 John Gore, Christopher's nephew, was president of the Boston Manufacturing Company.

23. Middlesex County Probate Records, Middlesex County Court House, CLVII, 181. Gore invested $2,000 in the Wolcott Woollen Manufacturing Company.
24. *The American Academy of Arts and Sciences, 1780-1940* (Boston, [1940]), pp. 1-5; "Fellows of the Academy," *Memoirs of the American Academy of Arts and Sciences*, new ser. (Boston, 1882), pt. 1, XI, 37.
25. Stephen T. Riley, *The Massachusetts Historical Society, 1791-1959* (Boston, 1959), pp. 10-19; Edward Stanwood, "The Massachusetts Election in 1806," Massachusetts Historical Society *Proceedings*, 2d ser., XX (January 1906), 15; William Bentley, *Diary of William Bentley* (Salem, 1911), III, 226; *Independent Chronicle* (Boston), May 5, 1806.
26. William Jenks, "An Account of the Massachusetts Historical Society," Massachusetts Historical Society *Collections*, 3d ser. (Boston, 1838), VII, 21; *Catalogue of the Social Law Library in Boston* (2d ed.; Boston, 1849), iii.
27. Samuel Eliot Morison, *Three Centuries of Harvard, 1636-1936* (Cambridge, 1936), pp. 187-91.
28. Josiah Quincy, *The History of Harvard University* (Cambridge, 1840), II, 302, 504; Harvard College Board of Overseers' Records, HUL, V, 199, 416; VI, 137; Morison, *Three Centuries of Harvard*, p. 211; *Independent Chronicle*, April 20, 1807.
29. Morison, *Three Centuries of Harvard*, pp. 211-12.
30. Morison, *Three Centuries of Harvard*, pp. 210-11.
31. King to Gore, June 5, 1820, Charles R. King, *The Life and Correspondence of Rufus King* (New York, 1900), VI, 345-46.
32. Gore to King, June 14, 1820, King Papers, NYHS.
33. Gore, Account Book, HBSL, pp. 60-62.
34. Gore to King, December 25, 1807, King, *Correspondence of King*, IV, 41.
35. *The Writings and Speeches of Daniel Webster* (National Edition; Boston, 1903), XVII, 19, 185, 194, 198.
36. *Writings and Speeches of Webster*, XVII, 21.
37. Charles Warren, *A History of the American Bar* (Boston, 1911), pp. 304-08.
38. *Independent Chronicle*, February 14, 1803.
39. *Boston Gazette*, August 4, 1806; *Independent Chronicle*, August 4, 1806; T. Lloyd and George Caines, eds., *Shorthand Report of the Trial of Thomas O. Selfridge* (2d ed.; Boston, 1807), pp. 32 ff.
40. Gore to King, August 5, 1806, King Papers, NYHS.
41. Theophilus Parsons, *Memoir of Theophilus Parsons* (Boston, 1859), p. 192; *Independent Chronicle*, December 4, 22, 1806.
42. Lloyd and Caines, *Shorthand Report of the Trial of Thomas O. Selfridge*, pp. 14, 116-28; Thomas Coffin Amory, *The Life of James Sullivan* (Boston, 1859), II, 180.
43. Lloyd and Caines, *Shorthand Report of the Trial of Thomas O. Selfridge*, pp. 52 ff.; Amory, *James Sullivan*, II, 186.
44. Gore to King, August 24, 1806, King Papers, NYHS.
45. *Independent Chronicle*, October 23, 1806; *Columbian Centinel* (Boston), March 28, 1807; Parsons, *Theophilus Parsons*, p. 255.
46. *Who Shall Be Elected Governor?* (Worcester, 1809).

Notes to Chapter VII

1. Gore to Rufus King, December 28, 1807, Rufus King Papers, NYHS.
2. Gore to King, November 1, 1803, King Papers, NYHS.
3. David Hackett Fischer, *The Revolution of American Conservatism* (New York, 1965), pp. 50-72; Gore to Bristol County Committee, March 25, 1807, MHS.
4. *Columbian Centinel* (Boston), April 9, 1806; Gore to King, April 15, 1806, King Papers, NYHS.
5. Journal of the Senate, Massachusetts Archives, State House, May 1806-February 1807, pp. 27, 50, 51; *Columbian Centinel,* June 11, 12, 16, 1806; Edward Stanwood, "The Massachusetts Election in 1806," Massachusetts Historical Society *Proceedings,* sec. ser., XX (January 1906), 12-19.
6. *Independent Chronicle* (Boston), January 29, 1807; *Columbian Centinel,* January 21, 31, 1807.
7. Bradford Perkins, *Prologue to War: England and the United States, 1805-12* (Berkeley, 1961), p. 29.
8. Gore to King, March 10, 1805, King Papers, NYHS.
9. Perkins, *Prologue to War,* pp. 23, 79-82.
10. Gore to King, March 26, 1806, King Papers, NYHS.
11. Gore to King, August 24, 1806, King Papers, NYHS.
12. *Columbian Centinel,* July 1, 4, 11, 18, 1807; Samuel Eliot Morison, *The Life and Letters of Harrison Gray Otis* (Boston, 1913), I, 276-78.
13. Gore to King, November 9, 1805, King Papers, NYHS. Although this quotation is out of context, it accurately represents Gore's opinion on whether Jefferson would go to war against England.
14. Louis M. Sears, *Jefferson and the Embargo* (Durham, 1927), chs. 1-3, *passim*; Perkins, *Prologue to War,* pp. 149-82.
15. Samuel Eliot Morison, *The Maritime History of Massachusetts, 1783-1860* (Boston, 1921), pp. 188-92; Robin D. S. Higham, "The Port of Boston and the Embargo of 1807-1809," *The American Neptune,* XVI (July 1956), 189-207; Perkins, *Prologue to War,* p. 61.
16. Morison, *Maritime History,* p. 191; Benjamin W. Labaree, *Patriots and Partisans; the Merchants of Newburyport, 1764-1815* (Cambridge, 1962), pp. 153-54; James Duncan Phillips, "Jefferson's 'Wicked Tyrannical Embargo,'" *New England Quarterly,* XVIII (December 1945), 468-73.
17. John Howe to Sir John Prevost, May 5, 1808, David W. Parker, ed., "Secret Reports of John Howe," *American Historical Review,* XVII (October 1911), 71-83.
18. Gore to King, December 8, 1808, King Papers, NYHS.
19. *A Letter from the Hon. Timothy Pickering . . . Addressed to His Excellency James Sullivan, Governor of the State* (2d ed.; Boston, 1808).
20. Gore to King, March 10, 1808, King Papers, NYHS.
21. Thomas Coffin Amory, *The Life of James Sullivan* (Boston, 1859), II, 280-81; George Cabot to Timothy Pickering, March 9, 1808, Henry Cabot Lodge, *Life*

and Letters of George Cabot (Boston, 1878), pp. 380-81; Abstracts of Vote for Governor and Lieutenant Governor, Massachusetts Archives, State House, 1805-1812.

22. John Quincy Adams to Harrison Gray Otis, March 31, 1808, Worthington C. Ford, ed., *The Writings of John Quincy Adams* (New York, 1914), III, 189-223.
23. Gore to King, April 8, 1808, King Papers, NYHS.
24. Gore to King, May 28, June 4, 1808, King Papers, NYHS; Worthington C. Ford, "The Recall of John Quincy Adams in 1808," Massachusetts Historical Society *Proceedings*, XLV (January 1912), 364-65.
25. John Quincy Adams to the Honorable Senate and House of Representatives . . . , June 8, 1809, Ford, *Writings of John Quincy Adams*, III, 237-38.
26. Gore to King, June 16, 1808, NYHS.
27. *Independent Chronicle*, May 30, 1808.
28. William W. Story, *The Life and Letters of Joseph Story* (Boston, 1851), I, 136; Journal of the House of Representatives, Massachusetts Archives, State House, May 1808-March 1809, pp. 34-37; *Columbian Centinel*, May 28, 1808.
29. Story, *Joseph Story*, I, 517.
30. Journal of the House of Representatives, Massachusetts Archives, State House, May 1808-March 1809, pp. 110-11; *Columbian Centinel*, June 4, 1809.
31. Gore to King, May 28, 1808, King Papers, NYHS.
32. Gore to King, June 4, 1808, King Papers, NYHS.
33. *Columbian Centinel*, November 16, 1808; Journal of the Senate, Massachusetts Archives, State House, May 1808-March 1809, p. 111.
34. Gore to King, June 16, 1808, King Papers, NYHS; Charles R. Brown, *The Northern Confederacy According to the Plans of the Essex Junto, 1796-1814* (Princeton, 1913), p. 51.
35. Gore to King, June 8, 1808, King Papers, NYHS.
36. Gore to King, June 16, 1808, King Papers, NYHS.
37. Gore to King, June 16, 1808, King Papers, NYHS.
38. Samuel Eliot Morison, "The First National Nominating Convention, 1808," *American Historical Review*, XVII (July 1912), 746, 755 ff.; Cabot to Pickering, August 10, 1808, Lodge, *Letters of George Cabot*, p. 397.
39. King to Gore, September 27, 1808, King Papers, NYHS; Noble E. Cunningham, Jr., *The Jeffersonian Republicans in Power; Party Operations, 1801-1809* (Chapel Hill, 1963), p. 9. In the summer of 1808 the Boston Federalists conducted an impressive funeral for Fisher Ames. The body lay in state in Gore's Park Street house, and the procession to King's Chapel included the governor, lieutenant governor, council, and president of Harvard. Gore was a pallbearer. —Elisha P. Douglass, "Fisher Ames, Spokesman for New England Federalism," American Philosophical Society *Proceedings*, CIII (October 1959), 693.
40. Gore to Pickering, December 20, 1808, Henry Adams, ed., *Documents Relating to New-England Federalism, 1800-1815* (Boston, 1877), pp. 375-76.
41. Pickering to Gore, January 8, 1809, Adams, *Documents of New-England Federalism*, pp. 376-78.
42. Gore to King, March 10, 1808, King Papers, NYHS.

43. Otis to Quincy, December 15, 1808, Morison, *Harrison Gray Otis,* II, 4-6.
44. Joseph Story to Joseph White, Jr., January 4, 1809, Story, *Joseph Story,* I, 174-75.
45. Jefferson to William Eustis, October 6, 1809, Paul Leicester Ford, ed., *The Writings of Thomas Jefferson* (New York, 1905), IX, 236-37.
46. Gore to King, December 26, 1808, King Papers, NYHS.
47. Herbert Heaton, "Non-Importation, 1806-1812," *Journal of Economic History,* I (November 1941), 191.
48. *Columbian Centinel,* January 25, 1809; *Boston Gazette,* January 26, February 2, 1809.
49. William T. Whitney, Jr., "The Crowninshields of Salem, 1800-1808," Essex Institute *Historical Collections,* XCIV (April 1958), 114; *The Patriotick Proceedings of the Legislature of Massachusetts, during their Session from January 26, to March 4, 1809* (Boston, 1809), p. 53.
50. *Patriotick Proceedings,* pp. 53, 63; *Columbian Centinel,* February 4, March 13, 1809.
51. *Patriotick Proceedings,* p. 110; *Boston Gazette,* February 27, 1809.
52. *Boston Gazette,* March 6, 9, 1809; Journal of the House of Representatives, Massachusetts Archives, State House, May 1808-March 1809, p. 357.
53. *Columbian Centinel,* January, February 1809; *Independent Chronicle,* January, February 1809; Herman V. Ames, *State Documents on Federal Relations* (Philadelphia, 1906), pp. 34, 36, 42, 44; Labaree, *Patriots and Partisans,* pp. 155-57.
54. Jefferson to William B. Giles, December 25, 1825, Andrew A. Lipscomb, ed., *The Writings of Thomas Jefferson* (Washington, 1905), XVI, 143-45; Perkins, *Prologue to War,* pp. 165-83.
55. *Columbian Centinel,* March 22, 25, 29, 1809.
56. *Boston Gazette,* March 20, 1809.
57. *Boston Gazette,* March 27, 1809.
58. *Boston Gazette,* March 30, 1809.
59. *Independent Chronicle,* March 30, 1809. Essex Junto was the conservative wing of the Massachusetts Federalists and in 1809 included Parsons, Cabot, Pickering, Lowell, Higginson, and Gore. In 1781 John Hancock conferred the name on merchants and lawyers of Essex County who had opposed the state constitution.
60. *Independent Chronicle,* April 3, 1809.
61. *Independent Chronicle,* March 16, 1809.
62. "Letters of John T. Kirkland," Massachusetts Historical Society *Proceedings,* XVII (June 1879), 113-14, 116.
63. Abstracts of Votes for Governor and Lieutenant Governor, Massachusetts Archives, State House, 1805-1812. Gore carried the counties of Washington, Hampshire, Cumberland, Essex, Bristol, Worcester, Suffolk.
64. William Sullivan, *Familiar Letters on Public Characters and Public Events* (Boston, 1834), pp. 370-71. Gore's suit is displayed at Gore Place, Waltham, Massachusetts.
65. *Acts and Resolves,* 1806-1810, 304-14.
66. Herman V. Ames, *Proposed Amendments to the Constitution of the United States*

during the First Century of its History, American Historical Association *Annual Report* (New York, 1896), II, 264.

67. Frank W. Grinnell, "The Constitutional History of the Supreme Judicial Court of Massachusetts from the Revolution to 1813," *Massachusetts Law Quarterly*, II (May 1917), 536-41; *Columbian Centinel*, June 17, 21, 1809; *Acts and Resolves*, 1806-1810, 356-57.
68. James Duncan Phillips, "Hamilton Hall," Essex Institute *Historical Collections*, LXXXIII (October 1947), 302; *Columbian Centinel*, August 16, 19, 1809; *New-England Palladium* (Boston), July 25, August 15, September 19, 1809.
69. Gore to King, August 15, 19, 1809, King Papers, NYHS.
70. *New-England Palladium*, August 4, 1809.
71. *Pittsfield Sun*, August 5, 12, 26, 1809; *Independent Chronicle*, August 7, 17, 21, 1809.
72. George Ticknor Curtis, *The Life of Daniel Webster* (3d. ed.; New York, 1870), I, 64 note.
73. *Boston Gazette*, February 26, 1810; Heaton, "Non-Importation, 1806-1812," *Journal of Economic History*, I (November 1941), 192-94.
74. "Letters of John T. Kirkland," Massachusetts Historical Society *Proceedings*, XVII (June 1879), 116.
75. Gore to King, February 7, 1812, King Papers, NYHS.
76. Morison, *Harrison Gray Otis*, I, 49.

Notes to Chapter VIII

1. Bradford Perkins, *Prologue to War; England and the United States, 1805-12* (Berkeley, 1961), pp. 92-93, 421-37; Roger H. Brown, *The Republic in Peril: 1812* (New York, 1964), pp. 36-43; Samuel Eliot Morison, *The Maritime History of Massachusetts, 1783-1860* (Boston, 1921), pp. 196-97; Alfred L. Burt, *The United States, Great Britain and British North America from the Revolution to the Establishment of Peace after the War of 1812* (New Haven, 1940), pp. 210-24, 290-98, 309-10; Clement C. Sawtell, "Impressment of American Seamen," Essex Institute *Historical Collections*, LXXVI (October 1940), 325-26.
2. Gore to King, October 5, 1812, Rufus King Papers, NYHS.
3. *Columbian Centinel* (Boston), July 1, 1812; *American State Papers, Military Affairs*, I, 319-25, 607-14; Herman V. Ames, *State Documents on Federal Relations* (Philadelphia, 1906), pp. 54-55, 57-59; *Acts and Resolves*, 1812-1815, 76, 149; Niles' *Weekly Register* (Baltimore), IV, 251-53.
4. King to Gore, March 7, 1813, Charles R. King, *The Life and Correspondence of Rufus King* (New York, 1898), V, 298.
5. King to Gore, February 14, 1813, King Papers, NYHS.
6. Strong to King, March 12, 1813, King, *Correspondence of King*, V, 298-99.
7. *Columbian Centinel*, May 28, 1813.
8. Claude M. Fuess, *Daniel Webster* (Boston, 1930), I, 151.

9. Mason to Mary Means Mason, January 23, 1814, George S. Hillard, ed., *Memoir and Correspondence of Jeremiah Mason* (Cambridge, 1873), p. 78.
10. *Acts and Resolves*, 1812-1815, 318, 331-42; *Annals of Congress*, Thirteenth Congress, 1st sess., p. 37.
11. *Annals of Congress*, Thirteenth Congress, 1st sess., p. 500, 2d sess., pp. 549, 603.
12. Henry Adams, *History of the United States of America, 1801-1817* (New York, 1891), VIII, 14-16; Matthew Carey, *The Olive Branch; or Faults on Both Sides* (10th ed.; Philadelphia, 1815), pp. 289-91; Ronald Copp, "Nova Scotian Trade during the War of 1812," *Canadian Historical Review*, XVIII (June 1937), 141-44.
13. *Annals of Congress*, Thirteenth Congress, 2d sess., p. 606.
14. *Annals of Congress*, Thirteenth Congress, 2d sess., pp. 607-11.
15. *Annals of Congress*, Thirteenth Congress, 2d sess., pp. 19-97; Daniel Webster to Ezekiel Webster, January 30, 1814, *The Writings and Speeches of Daniel Webster* (National ed., 1903), XVII, 240.
16. Gore to King, July 28, 1814, King Papers, NYHS; Copp, "Nova Scotian Trade during the War of 1812," *Canadian Historical Review*, XVIII (June 1937), 151; Niles' *Weekly Register*, VI, 182.
17. *Annals of Congress*, Thirteenth Congress, 2d sess., pp. 651-57.
18. *Annals of Congress*, Thirteenth Congress, 2d sess., pp. 694-706.
19. *Annals of Congress*, Thirteenth Congress, 2d sess., pp. 707-22.
20. *Annals of Congress*, Thirteenth Congress, 2d sess., pp. 742-59.
21. Gore to King, September 13, 1813, King Papers, NYHS.
22. *Columbian Centinel*, March 27, 1813.
23. *Columbian Centinel*, June 18, 1814.
24. Cary, *The Olive Branch*, p. 221; Adams, *History of the United States*, VII, 51, 68-70, 366; Samuel Eliot Morison, *The Life and Letters of Harrison Gray Otis* (Boston, 1913), II, 67-68.
25. Shaw Livermore, Jr., *The Twilight of Federalism; the Disintegration of the Federalist Party, 1815-1830* (Princeton, 1962), p. 11; Adams, *History of the United States*, VIII, 13; Benjamin W. Labaree, *Patriots and Partisans; the Merchants of Newburyport, 1764-1815* (Cambridge, 1962), p. 190.
26. Jefferson to Gerry, June 11, 1812, Andrew A. Lipscomb, ed., *The Writings of Thomas Jefferson* (Washington, 1903), XIII, 163.
27. King, *Correspondence of King*, V, 422-24.
28. Adams, *History of the United States*, VIII, 217-19, 264-80.
29. *Annals of Congress*, Thirteenth Congress, 3d sess., pp. 95-102; Irving Brant, *James Madison* (Indianapolis, 1961), VI, 349.
30. *Annals of Congress*, Thirteenth Congress, 3d sess., pp. 110, 141.
31. Gore to King, July 28, 1814, King Papers, NYHS; Report of John W. Eppes, Committee of Ways and Means, *American State Papers, Finance*, II, 854-55; Adams, *History of the United States*, VII, 14-16; N. S. B. Gras, *The Massachusetts-First National Bank of Boston, 1784-1934* (Cambridge, 1937), pp. 76, 93.
32. Niles' *Weekly Register*, VII, 270.
33. Gore to King, July 22, 28, 1814, King Papers, NYHS.

34. Report of Secretary George W. Campbell, September 26, 1814, *American State Papers, Finance*, II, 840-43.
35. *Annals of Congress*, Thirteenth Congress, 3d sess., pp. 150-60.
36. King, *Correspondence of King*, V, 451-53.
37. Morison, *Harrison Gray Otis*, II, 78-199; Ames, *State Documents on Federal Relations*, pp. 78-80, 83-86; Adams, *History of the United States*, VIII, 296-97.
38. Gore to Strong, January 14, 1815, Henry Cabot Lodge, *Life and Letters of George Cabot* (Boston, 1878), pp. 559-60.
39. Ames, *State Documents on Federal Relations*, pp. 86-88; Brant, *James Madison*, VI, 361-62.
40. Adams, *History of the United States*, VIII, 282-84.
41. Gore to Strong, January 22, 1815, Lodge, *Letters of George Cabot*, pp. 560-61; 25 *U. S. Stat.*, 193-94; Pickering to Lowell, January 23, 1815, Henry Adams, ed., *Documents Relating to New-England Federalism, 1800-1815* (Boston, 1877), p. 424.
42. Gore to Strong, February 18, 1815, Lodge, *Letters of George Cabot*, p. 563; Livermore, *Twilight of Federalism*, pp. 12-13.
43. Gore to King, April 24, 1815, King Papers, NYHS.
44. Gore to King, April 11, 1815, King Papers, NYHS.
45. Adams, *History of the United States*, VIII, 233-38; J. S. Martell, "A Side Light on Federalist Strategy during the War of 1812," *American Historical Review*, XLIII (April 1938), 553-66.
46. Gore to King, April 24, 1815, King Papers, NYHS.
47. *Annals of Congress*, Fourteenth Congress, 1st sess., pp. 300, 331.
48. Gore to King, June 6, 1816, King Papers, NYHS.
49. Mason to Mary Means Mason, April 6, 1816, Hillard, *Jeremiah Mason*, p. 141.

Notes to Chapter IX

1. Gore to King, May 29, June 6, November 22, 1816; December 17, November 3, 1822; December 29, 1825; March 26, 1826, Rufus King Papers, NYHS; Francis W. P. Greenwood, *Funeral Sermon on the late Hon. Christopher Gore* (Boston, 1827), p. 13; 5 *Pickering's Reports*, 370; Suffolk County Registry of Deeds, Suffolk County Court House, vol. 278, pp. 148-50.
2. Gore to King, September 21, 1821, King Papers, NYHS.
3. Gore to King, August 6, 1820, King Papers, NYHS.
4. Gore to Richard Henry Dana, June 26, 1821, Dana Papers, MHS. Gore's books that are owned by Harvard College Library are on loan to the Gore Place Society.
5. Gore to King, August 1, October 9, 1816, King Papers, NYHS.
6. Gore to King, November 23, 1817, King Papers, NYHS.
7. *New England Farmer and Horticultural Register* (Boston), December 17, 1830.
8. *Transactions of the Massachusetts Society for Promoting Agriculture* (Boston, 1858), new ser., I, 25, 43, 54, 81-85.

9. Gore to Mason, June 22, 1817, George S. Hillard, ed., *Memoir and Correspondence of Jeremiah Mason* (Cambridge, 1873), pp. 158-59.
10. Gore to Mason, July 4, 1817, Hillard, *Jeremiah Mason*, p. 173.
11. *Columbian Centinel* (Boston), July 12, 1817.
12. Gore to King, February 22, 1822, King Papers, NYHS.
13. Gore to King, June 2, 1822, King Papers, NYHS.
14. King to Gore, February 13, 1818, Charles R. King, *The Life and Correspondence of Rufus King* (New York, 1900), VI, 117.
15. Gore to King, February 24, 1818, King Papers, NYHS.
16. Gore to King, June 2, 1822, King Papers, NYHS.
17. Herman V. Ames, *State Documents on Federal Relations* (Philadelphia, 1906), p. 55.
18. Gore to King, January 28, 1820, King Papers, NYHS.
19. Gore to King, January 29, 1820, King Papers, NYHS.
20. Gore to King, January 28, 1820, King Papers, NYHS.
21. Gore to Mason, June 25, 1820, Hillard, *Jeremiah Mason*, pp. 247-48.
22. King, "The Substance of Two Speeches on the Missouri Bill . . . ," King, *Correspondence of King*, VI, 690-703.
23. Gore to Mason, January 9, 1820, Hillard, *Jeremiah Mason*, pp. 235-36.
24. Gore to King, March 9, 1820, King Papers, NYHS.
25. Gore to King, May 10, 1824, King Papers, NYHS.
26. Gore to King, June 2, 1822, King Papers, NYHS.
27. Gore to King, February 22, 1822, King Papers, NYHS.
28. Gore to King, November 23, 1817, King Papers, NYHS.
29. Gore to King, April 1, 1826, King, *Correspondence of King*, VI, 666-67; Shaw J. Livermore, Jr., *The Twilight of Federalism; the Disintegration of the Federalist Party, 1815-1830* (Princeton, 1962), pp. 106, 269-73.
30. Gore to King, September 28, 1822, King Papers, NYHS.
31. Notes by John Lowell in Greenwood, *Funeral Sermon*, p. 18.
32. Gore, Account Book, HBSL, p. 64.
33. Gore to King, October 27, 1818, King Papers, NYHS.
34. Gore to King, October 19, 1819, King Papers, NYHS.
35. Middlesex County Probate Records, Middlesex County Court House, CLVII, 421.
36. Josiah Quincy, *The History of Harvard University* (Cambridge, 1840), II, 430.
37. Quincy, *History of Harvard University*, II, 431-35, 599-601; Edmund Quincy, *The Life of Josiah Quincy* (Boston, 1867), p. 469; Samuel Eliot Morison, *Three Centuries of Harvard, 1636-1936* (Cambridge, 1936), pp. 211-12.
38. King to Gore, March 24, 1825, King, *Correspondence of King*, VI, 602.
39. Gore to King, March 31, 1825, King, *Correspondence of King*, VI, 603.
40. Gore to King, April 16, 1825, King Papers, NYHS.
41. King to Gore, May 18, 1825, King Papers, NYHS.
42. 5 *Pickering's Reports*, 370; *Columbian Centinel*, March 3, 1827.
43. Greenwood, *Funeral Sermon*, p. 13.
44. Notes by John Lowell, Greenwood, *Funeral Sermon*, p. 16. The city of Boston's records of the people buried in King's Chapel Burying Ground and in the Old Granary Burying Ground do not include Christopher Gore.

Index